THE MYTHOLOGY OF THE 'PRINCES IN THE TOWER'

THE MYTHOLOGY OF THE 'PRINCES IN THE TOWER'

JOHN ASHDOWN-HILL

AMBERLEY

This book is dedicated to

Glen Moran,
Elizabeth Roberts,
the Right Hon., the Earl of Derby,
and the University of Leuven Centre of Human Genetics,
for their help in revealing the mtDNA haplogroup of the so-called
'Princes in the Tower'.

First published 2018

Amberley Publishing
The Hill, Stroud
Gloucestershire, GL5 4EP

www.amberley-books.com

Copyright © John Ashdown-Hill, 2018

The right of John Ashdown-Hill to be identified
as the Author of this work has been asserted in
accordance with the Copyrights, Designs and
Patents Act 1988.

ISBN 978 1 4456 7941 9 (hardback)
ISBN 978 1 4456 7942 6 (ebook)

British Library Cataloguing in Publication Data.
A catalogue record for this book is available
from the British Library.

Origination by Amberley Publishing.
Printed in the UK.

CONTENTS

Introduction   1

1 Who were the so-called 'Princes in the Tower'?   9
2 Who invented the term 'Princes in the Tower', and when?   13
3 What does the term 'Princes in the Tower' imply?   18
4 What was young Edward really like?   22
5 What was young Richard really like?   25
6 How was young Edward brought up?   29
7 What provisions were made for young Richard?   35
8 When did King Edward IV die?   41
9 Were the two boys *captured* in April 1483?   46
10 What did their mother do?   51
11 Why were the 'princes' declared bastards?   60
12 What did Lord Hastings do?   68
13 What does the Cely Note mean?   75
14 Would Richard III have had the boys killed?   79
15 Did 'Edward V' attend Richard III's coronation?   86
16 What was the Duke of Buckingham up to?   90
17 Did young Edward die in 1483?   98
18 Did young Richard survive beyond 1483?   112
19 What did the Duke of Norfolk do in late
   July/August 1483?   117
20 Would Henry VII have had the boys killed?   125
21 What myths are told about 'Richard of England'?   133
22 What myths are told about 'Richard of Eastwell'?   145

23 When was the story of the murder of the 'princes in the
    Tower' put out?   152
24 How and why was the story promulgated?   157
25 How are the boys said to have been killed?   163
26 What bones were found at the Tower of London,
    and when?   171
27 What did the 1933 urn opening reveal?   177
28 Hypodontia?   187
29 Can DNA now reveal the truth?   194
Conclusion   210

Appendix 1   The Reign of Edward V   217
Appendix 2   Tanner   223
Appendix 3   The Meaning of the Latin Word *nuper*   258
Appendix 4   Leuven Reports   262
Abbreviations   267
Notes   268
Bibliography   296
Acknowledgements   303
Index   305

Ἀκούεις βοὰν ἀκούεις τέκνων;
(Do you hear the cry? Do you hear the children?)

Euripides, *Medea*

Ex iniquis enim somnis filii qui nascuntur, testes sunt nequitiæ
adversus parentes in interrogatione sua.
(For children born of unlawful unions are witnesses
of evil against their parents.)

Book of Wisdom, chapter 4, v. 6

INTRODUCTION

One of my fervent desires in my teaching or writing of ancient history is that the novice or reader will be confronted time and again by the factual evidence, as much or as little as it is. Read the scholar's or the novelist's romanticized version of the story and enjoy it fleetingly – then discard it, and turn to ferret out the truth.

Professor D. B. Redford, *Akhenaten:*
The Heretic King, p. 232

The widely used term 'princes in the Tower' contains two nouns. The first of them is the word 'princes'. A prince is the son, grandson or close male relative of a monarch. However, dictionary definitions of the word 'prince' often appear to omit one key point without which the word could not really be applied – namely the fact that the person in question has to be a *legitimate* member of the royal family. A male royal bastard is not accorded the title of prince. Later, in chapter 3, after the identity of the particular individuals characterised as 'the princes in the Tower' has been made clear, the issue of legitimacy – which is extremely significant in the case of the people in question – will be examined.

The second noun, 'Tower', refers to the Tower of London. Nowadays, of course, the Tower of London is chiefly a historic site visited by tourists. Curiously, however, the modern tendency seems to be to think that, in its past life, the Tower of London always functioned chiefly as a prison. As a result the popular label 'princes in the Tower' is generally seen as referring to two specific young members of the fifteenth-century English royal family who are thought to have been cruelly detained in the Tower as prisoners.

Nineteenth-century engraving of a fifteenth-century image of the Tower of London – the medieval equivalent of Buckingham Palace.

In the light of that popular perception it is very important to stress the fact that, in reality, in the Middle Ages, the Tower of London would not chiefly have been seen as a prison. Of course it was a castle, and because they were secure places, medieval castles were sometimes used to detain people. Indeed, Richard III himself refers in one surviving memorandum to detentions in 'the Toure of London or other prisone'.¹ However, in terms of its main function, in the Middle Ages the Tower of London was roughly the equivalent of the modern Buckingham Palace. 'If it had not been first and foremost a palace, Henry VII would hardly have sent his Queen there to have her last child.'²

In other words the medieval Tower of London functioned principally as the chief official residence of central members of the English royal family when they were *in* the capital city. Of course, like the modern royal family (which often resides at Windsor rather than in Buckingham Palace), medieval royalty often lived *outside* the London walls, in the nearby countryside – for example, at the Palace of Westminster. But naturally various members of the royal family – including princes – lived at the Tower at various times. For example in the year 1482, King Edward IV is recorded as having been at the Tower of London on seventy-four different dates.³ Often those dates are consecutive, so the king must have been living there. Also, significantly, at that period the Tower of London was regularly and traditionally employed as their residence by all new Kings of England who had succeeded to the throne, and who were making the preparations for their coronation. The normal practice was for such new monarchs to process from the Tower of London to Westminster Abbey for their coronation ceremony.

Another curious point is the fact that actually a certain number of significant princes (and princesses) found themselves held under guard at the Tower at different times. Considering the list of medieval male royalty ('princes') only, the record of possible people who could be given the label 'princes in the Tower' runs as follows. In the 1290s, John Balliol, former King of Scots, was held in the Tower. Half a century later, David II, King of Scots was also held there, as was Jean II, King of France. In the early fifteenth century James I of Scotland was imprisoned in the Tower, as was ex-King Henry VI of England in 1471. Henry VI died there, though the precise date and cause of his death are debatable. Edward IV's brother, George of York, Duke of Clarence, was also held in the Tower, and was executed there, in 1477–8.

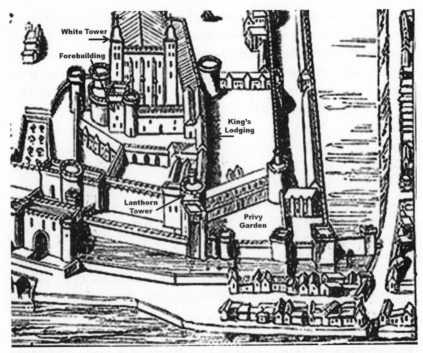

Sixteenth-century plan of part of the Tower of London, showing the royal residence and gardens. It also shows the White Tower and Forebuilding, which are usually associated in popular mythology with the discovery of the alleged bones of the 'princes in the Tower'. The King's Lodging is where Edward V and his brother were housed. Either the open space to the east of the King's Lodging, or the Privy Garden may be the area in which the boys were reportedly seen 'shotying and playyng' (an account written in about 1500). The Lanthorne Tower has been suggested as the possible location where the boys might have been housed following the bastardy decision.

As for King Edward V of England, in the summer of 1483 he and his brother, Richard, Duke of York were installed in the Tower palace. The reason why they went there is that it was part of the preparation for the coronation of that boy-king which was then being planned. It is normally assumed that the two of them may subsequently have been transferred to the Tower's prison cells. Yet the text of the Crowland Chronicle Continuations, compiled around April 1486, simply reports that after Richard III had been crowned king, and had left London on a royal tour, 'King Edward's two sons remained in the Tower of London under a certain appointed guard'.[4] This means that when their uncle had left the capital the two boys were left in London, and were guarded. All close relatives of the reigning monarch are normally guarded today. However, the wording of the Crowland Chronicle Continuations certainly does not suggest that the two boys had been moved into prison cells.

The only contemporary source which has sometimes been interpreted as implying that these two boys may have been *imprisoned* at the Tower seems to be a report written in December 1483, which states that

> He [Edward V], with his brother, was escorted into a remote building of the same Tower, they were rarely visible through the shutters and windows; thus they ceased to appear.[5]

This account seems to imply that they may have been removed from the 'King's Lodging'. It is not certain that such was the case, but probably the two boys were no longer residing in the royal apartments by the end of June 1483, because Edward had then ceased to be recognised as king. However, 'remote building' does not mean 'prison'. Thus, the true facts are far from clear in respect of how those two boys were treated after they had been officially removed from the line of succession and categorised as bastards.

Subsequently three Yorkist 'princes' were imprisoned at the Tower of London by King Henry VII. The first of these was considered to be the cousin of both Edward V and his brother, Richard, Duke of York – namely, the young lad who was officially recognised as Edward, Earl of Warwick (son of the executed Duke of Clarence). Actually, the Tower prisoner in question may not have been the genuine Earl of Warwick. He might have been a substitute, introduced as a baby by the Duke of Clarence to function as a royal impostor.[6] However, he was held at the Tower for about twelve years, until he was executed in 1499. From 1502 until 1539 another cousin, William de la Pole – nephew of Edward IV and Richard III, and one of the sons of their middle sister, Elizabeth, Duchess of Suffolk – was also held in the Tower. As for 'Richard of England' (alias 'Perkin Warbeck'), the young man who claimed to be Edward V's younger brother, Richard, Duke of York – and who may indeed have been a son of Edward IV, whom he reportedly resembled closely in height and facial appearance – his imprisonment at the Tower of London by Henry VII coincided from

1497 to 1499 with that of the titular Earl of Warwick. And 'Richard of England' also remained at the Tower until he was executed.

Given all these facts, it seems odd that, out of the total of no less than eleven possible royal males, the label 'princes in the Tower' seems actually to be applied exclusively to Edward V and Richard, Duke of York – the subjects of this present study. After all, leaving aside for the moment the point that those two boys had officially been defined not to be princes (a point which will be explored in detail later), and apart from the fact that we have no solid evidence to show that they were ever prisoners, we have now seen that some nine other medieval royal men could equally well be considered entitled to be categorised as 'princes in the Tower'!

Dates

In the modern English world 'new years' begin on 1 January ('New Year's Day'). In some other European countries that was also the norm in the past. In England, however, it was not. The English calendar was updated in the eighteenth century in that respect. Earlier, in England, 'new years' started on 'Lady Day' (the Feast of the Annunciation – 25 March). Thus English medieval records which refer to January, February or March *1484* (the first three months of that year in modern terms) would have their dates written as January, February or March *1483* (the last three months of that year in medieval terms). Therefore, in the present text both years dates will be used in the case of those three medieval months in the following way: 'March *1483/4*'.

Historical Sources

In respect of the mythology relating to the so-called 'princes in the Tower', some of the sources which have generally been accepted for the past five centuries are not contemporary with the events to which they refer. In the case of this particular story the problem in respect of source dates is that a key political change took place in England in 1485. That was the violent seizure of power by Henry VII. His regime then rewrote history in respect of the previous monarch, Richard III, whom Henry had ousted and whom his forces had killed in battle. That rewriting of political history from September 1485 onwards was very clearly and specifically documented by Henry VII in his first parliament, and his words on that occasion will be quoted later (see

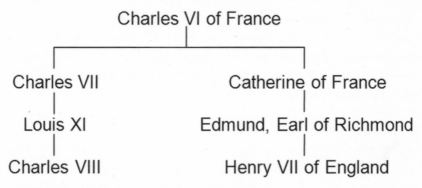

The French Royal Connections of King Henry VII.

below, chapter 20). For that reason, as far as possible, the present study will employ contemporary sources in respect of the so-called 'princes' and their story. Where later sources, written under the new regime of Henry VII and his dynasty, are referred to, that key date issue will be emphasised.

Also, in respect of source material the geographical location may be significant in this story. For example, sources from France – where Henry VII had lived in exile prior to his seizure of power in England, as a close blood relative of the French king – may reflect his influence.

On the other hand sources written in the Low Countries – inhabited by Richard III's sister, Margaret of York, dowager Duchess of Burgundy – are more likely to be uninfluenced by Henry VII.

Royal Surnames

Royal surnames are a problem. During the French Revolution, Louis XVI of France was amazed to hear himself called 'Louis Capet'. And at the time of the First World War, when King George V wished to abandon the use of any German surname, it actually proved difficult to establish what his German surname was!

In the present volume the popularly used alleged royal surnames, 'Plantagenet' and 'Tudor', will not normally be employed because, like so many alleged historical 'facts', they appear to be potentially mythological. The earliest solid contemporary evidence for the use of the name 'Plantagenet' dates from the 1450s, when it was adopted by Richard, Duke of York, father of Edward IV and Richard III. Subsequently it was used by *his* descendants.[7] There is also no authentic evidence to show that Henry VII ever used the name 'Tudor' – though that name was applied to him by Richard III in 1485, as part of the latter's attempt to show that Henry had no valid claim to the throne.

Portraits

Illustrations can also be mythological. Sadly many history books include the use of 'portraits' which are not contemporary, and which may be very misleading in terms of the features and complexion which they show. One reason for that is probably financial. Unfortunately permission to publish authentic medieval royal portraits can be rather expensive! Of course, some royal 'portraits' are not authentic. One key example is a famous depiction which is popularly thought to be of Henry IV – but which is actually an invention based on a fifteenth-century French royal portrait.[8] Also one published depiction of Cardinal Beaufort employs the image on his tomb in Winchester Cathedral. But unfortunately that was only created in the seventeenth century, after his original tomb image had been destroyed during the Civil War. The recreated image is not a genuine portrait. It also shows the cardinal wearing the red robes of that status, whereas his original image would have been more likely to represent him wearing Mass vestments.

In a similar way, many accounts of the so-called 'princes in the Tower' use the Canterbury Cathedral stained-glass images of the two sons of Edward IV. But once again, those had to be recreated after the original depictions had been smashed in the Civil War. In their present form they date from about the year 1800, and they bizarrely depict *both* boys wearing *kingly* crowns of that period! Of course, most of the existing depictions of the sons of Edward IV are simply nineteenth-century inventions. In the present volume, however, I have tried to focus on contemporary or near-contemporary depictions of the people who figure in this account.

I

WHO WERE THE SO-CALLED 'PRINCES IN THE TOWER'?

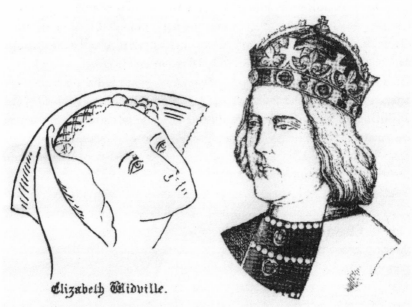

Elizabeth Widville.

The parents: Edward IV, redrawn from an image produced in the 1470s, and Elizabeth Widville, from a nineteenth-century engraving of a depiction of her in a fifteenth-century stained glass window.

The two boys who are normally referred to nowadays as the 'princes in the Tower' were the sons of Edward IV and Elizabeth Widville.[1] The names they bore were Edward and Richard. Their father, who had initially held the title of Earl of March, and who later became King Edward IV, had been born at Rouen in France at an unknown date, probably in 1442.[2] *His* father, Richard, Duke of York, a cousin of King Henry VI, had then been serving as the governor of the English possessions in France. It was about seventeen years after the birth of his son, Edward, that the Duke of York had put forward the Yorkist claim to the English crown. And although he himself was killed in the ensuing conflict, his son, the Earl of March, subsequently claimed the throne and became King Edward IV.

Edward IV was still quite young when he became king, and was not married. However, he seems to have met an attractive noble widow, Lady Eleanor Talbot (daughter of the Earl of Shrewsbury and widow of Sir Thomas Boteler, the son and heir of Lord Sudeley), whom he was later said to have secretly married. Such a secret marriage could have taken place at one of Eleanor's Warwickshire manors on about 8 June 1461.[3]

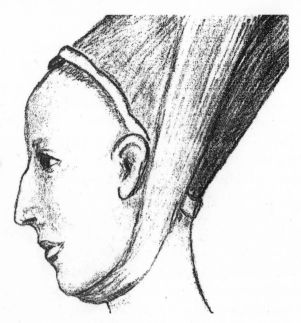

Lady Eleanor Talbot, a facial reconstruction, produced by the author in 1996, of a skull in Norwich which may be hers.

Unfortunately, the relationship between Edward and Eleanor proved unproductive, and it was never formally acknowledged by the young king. Indeed, he subsequently seems to have become involved in a same-sex relationship with the lovely Eleanor's handsome first cousin, Henry Beaufort, Duke of Somerset![4]

But by 1464 Edward was involved with another attractive widow, Elizabeth Widville, Lady Grey. He secretly married her on 1 May 1464. As in the earlier case of Eleanor Talbot, the Widville marriage was initially not made public. But in the autumn of 1464 Edward IV astonished the world by formally recognising Elizabeth as his consort. Probably the young king publicly recognised his union with Elizabeth at that point because, as a contemporary source states, she then told him that she was expecting his child.

> *Questo acto occulto per ogni rispecto*
> *tene 'l re un tempo; el matrimonio infine,*
> *gravida facta lei, mandò ad effecto.*

> (This contract the king kept in every respect
> concealed for a time; finally, the marriage
> made her pregnant, and was acknowledged.)[5]

But obviously if that really was the case, then the child in question must subsequently have been miscarried. Certainly for some reason Elizabeth's coronation as queen consort at Westminster Abbey was postponed until the following year. That might well have been because during the intervening months she had been pregnant.

The legality of Edward IV's relationship with Elizabeth Widville appears to have been questioned from the very beginning in some quarters – notably by certain members of the royal family, possibly including the king's mother, Cecily, Duchess of York, and certainly including his brother, George, Duke of Clarence, who had hitherto been the heir presumptive to Edward IV's throne. However, the Widville relationship proved very productive in terms of offspring. Initially the children that Elizabeth bore Edward were female. It was only six years after their secret marriage that she first produced a son for the king.

Edward V was born, not in a royal palace, but in the sanctuary at Westminster Abbey in November 1470.

This yere, the iij^de day of November, prince Edward the Son of kyng Edward the iiij^th, his fader then beyng ffled into fflaunders, was borne at Westmynster w^t in the Sayntuary; and Christyned in thabbey, whos Godfaders were the abbot and the pryour of Westmynster, and the Lady Scrope, Godmoder.[6]

The boy's own mother had then taken refuge at the abbey because at that time his father had been deprived of the English crown. Edward IV was in exile in the Low Countries when young Edward (V) came into the world, because the Lancastrian Henry VI had then been briefly re-proclaimed King of England. However, Edward IV returned home in 1471 and reclaimed the English crown. He then encountered his newborn son, who was created Prince of Wales and acknowledged by his father as the new heir to the English throne.

Edward V's younger brother, Richard, was born at Shrewsbury in August 1473. In addition to their numerous sisters, the two boys also briefly had one younger brother, called George. However, like some of the other children produced by his parents, George seems to have been a sickly child. He died very young, at the age of only two.

The known children of Edward IV and Elizabeth Woodville

NAME	MARRIED
Elizabeth	Henry VII
Mary	-
Cecily	1. Ralph Scrope; 2. John Welles, 1st Viscount Welles; 3. Thomas Kyme or Keme.
Edward	(betrothed 1480 to Anne of Brittany)
Margaret	-
Richard	1. Anne Mowbray; [? & *possibly* 2. Lady Catherine Gordon?]
Anne	Thomas Howard, 3rd Duke of Norfolk.
George	-
Catherine	William Courtenay, 1st Earl of Devon.
Bridget	(nun)

2

WHO INVENTED THE TERM 'PRINCES IN THE TOWER', AND WHEN?

Fifteenth Century
Not a shred of evidence exists to suggest that either Edward or Richard would ever have heard themselves referred to as 'the princes in the Tower'. Of course Edward, who then held the title Prince of Wales, was referred to as a prince during the reign of his father, King Edward IV. In his case that means that he was definitely assigned the princely title shortly after his birth – in 1471, when his father returned to the English throne – and he retained that title until April 1483, when his father passed away, and he himself was proclaimed king. Clear contemporary evidence for this survives. One good example is the will which his father put together on 20 June 1475.

In that will, King Edward IV sometimes refers to his elder son and heir as 'oure son Edward the Prince'. However, he does not always apply to the boy the princely title, for he also refers to him simply as 'oure said son Edward'.[1] In his will Edward IV does not group his two sons together, or use the common modern labelling term for the two of them. Indeed, he does not refer to his younger son as a prince. Instead he applies to that son the ducal title which had been bestowed upon the boy in May 1474, when he was nine months old. In the will his father refers to him consistently as 'oure son Richard Duk of York'.[2]

Other contemporary fifteenth-century documents also show clearly that the term 'princes in the Tower' was never employed at that time. For example, the account written in 1483 by the Roman priest Domenico Mancini for Archbishop Angelo Cato (Catho de Supino) of Vienne, the astrologer, doctor and almoner of King Louis XI of France,[3] mostly speaks about the elder of the two boys.

Fifteenth-century medallion of Archbishop Angelo Cato, King Louis XI's doctor and astrologer, who commissioned the 1483 report of Domenico Mancini.

However, Mancini does acknowledge that 'at his death Edward [IV] left two sons: … Edward the eldest, who had already some time before been proclaimed prince of Wales … [and] his second son called the duke of York'.[4] He refers to the Duke of York as the potential heir to the throne during the reign of his elder brother.[5] But like Edward IV, in his will, Mancini never employs for the two boys the modern label 'princes in the Tower'. There is no indication in his text that Mancini ever knew or used that term.

The update to the Crowland Abbey Chronicle, which was probably written in 1486, refers to Edward as 'the new king'.[6] It also mentions that his younger brother, Richard, came 'to the Tower for the comfort of his brother, the king'.[7] It then states that thereafter 'the two sons of King Edward remained in the Tower of London with a specially appointed guard.'[8] However, it never employs the term 'princes' for the two of them, let alone 'princes in the Tower'.

The New Dynasty and the Sixteenth Century

Some features relating to the story of the two sons of Edward IV were updated under the new dynasty of Henry VII and his son, Henry VIII, as part of the political rewriting of history which then took place. This included the invention of a fictional character named as 'Elizabeth Lucy', who was then said to be the person whom Richard III had claimed was the legitimate wife of Edward IV (thus leading to the bastardisation of Edward's children by Elizabeth Widville). However, it was also asserted that 'Elizabeth Lucy' had never really been married to Edward IV.

Despite this significant fabrication in respect of what had actually taken place in 1483, historians of the reigns of Henry VII and Henry VIII still did not employ the term 'princes in the Tower'. Obviously that label had not yet been invented. For example, Polydore Vergil referred to the sons of Edward IV as 'those babes of thyssew royall'. Ironically he then refers to them as 'Prince Edward and Richarde his brother', thus apparently ignoring Edward V's alleged kingship. Also when he speaks of the two boys, he does not refer to them as both being princes. Rather, he calls the two of them 'these sely [= innocent] chyldren'.[9] Later Sir Thomas More also called the two boys 'the prince and his brother', and 'the sely [= innocent] children',[10] but he does not refer to both of them as princes, and never employs the label 'princes in the Tower'.

Obviously Shakespeare made use of the story of the sons of Edward IV, particularly in the last decade of the sixteenth century, in his famous play entitled *Richard III*. He was a playwright, not a historian, and he is known to have invented a number of features of what he presented on stage as part of his dramatisation of the story of what had taken place. Nevertheless, like the earlier writers, he never employed the label 'princes in the Tower' for the sons of Edward IV.

Seventeenth and Eighteenth Centuries

A little later, in the seventeenth century, when George Buck wrote *The History of the Life and Reigne of King Richard the Third*, he published for the first time the legal evidence of the 1484 act of parliament, which had been concealed under the previous dynasty, but which shows clearly that it had been formally adjudged that Edward IV's lawful wife was Eleanor Talbot, and that the king's sons by Elizabeth Widville had therefore been bastards. In spite of his presentation of that important evidence, Buck does still refer to 'those two Princes'. He also speaks fully of 'Edward the fifth King in hope, and Richard of Shrewsbury, Duke of Yorke and Norfolke his younger brother'.[11] Like the earlier writers, however, Buck never employs the label 'the princes in the Tower'.

Similarly, sixty years later, in the early years of the eighteenth century, *A Genealogical History of the Kings and Queens of England* was published by Francis Sandford, Rouge Dragon Pursuivant at the College of Arms.[12] Sandford ignored the secret marriage between Edward IV and Eleanor Talbot (the evidence in respect of which had been published earlier by Buck). And he mentions the fictional 'Elizabeth Lucy', though he does not repeat the claim which had been made a century earlier, which falsely suggested that she had been said by Richard III to have been the legal wife of Edward IV. In respect of the sons of Edward IV and Elizabeth Widville, Sandford refers to 'the Issue of King Edward (IV)' and calls them 'these Two innocent Princes'. He also tells the story of the then recent burial at Westminster of bones found at the Tower in 1674, and believed to belong to Edward and Richard. (The evidence in respect of those bones will be explored later – see below, chapter 26 onwards.) However, once again, he never uses the term 'princes in the Tower'.

Francis Sandford.

In the mid eighteenth century the historian Horace Walpole produced his significant *Historic Doubts on the Life and Reign of Richard the Third* (1768). Walpole questioned the widely believed mythology concerning Richard III. Naturally, in his account he refers to 'both the princes'. However, like all his predecessors, he makes no use of the term 'the princes in the Tower'.

Nineteenth Century Onwards

The same is also true of Caroline A. Halsted (Mrs Atthill, 1803/4-1848), in her extensive, two-volume, early nineteenth-century *Richard III as Duke of Gloucester and King of England*. Likewise, in his *Letters and Papers of the Reigns of Richard III and Henry VII*, published in 1861, James Gairdner simply refers to 'Richard III's nephews'.

Curiously, however, later, in his *History of the Life and Reign of Richard the Third* (1898) Gairdner does employ the term 'the two young princes in the Tower'. This appears to show that the term was finally invented in the 1890s. Perhaps the label was invented by James Gairdner himself. The other possibility is that someone else had recently invented it and that Gairdner picked it up and also employed it.

Subsequently the label seems rapidly to have become very popular. Agatha G. Twining (1872–1962), in *Our Kings and Westminster Abbey* (1907), speaks of 'the little princes of the Tower, as they are so often called'. Also, in his report of the examination of the bones found at the Tower of London, which was read on 30 November 1933, Lawrence Tanner described his work as 'Recent Investigations regarding the fate of the Princes in the Tower'.[13]

3

WHAT DOES THE TERM 'PRINCES IN THE TOWER' IMPLY?

As has already been seen in the Introduction, as it is normally now employed, the label 'princes in the Tower' refers to two specific members of the house of York who are believed to have been held at the Tower as prisoners (though actually there is no real evidence in that respect). However, the term also bears a number of other significant implications.

Princes?

First, the use of the word 'princes' implies that the two boys in question were legitimate members of the royal house who had a valid claim to the throne. That had indeed been the status accorded to Edward and Richard by their father, King Edward IV, during his lifetime. However, it was a status which was cast into question by Bishop Stillington in June 1483 (see below, chapter 11). The fact that Stillington produced the key evidence which led to the official decision that the children of Edward IV and Elizabeth Widville were illegitimate is cited in Henry VII's legal records of January 1485/6,[1] and by sources dating from the 1490s and the 1530s (see below). Although he had hitherto remained silent on the matter, on 9 June 1483 Robert Stillington, Bishop of Bath and Wells, told a royal council meeting which was working on preparations for the coronation of the boy-king Edward V that the coronation could not proceed because the boy was illegitimate. Stillington said that he himself had married Edward IV to Eleanor Talbot (Lady Boteler).[2] Although Eleanor had died in 1468,[3] she had still been alive in 1464, when Edward IV contracted a second secret marriage with Elizabeth Widville (Lady Grey).[4]

Stillington's evidence was then presented to the three estates of the realm. These were members of the clerical and temporal Lords, and members of the Commons, who had been summoned to the capital to constitute a new parliament. However, a formal parliament could not then be opened because there was as yet no crowned king in England. So instead of meeting at the Palace of Westminster as a formal parliament, the three estates of the realm met informally at the London Guildhall. There they heard the evidence, and they then confirmed that the marriage between Edward IV and Elizabeth Widville had been invalid, and that therefore the children of that alleged marriage were all illegitimate and had no rights to the English crown. The crown was then offered by the three estates to Edward IV's surviving younger brother, Richard, Duke of Gloucester, who thus became King Richard III.[5] As a result of the decisions reached by the three estates of the realm, by the end of June 1483 neither Edward V nor Richard of Shrewsbury had the legal status of a prince.

Indeed, evidence exists which clearly shows that in the autumn and winter of 1483 Edward V was described in local and national government records as an 'illegitimate king' – in Latin *Regis Bastardi* (see below, chapter 17). This does not correspond with the terminology employed earlier in respect of the English kings of the ousted Lancastrian dynasty. The formula employed by the government of Edward IV to describe Henry IV, Henry V, and Henry VI was *rex de facto, non de iure* ('king in fact but not in law').[6] But of course, the *personal legitimacy* of Henry IV, Henry V and Henry VI had never been questioned. It was only their right to the crown which had been in dispute. On the other hand the new situation was entirely different. Yet in the autumn and winter of 1483 it would have been very difficult to ignore the fact that Edward V had for some weeks been recognised as England's king earlier in that year, because official government documents had been issued in his name. Thus the term 'illegitimate king' would have covered the situation confronting local and national government officials in respect of such paperwork.

Edward V and Richard of Shrewsbury then remained illegitimate children of Edward IV – and therefore commoners – until 1485. However, after Richard III had been defeated and killed at the battle of Bosworth, the formal decision made by the three estates of the realm in 1483 – which had subsequently become a formal act of parliament in 1484 – was repealed by Henry VII, who also attempted to wipe the story of what had been done – and why – out of history. The motive of Henry VII was his own intended marriage to Elizabeth of York (daughter of Edward IV and Elizabeth Widville), and his claim that she should be seen as the Yorkist heiress.

Nevertheless, Henry VII presented not one single shred of new evidence regarding the Edward IV marriage question. He simply attempted to destroy what had been said in respect of Eleanor Talbot. Although his policy may have worked in England, in parts of Europe which lay outside his control, the illegitimacy of the children of Edward IV and Elizabeth Widville continued to be accepted well into the sixteenth century.

Eustace Chapuys.

For example, surviving letters exist written in the 1530s by Eustace Chapuys, ambassador of the Holy Roman Emperor Charles V. These state that Henry VIII's mother, Elizabeth of York, the elder sister of Edward and Richard

> was declared by sentence of the bishop of Bath (Stillington) a bastard, because Edward [IV] had espoused another wife before the mother of Elizabeth of York.[7]

Thus the authentic royal status of Edward and Richard remains questionable.

In the Tower?

Secondly, the term 'Princes in the Tower' implies that the two boys were both fundamentally linked to the Tower of London. As we saw in the Introduction, that is often now seen as primarily a prison, and presumably the use of the word Tower in the appellation 'princes in the Tower' is intended to convey the picture that the two royal boys were prisoners. However, it is important to remember that, in the fifteenth century, the Tower of London was, in effect, the equivalent of Buckingham Palace in modern London. In other words, at that time the Tower was the official residence of English royalty in the capital city. It was the residence normally used for preparations for a coronation, and that is why the boy-king Edward V was initially moved there in 1483.

It is quite clear that at that time Edward was not a prisoner. As for his younger brother, Richard, he was released by their mother from sanctuary in Westminster Abbey, and sent to the Tower to join his elder brother. It is highly improbable that Elizabeth Widville would have decided to send her younger son from safety to prison. Her action therefore shows very clearly that she did not in any way perceive the Tower of London as a prison when she sent Richard there to join Edward.

United?

Thirdly, the appellation implies that the two boys were united in some way, and should be perceived as a single unit. That is very odd. The two brothers had definitely not grown up together in the same place. Edward had lived mostly at Ludlow Castle, under the guardianship of his maternal uncle Earl Rivers. However, Richard of Shrewsbury, Duke of York, seems to have lived mostly in and around London, Westminster, Windsor and royal manors, with his parents and his sisters. Thus in geographical terms the two boys had not really been united for most of their lives.

They also differed in other ways. As the Prince of Wales, Edward V seems to have been thought of as possibly sickly. On the other hand, Richard, Duke of York, was apparently regarded as a healthy child. Contemporary accounts also imply that the boys' characters were seen to be different. Edward was apparently thought to be depressed, whereas Richard was seen as a cheerful boy. They may also have had hair of different colours. Detailed evidence in all these respects will be presented shortly (see chapters 4, 5, 17 and 18).

4

WHAT WAS YOUNG EDWARD REALLY LIKE?

Appearance?

Edward, Prince of Wales/King Edward V (left), redrawn from a manuscript illustration commissioned by his maternal uncle, Earl Rivers (see plate 1); (right) redrawn from a nineteenth-century engraving based on the panel at St George's Chapel, Windsor (see plate 3).

Edward V is depicted in one surviving fifteenth-century representation of him, which was made during his lifetime, as a boy with ginger hair (plate 1). One posthumous fifteenth-century image shows fair hair (plate 2), though two other posthumous fifteenth-century images show auburn hair (plates 3 and 4). However, all those images show Edward with dark eyes. It therefore appears that his hair colour may have been somewhat lighter than that of his father, King Edward IV, particularly when he was very young, and that it probably had a reddish tinge.

Sickly?

It also seems possible that Edward was always known by his intimate family to be a sickly child. Indeed, in that respect he could well have resembled his youngest brother, George (who died at the age of two) and also two of his sisters: Margaret, who had died at the tender age of eight months, in December 1472, and Mary, who died at the age of fourteen, about a year before her father, in May 1482. Given that at least three other children of Edward IV and Elizabeth Widville are known to have died young, and of natural causes, the idea that Edward V may have suffered a similar fate is certainly plausible. What is more, in chapter 17 specific evidence will be considered which supports the view that Edward V may well have died in 1483.

Death ages of all known children of Edward IV and Elizabeth Widville

Their average life expectancy, based on those eight children whose age at death is on record, would have been 26.6 years.

Elizabeth	age 37
Mary*	age 14
Cecily	age 38
Edward*	age 12?
Margaret*	age 8 mths
Richard	age ??
Anne	age 36
George*	age 2
Catherine	age 48
Bridget	age 37

*Three (possibly four) of the children died naturally below the age of 15.

Possible evidence that his family knew Edward to be a sickly child can be found in the will which his father drew up in 1475, prior to his departure to France. In that will King Edward IV refers specifically to 'oure son Edward the Prince or *such as shall please almighty God to ordeigne to bee oure heires and to succede us in the Corone of England*'.[1] That phrase definitely appears to take account of the possibility that young Edward could well predecease his father. Later, Edward IV repeats the notion that some other heir might succeed him on the throne, speaking of 'oure said son Edward *or to such as shall please God to ordeigne to bee oure heire*'.[2]

The king also speaks of 'oure said son Edward and his heires'.[3] That can be interpreted in one of two different ways. First, it might be thought to imply that young Edward could possibly survive and have children of his own. However, it could also be understood as implying once more that young Edward may not outlive his father.

Overall, the king's choice of wording in his will is intriguing. It does appear to strongly suggest that he felt rather uncertain in 1475 that his eldest son would survive long enough to succeed to the English throne. However, there is also another very significant possible explanation for Edward IV's wording of his will in this respect. It seems that by 1475 both Edward IV and Elizabeth Widville were very well aware of the fact that the validity of their marriage was a matter for dispute. Thus it could also be that Edward IV felt unsure whether his son, the Prince of Wales, would actually be acknowledged as his legitimate heir when he himself was no longer around.

Depressed?

It also seems that Edward V may have been depressed. In chapter 17 evidence will be presented from a report written in 1483 which shows that in about June or July of that year the boy was frequently making confessions. Also in chapter 17 further contemporary evidence will be offered which suggests that Edward was then known to be in need of cheering up.

Religious?

However, another motive to inspire his reported frequent confessions could have been the fact that Edward V seems to have been brought up as quite a religious boy. According to the instructions given by his father, King Edward IV, to Lord Rivers, maternal uncle and governor of the young Prince of Wales, the boy was brought up to rise each morning 'at a convenient hour, according to his age', and immediately take part in morning prayer in his chamber. Then as soon as he was dressed he was to go to Mass in the chapel. Only after Mass could the boy have his breakfast. In the late afternoon every day he was then required to attend vespers before having his supper and going to bed at eight o'clock.[4] Also a Book of Hours seems to have been produced for young Edward in Ghent in about the year 1480. That was possibly commissioned as a gift for the Prince of Wales by Lord Hastings.[5]

5

WHAT WAS YOUNG RICHARD REALLY LIKE?

Appearance?

Although several contemporary images do survive of young Edward V, I can find only one fifteenth-century image of his younger brother, Richard of Shrewsbury, Duke of York. The image in question is not really a contemporary *portrait* of the younger brother. It was simply added as a small illustration in a royal family tree which was produced during the reign of King Henry VII. Nevertheless, the illustration is interesting, because it depicts Richard with dark hair, similar to that of both his father, King Edward IV, and his maternal uncle Anthony Widville, Earl Rivers. On the other hand, as we have seen, his elder brother, Edward V, is depicted, both in the family tree and in other fifteenth-century representations of him, as having hair of a lighter colour than that of his father, and hair which had a reddish tinge.

The only surviving fifteenth-century image of Richard of Shrewsbury which I have been able to find. Redrawn from a family tree produced in the reign of Henry VII (see plate 4).

Sadly, the images of young Richard which are usually depicted nowadays are all mythological. They include a stained-glass window 'portrait' from Canterbury Cathedral. That was originally a contemporary image, and therefore presumably authentic. Subsequently, however, it was smashed during the seventeenth-century civil conflict. Later it was restored, but in a manner which apparently bears little reflection of the lost original version. For example, the restored image depicts the younger son of Edward IV wearing a king's arched crown. It also attributes fair hair to Richard.

Most of the other images we have of him merely form part of the nineteenth-century and later imaginary depictions of 'the princes in the Tower'. Nevertheless, a certain amount of documentary material does survive which allows us to form an impression of what Richard was like in some other respects.

Healthy?

For example, in the previous chapter, we considered the text of the will written by Edward IV in 1475 in respect of what it possibly shows about that king's view of his elder son, the future Edward V. However, the text of the will also offers evidence in respect of the king's younger son, Richard of Shrewsbury. In Richard's case his father's wording implies that Edward IV definitely expected his younger son to survive. The logical conclusion would be that, even though when the will was written Richard had not yet attained his second birthday, he may already have appeared to be quite a strong and healthy child.

What implies that the king expected Richard to survive is the fact that he repeatedly speaks of what should happen when the little boy has attained the age of sixteen. For example, Edward IV wrote:

> after that oure son Richard Duk of York come to the age of xvj. yeres thay make estate unto him of the Castell Lordshippes Manoirs lands and tenements of Fodrynghay Staunford and Grantham with thair appertenances and of all other Manoirs lands and tenements in the Shires of North't' Rutland and Lincoln which were in the possession of my said Lord and Fader.[1]

Only once does Edward IV's will mention what should be done if his younger son happens not to survive. On that one occasion the boy's father simply says that 'if it fortune the same oure son the Duk of York to deceasse, as God forbede, without heires masle of his body commyng and afore the said age of xvj. yeres, then we wol the revenues of all the premises expressed in this article be applied by oure Executours to the paiement of our said debtes and restitutions making.'[2]

Other possibly significant evidence also exists in respect of how Richard was perceived in this respect. For example, two writers in the reign of Henry VII asserted that in 1486–7 it was claimed that Richard of Shrewsbury was then still alive. The writers in question are Bernard André and Polydore Vergil, both of whom say that initially the boy who was crowned at Dublin Cathedral as a Yorkist prince claimed the identity of Richard of Shrewsbury. In point of fact their assertion in that respect seems entirely false, because very clear evidence exists which shows that the boy crowned in Dublin assumed the royal name and number of 'King Edward VI'.[3] It is therefore clear that – as was reported in Ireland and other parts of Europe outside the control of Henry VII and his government – actually the 1486–7 Yorkist pretender claimed to be Edward, Earl of Warwick, son of George, Duke of Clarence.

Survived to Adulthood?

Nevertheless, genuine evidence does also exist which shows that some late fifteenth-century Yorkists believed that Richard, Duke of York, was still alive after 1485. That is why some of them supported the second Yorkist pretender.

The young man in question is usually referred to by later writers as 'Perkin Warbeck'. However, he himself gave his name as 'Richard

'Richard of England' (alias 'Perkin Warbeck'). Redrawn from the fifteenth-century portrait at Arras.

of England'. Clearly that pretender claimed to be the younger son of Edward IV and Elizabeth Widville.

There can be no doubt regarding the royal identity which this second Yorkist claimant professed, because he employed a royal seal upon which he was named as 'Richard IV, King of England and France, and Lord of Ireland'. The seal displayed the royal arms of fifteenth-century England (the fleurs-de-lis of France in quarters 1 and 4, and the three leopards of England in quarters 2 and 3), surmounted by a closed crown, the arches of which rose from a circle of fleurs-de-lis. The shield was supported by crowned royal lions, holding plumes (see plate 8).[4]

The fact that 'Richard of England' received support from some Yorkists in England confirms that, at that time, they had no difficulty in believing that the boy, Richard of Shrewsbury, could still be alive, having survived beyond his late teens. Thus when the little boy in question had been growing up in and around the court of his father, King Edward IV, he may well have been known to be a healthy individual.

Cheerful and Active?

It also appears that Richard was known to be a cheerful and active boy. Evidence in respect of his cheerfulness exists in the form of a letter about him written in London, and also in the form of a slightly later account written on the mainland of Europe. This evidence is presented in full in chapter 18.

6

HOW WAS YOUNG EDWARD BROUGHT UP?

On Saturday 20 February 1472/3 Edward IV appointed

the king's consort, Elizabeth, queen of England,
the king's kinsman, Thomas, cardinal archbishop of Canterbury,
the king's brothers, George, duke of Clarence, and Richard, duke
of Gloucester, Robert [Stillington], bishop of Bath and Wells and
chancellor,
L[awrence Booth], bishop of Durham,
E[dward Story], bishop of Carlisle,
J[ohn Alcock], bishop of Rochester,
the king's kinsmen John [Talbot, third] earl of Shrewsbury, and
Anthony, earl of Ryvers,
Thomas [Millyng], abbot of Westminster, chancellor of the king's
firstborn son Edward, prince of Wales,
William Hastynges of Hastynges, knight, the king's chamberlain,
Richard Fenys [Fiennes] of Dacre, knight,
Walter Devereux of Ferrers, knight,
John Fog [Fogge], knight,
John Scot [Scotte], knight,
Thomas Vaghan [Vaughan], chamberlain of the said prince,[1]
John Nedeham, knight,
Richard Chokke, knight,
Richard Fowler,
Master Richard Martyn, clerk,
William Allyngton,

Richard Haute,
John Sulyard[2]
and Geoffrey Coytemore
as tutors and councillors of the said prince until he shall be of
the age of fourteen years.[3]

His son the Prince of Wales was then two years and three months old.
Obviously, Elizabeth Widville, Cardinal Bourchier, Earl Rivers and
Lord Hastings figure elsewhere in the present volume, as does Robert
Stillington, Bishop of Bath and Wells – the man whose subsequent
revelation in respect of Edward IV's bigamy led to the ruling that young
Edward (V) was a bastard (see below, chapter 11). However, most of
the other individuals who figure in the list can also be identified and
some information is available in respect of them, as follows:

Lawrence Booth, Bishop of Durham (1457–76), was the former
   chancellor of Margaret of Anjou, and had been the tutor and
   guardian of *her* son, Edward of Westminster, Prince of Wales. He
   was later appointed Archbishop of York.
Edward Story, Bishop of Carlisle (1468–78), was the chaplain of
   Elizabeth Widville, and chancellor of the University of Cambridge.
   He was later appointed Bishop of Chichester.
John Alcock, Bishop of Rochester (1472–6), was Dean of St Stephen's
   Chapel, Westminster, and Master of the Rolls. He was later
   appointed Bishop of Worcester, and finally became Bishop of Ely.
John Talbot, third Earl of Shrewsbury, was distantly related to the
   king in various ways. However, he was also a nephew of Lady
   Eleanor Talbot. William Worcester described him as 'more devoted
   to literature and the muses, than to politics and arms'.[4] He died in
   1473, at the very young age of twenty-four, but the cause of his
   youthful demise is unknown.
Thomas Millyng, Abbot of Westminster (1469-1474), was one of
   young Edward's godfathers. In 1474 he was appointed Bishop of
   Hereford.
There was more than one Richard Fiennes of Dacre living in 1472/3.
   The elder of them had acquired the title of Lord Dacre by right of
   marriage to the heiress, Joan Dacre (a maternal line first cousin of
   King Edward IV).[5] Possibly the 'Richard Fenys' who was appointed

as tutor and councillor of the Prince of Wales – and who is not referred to as 'Lord Dacre' – was the third son and namesake of the holder of that title. However, the elder 'Richard Fenys lord Dacre' is mentioned in connection with the Prince of Wales and his younger brother, Richard of Shrewsbury on other occasions,[6] so probably he was appointed tutor and councillor, and his title of lord is omitted because he held it *iure uxoris*.

Similarly, 'Walter Devereux of Ferrers' must presumably have been Lord Ferrers. But like 'Richard Fenys of Dacre', he held the title of lord as a result of marriage with the Ferrers heiress. Walter, Lord Ferrers, was a loyal Yorkist, and a member of Edward IV's inner circle, who later died fighting for Richard III at Bosworth.[7]

Sir John Fogge, *c.* 1417–1490, lord of the manor of Repton.

Sir John Fogge of Ashford in Kent was treasurer of the king's household.[8] A former Lancastrian, he had switched to Yorkism. His second wife, Alice Lady Fogge (*née* Haute), was a first cousin of Elizabeth Widville, whom she served as a lady-in-waiting. Fogge seems to have links with Lord Hastings, and it seems that, like Hastings, he later opposed the removal of Edward V from the throne on the grounds of bastardy. He then became involved in what is generally known as 'Buckingham's Rebellion' by supporting Richard Guildford in Kent.[9] The aim of Guildford's movement seems to have been the reinstatement of Edward V (see below, chapter 16). Initially Fogge was attainted for that rebellious action by Richard III. And although Richard granted him a pardon,[10] Fogge subsequently supported the claim to the throne of the 'Earl of Richmond' (Henry VII).[11]

Sir John Scot[te] of Smeeth and Brabourne, Kent, 'served as Comptroller of the Household to Edward IV, and lieutenant to the Lord Warden of the Cinque Ports'.[12] He later appears to have been loyal to Richard III, who confirmed an earlier grant which Edward IV had made to him.[13]

Thomas Vaghan [Vaughan] had been the young Edward's chamberlain since before 6 August 1471.[14] He died in 1483.[15]

Sir John Nedeham was a lawyer and King's Bench judge.[16]

Sir Richard Chokke was a lawyer, justice of assize, and Common Bench judge.[17] He died in 1484, and his widow, Margaret, was granted permission by Richard III to found a chantry for the repose of his soul at Long Ashton in Somerset.[18]

Master Richard Martyn, clerk, was a priest who was serving as the Archdeacon of the London diocese in February 1472/3.[19] On 9 March 1472/3 he was designated as Bishop of Waterford and Lismore in Ireland, but he was never confirmed in that post, which was granted to another candidate in 1475. In April 1482, Richard Martyn was appointed Bishop of St David's in Wales. This time he was consecrated in that post, but he died in that office about a year later (May 1483).

In 1475 William Allyngton, esquire, served as 'Speaker of this Parliament'.[20]

Richard Haute, esquire, of Danbury in Essex, and Ightham in Kent, first cousin of Elizabeth Widville, was later commissioned by Edward IV in March 1482/3 to work with members of the Widville, Grey, and Twynyho families.[21] Haute seems to have sometimes been united in business with his brother-in-law, Sir John Fogge.[22] Apparently he also joined Fogge in the 1484 attempt to reinstate his young cousin, Edward V, as king. Thus he was attainted in 1484.[23] However he was pardoned by Richard III in March 1484/5.[24]

Trained at Lincoln's Inn, John Sulyard of Wetherden in Suffolk became a lawyer in the service of the Mowbray Dukes of Norfolk, of their cousin, Sir John Howard (later Duke of Norfolk), and of Richard, Duke of Gloucester, and he was appointed *Legisperitus* for the borough of Colchester in 1473.[25] He was also a Justice of the King's Bench.

In 1473 young Edward, Prince of Wales, was sent to the Welsh marches as part of the king's attempt to secure the loyalty of that region.[26] By – or soon after – his third birthday he had been based at Ludlow Castle. On Wednesday 10 November 1473 Bishop John Alcock of Rochester was appointed 'teacher of the king's son, the prince, that he may be brought up in virtue and cunning'.[27] Alcock was also made president of the prince's council. And young Edward's maternal uncle Anthony Widville, Earl Rivers, was appointed guardian of the prince on that same day, 'that he may be virtuously, cunningly and knightly brought up'.[28]

Earl Rivers dwelt with young Edward at Ludlow Castle from 1473 onwards. However, given the various other roles they had to fulfil, it seems impossible that all the 'tutors and councillors' who figure in Edward IV's list of such appointments could have also gone to dwell at Ludlow. Elizabeth Widville certainly did not reside with her son and her brother in Shropshire. As for John Sulyard, he seems to have served continuously as Colchester's Legisperitus from 1473 until 1482,[29] so presumably he remained in residence not far away from Colchester, at his home in Suffolk. Also on 28 June 1473 John Talbot, third Earl of Shrewsbury, who did hold government posts in Shropshire and north Wales, passed away at the age of only twenty-four. It is therefore difficult to ascertain to what extent Elizabeth Widville, John Sulyard and others named in the list actually figured in the upbringing and education of the Prince of Wales, and it is certain that the Earl of Shrewsbury cannot have played any significant role in that respect, because of his early demise.

On the other hand the appointment of Bishop John Alcock as the boy's tutor in November 1473, coupled with his subsequent transference from the see of Rochester to the see of Worcester – next door to the diocese of Hereford in which Ludlow was situated – in the summer of 1476, clearly mean that he played a role in Edward's upbringing. Probably so too did the boy's godfather, Thomas Mylling, formerly the Abbot of Westminster but appointed Bishop of Hereford in the summer of 1474. As for Bishop Robert Stillington, who had been serving as Edward IV's chancellor from 1467, he lost that office in 1473 and appears then to have left the capital (see below, chapter 11). Presumably thereafter he was mainly based in his Bath and Wells diocese, which in that pre-Reformation period was the next-door neighbour of the diocese of Hereford and the diocese of Worcester. So despite the action he took later to remove Edward V from the English throne, Stillington may also have played some role in the boy's education!

The instructions provided by the king in respect of his son's upbringing included regular religious observance (see above, chapter 4). He was to have 'such virtuous learning as his age shall suffer to receive', and while eating his dinner he was to hear the reading of 'such noble stories as behooveth to a prince to understand and know'. He was also to have 'convenient disports and exercises'. At eight o'clock in the evening he was to be put to bed. A doctor and a surgeon were always to be in his service.[30] Possibly his doctor was already John Argentine (see below, chapter 17). The boy also had a nurse. Her name was Avice Welles (Wellis), and she is named as Edward's nurse in surviving records from 1472 to 1481.[31]

A medieval nurse and child.

7

WHAT PROVISIONS WERE MADE FOR YOUNG RICHARD?

The greatest provision for young Richard was the attempt made by his parents to secure for him the Mowbray inheritance of the Duke of Norfolk. Those lands and titles had previously been held by Edward IV's cousin John Mowbray, fourth Duke of Norfolk. He was married to Elizabeth Talbot, the younger daughter of the first Earl of Shrewsbury and thus the loving sister of Eleanor Talbot. Eleanor had died young and unexpectedly in the summer of 1468. At the time of her death all of Eleanor's living relatives had been out of the country. They had been required to form part of the entourage of Margaret of York (the king's sister) for her splendid marriage with Charles the Bold, Duke of Burgundy, the ceremonies of which were chiefly organised by Elizabeth Widville. Possibly their appointments in that respect formed part of a plan to ensure that Eleanor was unprotected and could be removed.

In December 1475 the Duke and Duchess of Norfolk seem to have spent the Christmas season in Norwich. The duke himself then returned to their chief residence, Framlingham Castle in Suffolk. But he left his pregnant wife in Norwich. Sir John Paston II waited on the duke at Framlingham, and he tells us what happened next:

> It is so fortunyd that wher as my lorde off Norffolke yisterdaye beyng in goode heele, thys nyght dyed a-bowte mydnyght; wherffor it is alle that lovyd hym to doo and helpe nowe that that may be to hys honoure and weel to hys sowele'.[1]

Sir John gives no hint as to what had caused the sudden and unexpected death of the young duke, early on the morning of Wednesday 17 January 1475/6 – about two and a half years after the youthful death of his wife's nephew, John Talbot, third Earl of Shrewsbury. However, Paston makes it clear that the event had come as a shock, because he says that the previous day the duke had been in good health.

After the sudden death of the Duke of Norfolk – which also might possibly have been a killing – rapid plans were made by Edward IV and Elizabeth Widville in an attempt to secure the Mowbray inheritance for their younger son, Richard of Shrewsbury. On Saturday 27 January Sir John Paston wrote again to his younger brother, discussing the fact that Edward IV was now seeking to marry his two-and-a-half-year-old younger son to Lady Anne Mowbray (plate 5).

Young Anne was the only living child of the late duke, and therefore his potential heiress. However, at the time of the Duke of Norfolk's death the status of his daughter, Anne, could still possibly have changed. That was because her mother was pregnant at that time. It seems that Sir John Paston was worried about the royal marriage plan for Anne. He therefore proposed to his younger brother 'late vs alle preye God sende my lady off Norffolke a soone'.[2]

Elizabeth Talbot may also have been hoping to bear her late husband a son. If she had done so, at his birth the baby boy would immediately have become the new Duke of Norfolk. However, it appears that she must have miscarried by 12 June 1476, for by that date she seems to have agreed in principle to the proposed royal marriage for her daughter, who was the only direct heiress to the Mowbray estates and titles. On Wednesday 12 June the title Earl of Nottingham was granted to Anne's prospective bridegroom, the young Duke of York. The earldom of Nottingham had been one of the Mowbray titles, but the granting of it to the king's own younger son could only have meant that there was no longer any possibility that the Duchess of Norfolk would bear her late husband a posthumous son and heir.

About six months later, around the anniversary of her husband's death, Elizabeth Talbot's negotiations with the king had obviously progressed even further. On Friday 7 February 1476/7 the titles of

Duke of Norfolk and Earl Warenne were both bestowed on the young Duke of York, who, in token of his new status – and in spite of his extreme youth – was also granted his own council chamber. He was, at the time, only three and a half years old.[3]

Through their common Neville ancestry – Anne being the great-granddaughter of Catherine Neville, and Richard being the grandson of Catherine's younger sister Cecily – the two children were related within the prohibited degrees. Thus they could not be married without a papal dispensation. Edward IV duly made application to the curia in Rome, and on Monday 12 May 1477 Pope Sixtus IV dispatched

> dispensation at the petition of the king, and also of his son Richard, Duke of York, of the diocese of Coventry and Lichfield, and Anne de Mowbray, of the diocese of Norwich, infants, for the said Richard and Anne, who have completed their fifth and fourth years of age respectively, to contract espousals forthwith, and as soon as they reach the lawful age, to contract marriage, notwithstanding that they are related in the third and fourth degree of kindred.[4]

The marriage date was fixed for January 1477/8. Meanwhile Edward IV, while recognising that, in respect of the Norfolk estates, Elizabeth Talbot 'was entitled to divers possessions by reason of her dower and jointure', spent his time trying to persuade the dowager Duchess of Norfolk 'to forbear and leave a great part thereof', in order to maximise the holdings which his son, the new Duke of Norfolk, would enjoy. Finally an agreement was reached between them on these matters, and 'it was appointed between the king and herself [Elizabeth Talbot] that she should have divers specified possessions for life'.[5]

On Wednesday 14 January 1478 the five-year-old Anne Mowbray, accompanied by her young bridegroom's maternal uncle Earl Rivers, was escorted into the king's great chamber in the Palace of Westminster. There she dined in state in the presence of a large assembly of the nobility and gentry of the realm.[6] On the following morning the little girl was prepared for her wedding ceremony in the chamber of Elizabeth Widville. Once again she was escorted by her young husband's maternal uncle Earl Rivers, and this time also by Richard's first cousin, John de la Pole, Earl of Lincoln, who was then aged about fifteen. Those two earls led Anne through the king's chamber and the White Hall to St Stephen's Chapel (now the site of the House of Commons). The Chapel Royal, brightly painted and gilded more than a century earlier by King Edward III, was adorned on this occasion with rich hangings of royal blue, powdered with golden fleurs-de-lis.

St Stephen's Chapel, Palace of Westminster.

In St Stephen's Chapel, under a canopy of cloth of gold, the royal family awaited the little bride. Edward IV and Elizabeth Widville were there, accompanied on this occasion by both their sons and by three of their daughters (Elizabeth, Mary and Cecily), and also by the king's mother. Anne's local ordinary, Bishop James Goldwell of Norwich, awaited the little bride at the chapel door. However, her procession was halted by Dr Coke, who announced that the ceremony could not proceed without a papal dispensation. Then Dr Gunthorpe, Dean of the Chapel Royal, read aloud the papal dispensation. After he had done so the Bishop of Norwich led the little bride into the chapel and asked who was giving her away. It was the king himself who then stepped forward to play that role. When celebration of the nuptial mass had been completed, the king's youngest brother, Richard, Duke of Gloucester, distributed largesse to those present. Then the bride was escorted to her wedding banquet by Gloucester and his cousin the Duke of Buckingham.

The wedding banquet was held in St Edmund's Chapel. At the high table, with the little bride and groom, sat the Duke of Buckingham, together with his Widville wife, and also his first cousin, Anne Mowbray's widowed mother (for Buckingham's relationships see below, chapter 16). Elizabeth Talbot was escorted on this occasion by Richard, Duke of Gloucester, who was the husband of her first cousin Anne Neville. There were also two side tables, and they were presided over by the Marquess of Dorset (eldest son of Elizabeth Widville), and by the Countess of Richmond (mother of the future Henry VII).

The wedding celebrations lasted for several days, and included the award of honours, and three types of jousting. Young Anne Mowbray, now the Duchess of York and Norfolk, awarded their prizes to the victors in the jousting. But her mother seems to have played no further role in the wedding festivities. After the wedding banquet her name is no longer mentioned in the surviving records.

The senior of Edward IV's two younger brothers, George, Duke of Clarence – cousin and long-time friend of the bride's father, the late Duke of Norfolk, and also the husband of Elizabeth Talbot's recently deceased young cousin Isabel Neville – was also absent from all the marriage celebrations. Thanks to Elizabeth Widville (whom George himself may have suspected of having arranged the poisoning of his late wife),[7] George was imprisoned at the Tower of London at the time of the royal wedding and its subsequent festivities!

It was probably also thanks to Elizabeth Widville that Edward IV enacted dubious legislation to ensure that his young son Richard should retain the Mowbray inheritance whatever happened.

The legal position was that, under normal circumstances, and in default of a direct Mowbray male heir, the last Mowbray duke's only daughter Anne Mowbray (and by extension, *iure uxoris*, Anne's husband) would have a right to inherit Mowbray *lands* (including reversionary rights to those held in dower by Anne's widowed mother and great grandmother, the dowager duchesses of Norfolk) and to pass them on to their eventual offspring. Failing future offspring, all such lands should subsequently have reverted, on Anne Mowbray's death, to the Mowbray collateral heirs (who in this case were Lords Howard and Berkeley). ... However, Edward IV enacted legislation in respect of the Mowbray *lands*, whereby the collateral heirs by blood were deprived of their right to inherit, in favour of his own younger son, who was to retain the Mowbray lands even if Anne died without producing children (as in fact she did). This legislation, which anticipated Richard of Shrewsbury's marriage to the Mowbray heiress (but actually preceded that marriage) was of such dubious legality that the king thought it as well to have Parliament enact it twice: first in 1478 (when Anne Mowbray was still alive), and again in 1483 (when she was dead). Moreover the king sought to augment the immediate holdings thus accruing to his younger son by trying to 'persuade' the junior dowager duchess, Elizabeth Talbot, to surrender her jointure. ... It seems clear that Edward IV's legislation in respect of the Mowbray lands was widely perceived at the time as unjust.[8]

8

WHEN DID KING
EDWARD IV DIE?

Do we know the precise date?
Generally it is claimed by historians that the death date of King
Edward IV is known exactly. Unfortunately, that claim is simply one
of the many mistakes. The standard version in respect of the death
date of the father of Edward V and Richard of Shrewsbury asserts
that he passed away in the early hours of the morning on Wednesday
9 April 1483.[1] Clearly 9 April was the date on which Edward IV's
death was *announced to the world*.[2] However, that does not prove
that he *died* on that date, which was recorded – but also questioned
– in the contemporary diary of the pope's secretary.[3]

For example, sixty-eight years later, in July 1553, the death of
Edward IV's great grandson and namesake, King Edward VI, was
concealed for four days. That concealment definitely formed part
of an attempted political coup which sought to enthrone Lady Jane
Grey, in order to ensure that her father-in-law, John Dudley, Duke of
Northumberland, should remain in power. It is perfectly possible that
something similar was done on behalf of Elizabeth Widville in 1483.

Contemporary York Records suggest that Edward IV might well
have died slightly earlier than 9 April. If so, the news could easily
have been dispatched promptly to York Minster by the archbishop,
who could have sent a messenger to his dean. The point is that the
Archbishop of York, Thomas Rotherham, was serving in London as the
Lord Chancellor. And later he himself celebrated Edward IV's funeral
Mass. Depending on whether Edward IV's York Requiem Mass was

John Dudley, Duke of Northumberland, who, as part of an attempted political coup, concealed the death of King Edward VI for four days in 1553.

celebrated on the seventh or the third day after his decease, the king could perhaps have died on either Tuesday 1 April or on Saturday 5 April.[4] Subsequently Jean Molinet reported that 'he died on the fourth day after Easter'.[5] Since Easter Sunday that year fell on 30 March, Molinet's account suggests that Thursday 3 April was Edward IV's death date (for details of Molinet, see below, chapter 18). Also Thomas Basin, Bishop of Lisieux, reported that Edward had fallen ill on Good Friday (28 March) and died within a week (i.e. by Friday 4 April).[6]

As for Domenico Mancini's account (which was written in the year of Edward IV's death, but some six months after that event occurred) it states that Edward IV died on Monday 7 April.[7] And, as will be seen in detail later, contemporary local government records relating to both Colchester and Bristol clearly record Edward IV's death date as Tuesday 8 April.

Ironically, an addition to the Anlaby Cartulary which was inserted in about 1510 (after the death of Henry VII) implies that actually Edward IV had died about a week after the date which is usually claimed, namely on Tuesday 15 April.[8] However, the Anlaby Cartulary is not a *contemporary* record. Moreover, no *contemporary* evidence exists to support the cartulary's later assertion. Thus, in respect of Edward IV's death date, the Anlaby Cartulary is obviously in error – as it also is in respect of other fifteenth-century dates.

Nevertheless, as we have seen, the surviving *contemporary* records penned by Mancini and others, including local government officials, give various slightly different dates for the king's death. Because those are contemporary accounts, the dates which they state cannot simply be dismissed as fabrications. We cannot pretend that the precise death date of King Edward IV is known for certain.

Is the confusion due to Elizabeth Widville's plot?

The confusion in respect of his death date could well be a result of the deliberate policy of his bereaved partner, the boys' mother, Elizabeth Widville. There seems to be little doubt that she was a potentially ambitious and manipulative woman. We know from Mancini's account that she had been aware for some years that the validity of her royal marriage was questioned in certain quarters.[9] As a result she became worried about the future of her children. She was determined to try to ensure that her royal son, Edward (V), should succeed to the throne. As a result she had found herself in conflict with the former Yorkist heir presumptive, Edward IV's brother George, Duke of Clarence. In the end it was Elizabeth Widville who had pushed Edward IV to execute George for treason. And she may well have plotted in other ways.

What happened when he died?

When Edward IV died, obviously many things happened in respect of preparations for his funeral. However, those details are not really relevant in terms of the present study. We shall therefore concentrate here on what was done in respect of installing a new English sovereign.

As we have seen, the Prince of Wales was living at Ludlow Castle, with his guardian and maternal uncle Earl Rivers. As for his younger brother, Richard, he was living with their mother at Westminster. Elizabeth Widville wished to have her brother, Anthony, bring the elder of the two boys to London, so that he could be crowned as king at the earliest possible convenience. Initially she seems to have planned for that coronation to take place less than a month after the announcement of Edward IV's death (which appears to confirm that the date on which his death was announced cannot have been the date on which he died). The date she proposed was Sunday 4 May.[10] Meanwhile, her prime objective was to ensure that she herself should take control of the political situation in the capital. One result of her plotting in that respect could well have been to keep the king's death unannounced for a brief time, in order to allow her to begin getting her own plans for the future into place.

The news of his father's death reached Edward V on Monday 14 April.[11] However, he did not set off immediately for London. Instead, he remained in Ludlow to celebrate the feast of St George nine days later, on Wednesday 23 April. It was on the day after that feast that young Edward set off on his journey back to the capital accompanied by his uncle Earl Rivers.[12] After all, the personal presence of the young king in the capital was not urgently needed by his mother. She herself was already there. She simply needed to put herself firmly in power and plan her son's crowning ceremony. As for the route of Edward V's journey from Ludlow to London, that was planned by his uncle Lord Rivers. And they went via Northampton, presumably because Rivers then intended to meet up en route with the young king's paternal uncle the Duke of Gloucester.

Meanwhile, in London, government was already in progress in the new sovereign's name. Elizabeth Widville's plans were chiefly aimed at putting herself in the role of regent for her young son until he reached maturity (see below, chapter 10). That was something which would by no means have been normal practice in England – though it was probably familiar to Elizabeth from the European mainland, where her mother had been born. In England, however, the norm in the fourteenth and fifteenth centuries (as can be seen in the cases of Edward III, Richard II and Henry VI) had been to give such powers not to the mother of the young kings but to their closest royal male relatives. Logically, in the case of Edward V that would mean that the 'lord protector of the realm' during the boy's minority should be his surviving paternal uncle, Richard, Duke of Gloucester.

On Monday 21 April, various government appointments were made in London.[13] And Sunday 27 April saw the issue of a number of royal commissions. Prominent among the men named in them were Thomas, Marquess of Dorset (Elizabeth Widville's eldest son by her first marriage) and her eldest brother, Anthony, Earl Rivers.

Anthony Widville, Earl Rivers.

44

Edward IV's distant cousin and supporter Lord Howard was also named in respect of the royal commission for the county of Kent. Curiously, however, he was not addressed as 'Lord' – a title which Edward IV had granted him some twelve years previously. Instead, he was simply referred to as 'Sir John Howard, knight'.[14] This is very interesting given the fact that previously Elizabeth Widville had been busy ousting Howard from the inheritance of his close maternal relatives, the Mowbray dukes of Norfolk. Her aim had been to ensure that nothing should pass to Howard. Instead, the entire Mowbray inheritance was to pass to Elizabeth Widville's own youngest living son, Richard of Shrewsbury, whose marriage she had arranged to the Mowbray heiress, Anne. It therefore seems probable that addressing Howard now without using his title may have been intended by Elizabeth as a deliberate insult. As she had been earlier with the Duke of Clarence (see above), and more recently with Lord Hastings (see below, chapter 10),[15] it seems that Elizabeth Widville may also have been in conflict with Lord Howard.

Her insult to Howard was not her only questionable conduct in April 1483. She appears to have sent no official notification of Edward IV's death to his brother, the Duke of Gloucester, at Middleham. Moreover, although Gloucester was the Lord Admiral of England, Ireland and Aquitaine, and therefore held official command of the English navy, it was Elizabeth Widville's brother Edward who put to sea on Tuesday 29 April in command of a fleet of twenty vessels, carrying off part of the royal treasure.[16] The excuse for this action was the fact that

> no sooner had the death of King Edward [IV] become known, than the French not only made the seas unsafe, but even bore off prizes from the English shores.[17] … Therefore in the face of threatened hostilities a council, held in the absence of the Duke of Gloucester, had appointed Edward [Widville]: and it was commonly believed that the late king's treasure, which had taken such years and pains to gather together, was divided between the queen, the marquess [of Dorset] and Edward [Widville].[18]

As Armstrong notes in his published edition of Mancini's text, splitting up the royal treasure between Widvilles was a serious offence, and Mancini's report of what was done in that respect comprises damaging evidence against Elizabeth and her family.[19]

9

WERE THE TWO BOYS
CAPTURED IN APRIL 1483?

As we have seen, when Edward IV died his youngest brother, Richard, Duke of Gloucester, was still living (and had been acting very loyally on behalf of his brother, the king) in the north of England. As we have also seen, based on the English precedents, Gloucester was logically the person who ought to act as 'lord protector' for his nephew, the new king, Edward V. However, it seems that in April 1483 he received no official notification of his elder brother's death from Elizabeth Widville – who also did not approach him in respect of the urgently required naval defence of the kingdom.

News of the king's death did reach Gloucester at Middleham Castle by about 20 April. However, it seems that the prime source for that information was the late king's chamberlain, Lord Hastings. Hastings had apparently not been close to, or got on well with, Elizabeth Widville and her family. Polydore Vergil later wrote that 'Lord Hastinges ... bare privy hatryd to the marquis [of Dorset] and others of the queens syde'.[1] Full details of the reason for the animosity between Lord Hastings and the Marquess of Dorset will be revealed later (see below, chapter 12).

As for Vergil's account in respect of fifteenth-century English history, that is, of course, not always to be trusted, having been penned under the next dynasty. Nevertheless, earlier, in 1486, the continuator of the Crowland Chronicles had also reported that Hastings now feared that if supreme power fell into the hands of the queen's relatives they would then sharply avenge the alleged injuries done to them by that lord [for] much ill-will ... had long existed between Lord Hastings and them.[2]

It therefore seems to be beyond question that conflict existed between Hastings and the Widville family. Apparently it was because Hastings felt worried about what Elizabeth was doing following Edward IV's death that he chose to send a message north, to the Duke of Gloucester.[3] It appears that Lord Hastings may also have contacted Edward IV's cousin the Duke of Buckingham about what was going on in London. Like the members of the house of York (and the house of Lancaster) Buckingham was descended from King Edward III – though in his case that royal descent was in a junior line.

When he received the news of his brother's death from Lord Hastings, the Duke of Gloucester set off from Middleham for the city of York. There he exacted oaths of fealty to his nephew, the new king, Edward V, from the city magistrates.[4] His actions in York indicate clearly that at that stage he had no questions in his mind in respect of who should be the next English monarch. And although he had not heard from Elizabeth Woodville, 'Gloucester wrote the most pleasant letters to console the queen', and to offer his fealty to his nephew as the new sovereign.[5]

Gloucester remained in York until St George's Day. He then set off towards London.[6] On his journey southwards, the Duke of Gloucester paused briefly at Pontefract. He arrived at Nottingham on 26 April. From there he rode on to Northampton, where he arrived on Tuesday 29 April.[7] At Northampton he apparently met both his cousin the Duke of Buckingham and Elizabeth Widville's brother Earl Rivers. However, the precise sequence of events is somewhat confused, because the Crowland Chronicle continuations contain two conflicting accounts.

The first version states that when the Duke of Gloucester reached Northampton 'the Duke of Buckingham joined him, [and] there arrived to pay their respects, Anthony, Earl Rivers, the king's maternal uncle, Richard Grey ... uterine brother to the king and others'.[8] That would mean that Buckingham had joined Gloucester before

Earl Rivers arrived. Later, however, it is claimed that Rivers and his companions arrived first, and dined with Gloucester. 'They passed the whole time in very pleasant conversation. Eventually Henry, Duke of Buckingham also arrived, and because it was very late, they went off to their various lodgings.'[9]

On the following day Lord Rivers, his nephew Richard Grey, and Sir Thomas Vaughan were all arrested and sent to the north. Meanwhile both Gloucester and Buckingham rode on to meet up with Edward V at Stony Stratford.[10] Reportedly, when he met his uncle and his distant cousin, Edward V spoke to them of his deep trust both in the peers of the realm and in his mother, Elizabeth Widville.

On hearing the queen's name the duke of Buckingham, who loathed her race, then answered, it was not the business of women but of men to govern kingdoms, and so if he [Edward V] cherished any confidence in her he had better relinquish it.[11]

The above image is of a plaque which was put up on a former inn in Stony Stratford. It contains three errors. First, there is no evidence to prove that the Duke of Gloucester and his nephew, Edward V, met at the Rose and Crown Inn (though that did exist in 1483). Second, Richard did not *capture* Edward V. Third, there is no proof that Edward V was murdered.

Since Buckingham was yet another nobleman who loathed the Widville family, he may have been the person responsible for the decision which was made to imprison (and later to execute) Elizabeth Widville's eldest brother, Anthony, together with one of her sons by her marriage to Sir John Grey (see below). Initially, when he met Earl Rivers on 29 April, the Duke of Gloucester appears to have treated him in a friendly way. But apparently that was before Buckingham had arrived on the scene. As we have seen, one contemporary account relates that 'eventually Henry, Duke of Buckingham, also arrived [when] ... it was late'.[12] And it seems that it was only after Buckingham's arrival that Rivers found himself arrested – on the morning of 30 April.

However, no contemporary account suggests that the young king himself was arrested at Stony Stratford. Unfortunately Domenico Mancini's report (as translated by Armstrong) does make the erroneous statement that 'Richard, the queen's other son, who was quite young, and but a little before had come from London to the king, was arrested with him in the same village [Stony Stratford]'.[13] Armstrong's translation of Mancini's Latin text contains some inaccuracies, and in this case Mancini did not actually use the term 'arrested'. His original text reads *detentus est*, which means 'was detained'.

But of course, even Mancini's original Latin text is in error at this point, because Richard, Duke of York, was definitely not with his brother at Stony Stratford when Edward V was met by his uncle the Duke of Gloucester and his cousin the Duke of Buckingham. Indeed, Mancini himself subsequently acknowledges that the situation had been different, because elsewhere in his report he states correctly that the Duke of York was with his mother and sisters at Westminster, where the family took refuge at Westminster Abbey.[14]

The probability is that Mancini had heard some of his sources refer to something like 'the arrest of the young King's brother, Richard', and that he then misunderstood what that statement really meant. In reality it was Edward V's *older half-brother*, Sir Richard Grey, who was arrested at Stony Stratford, together with his uncle Earl Rivers. But, for example, the continuator of the Crowland Chonicles states in his account that 'they arrested Earl Rivers and his nephew, Richard, the king's brother.'[15] Such a statement could very easily be misunderstood as referring to Richard of Shrewsbury rather than the person it really means – Sir Richard Grey. It is interesting to note that, in spite of being a contemporary source (writing in December 1483), Friar Domenico Mancini did not always know precisely what he was talking about!

Probably Edward V and Richard, Duke of Gloucester did not know each other very well. They may have met in London on occasions but, for the most part, in recent years Gloucester had been living at Middleham Castle and his nephew had been living at Ludlow Castle. Nevertheless, Gloucester now assumed control of the royal party, which eventually continued southwards to London to install the young king in his capital city and to complete the plan for his coronation.

Initially, however, his paternal uncle took Edward V *northwards*, returning the short distance from Stony Stratford to Northampton. And the party must have stayed at Northampton on the night of 1/2 May, because on Friday 2 May, Edward V wrote a letter from Northampton to his cousin the Cardinal Archbishop of Canterbury:

> Most reverend ffader in God and right entirely beloved cousin. We grete you hertely wele and desire and pray you to see for the saufegarde and sure keping of the gret seale of this our realme unto our coming to our cite of London. Where by your good advice and others of our counsaill the same ferther may be demeanded for the weele of us and our said realme; and that it woll like you to call unto you the lords there and provide for the suerte and saufegarde of our toure of London and the treasure being in the same in all diligence, and our faithfull trust is in you. Geven under our signet at our towne of Northampton, the second day of May
> Edward[16]

Presumably the young king was asked to send the cardinal this message by his paternal uncle the Duke of Gloucester, the aim being to peacefully re-establish control of affairs in the capital. Nevertheless the letter itself and all the other evidence make it clear that Edward V had not been *captured*. As for his younger brother, at this stage Richard of Shrewsbury was still in the Westminster sanctuary with his mother and sister.

10

WHAT DID THEIR MOTHER DO?

Widville Plotting?

As we have seen, it was at Stony Stratford, on Wednesday 30 April, that Richard, Duke of Gloucester assumed the guardianship of his nephew Edward V. In London, Elizabeth Widville received the news of what had happened – including the arrests of her brother Earl Rivers and of her son Sir Richard Grey – on Thursday 1 May. She had been hoping to make herself and her family the new English rulers. It seems that her aims had been 'to form a regency resembling the government established by Edward IV during his absence on the French expedition of 1475. The prince of Wales was then created Keeper of the Realm, brought to London, and installed in the household of his mother.'[1]

However, when Elizabeth heard how things had gone at Northampton and Stony Stratford, she realised that her attempt to seize regency powers appeared to be failing. Initially, therefore, she and her eldest son, Thomas Grey, Marquess of Dorset,

> who held the royal treasure, began collecting an army, to defend themselves, and to release the young king from the hands of the dukes.[2] But when they had exhorted certain nobles who had come to the city, and others, to take up arms, they perceived that men's minds were not only irresolute, but altogether hostile to themselves. Some even said openly that it was more just and profitable that the young sovereign should be with his paternal uncle than with his maternal uncles and uterine brothers.[3]

Consequently, that evening Elizabeth finally abandoned the Palace of Westminster, and fled into sanctuary at Westminster Abbey. She was accompanied by her brother Lionel, Bishop of Salisbury, her eldest son, Thomas, Marquess of Dorset, all of her daughters by Edward IV and her youngest surviving son, Richard of Shrewsbury, Duke of York.[4]

The Crowland Chronicle continuator reports that the existence of two opposing factions was now openly displayed in the capital. 'Some collected their associates and stood by at Westminster in the name of the queen, others at London, under the protection of Lord Hastings.'[5] And it seems that other members of the Widville family also understood now that their attempt to seize power had failed, so they felt that they were in potential danger. For example, Edward Widville (Elizabeth's youngest brother – more than twenty years younger than his sister), whom she had placed in naval command, and to whom she had given part of the royal treasury, did not join Elizabeth and their brother Lionel at Westminster Abbey. Instead Edward escaped to Brittany with all the bullion and ships he held. There he linked up with the self-styled 'Earl of Richmond' (who later assumed another English title by proclaiming himself King Henry VII).

Edward V's arrival in London

Meanwhile young Edward V, travelling now with his uncle the Duke of Gloucester and his cousin the Duke of Buckingham, continued his journey to London. On Saturday 3 May that royal party reached St Albans. There they spent the night at *that* Benedictine abbey.[6] On the following morning (Sunday 4 May – the date which had originally been planned for his coronation) the young king left St Albans Abbey and set off on the last stage of his journey to London.[7]

He and his uncle the Duke of Gloucester were welcomed into the city that afternoon by its dignitaries.[8] The young king was taken directly to the Bishop of London's palace, next to St Paul's Cathedral.[9] There, the Duke of Gloucester once again had oaths of fealty taken to Edward V. The repeated practice of Richard, Duke of Gloucester in respect of the administration of such oaths of fealty clearly shows that in April and May 1483 his honest intention was to have his nephew crowned as king of England. As for his aim in respect of *himself*, that was simply to act for the young monarch, and to serve him until Edward came of age. Gloucester had never planned to seize the throne of England, and he was not now planning to oust the young king, his nephew.

Edward V stayed at the Bishop of London's palace at least until Friday 9 May. It was a convenient residence for him, because it stood just a few minutes' walk to the north of Baynard's Castle. That was the London home of his grandmother, the dowager Duchess of York (Cecily Neville). And it was at Baynard's Castle that the Duke of Gloucester seems to have stayed – with his mother – after he arrived in London. (See below, chapter 14, for the evidence in that respect.)

Significantly, on Friday 9 May and the following day Lord Howard sent thirty-four of his retainers back home from London.[10] Howard's action at that point, to divest himself of men who would have been his potential supporters in the event of a crisis, clearly implies that *he* then foresaw no further problem in respect of the political situation in England. It suggests that at the end of the first full week of the month of May he was assuming that everything had effectively been sorted out in respect of the new English sovereign's reign and government. Presumably Howard was not the only person who saw things that way.

The Lord Protector

Edward V was now definitely established as the new king. As for his royal uncle, Richard, Duke of Gloucester – who had been famous for his loyal service to the late king, Edward IV – he was now formally acknowledged as the lord protector of the kingdom during the minority of the young monarch. Thus he 'received that solemn office which had once fallen to Duke Humphrey of Gloucester who, during the minority of King Henry, was called protector of the kingdom. He exercised this authority with the consent and good-will of all the lords.'[11]

Significantly, Gloucester 'does not appear to have assumed [the] office [of lord protector] until chosen and appointed by the council after his arrival in London with Edward V'.[12] Thus he behaved in every respect modestly, correctly and respectfully. Yet Gloucester's tenure of the role which had now been formally assigned to him by the royal council is described by many historians as a 'coup'! It seems that the writers in question have no understanding either of that royal duke or of his personal plans and intentions. Nor do they seem able to grasp the significance of the relevant fourteenth- and fifteenth-century legal precedents in respect of the tenure of protectorship in England during the reign of a minor, and how that office was always assigned to the individual who held it.

Where should Edward V live?

As we saw earlier, it may have been the Duke of Buckingham who had been responsible for the arrest at Stony Stratford of Earl Rivers. Now it was definitely the Duke of Buckingham who proposed that the most appropriate residence for the boy-king in the lead-up to his coronation would be the Tower of London. 'There was talk in the Great Council about the removal of the king [from the Bishop of London's palace] to some other, more spacious, place; some suggested the Hospital of St John, some Westminster, but the duke of Buckingham suggested the Tower of London' and his proposal was accepted.[13]

Why did Elizabeth Widville send her youngest son to the Tower?

Buckingham was also a leading member of a delegation which, on Monday 16 June, was sent by boat a short distance up the Thames to Westminster Abbey, to try to persuade Elizabeth Widville to release her younger son, Richard, Duke of York, from sanctuary, and send him to join his elder brother at the King's Lodgings in the Tower. However, the person who actually led the deputation into the sanctuary at Westminster had to be a priest. Therefore the group was led by another royal cousin, Cardinal Bourchier, Archbishop of Canterbury.

An imaginary nineteenth-century engraving, showing Elizabeth Widville handing over her younger son, who is misnamed in the title as Edward, Duke of York.

Plans in respect of persuading Elizabeth Widville to give up her own residence in sanctuary seem to have begun earlier, on Friday 23 May.

> That day an oath was read of Richard, Duke of Gloucester, Protector of England, Thomas, Archbishop of Canterbury, Thomas, Archbishop of York, Henry, Duke of Buckingham, who had lately been given charge of our lord the King.

> Item: oath that, if the same lady is willing, the said lords wanted the lady Elizabeth, Queen of England, who is now living in the sanctuary of St Peter of Westminster, to give up the privileges of that same place.[14]

Of course, Elizabeth herself did not leave the sanctuary in May.

However, on 16 June she seems to have been very easily and rapidly persuaded by the delegation she received there to send out her youngest son. Mancini later suggested she may have been swayed by the fact that an armed force had been sent to surround her sanctuary. However, even he acknowledged that she trusted the word of the cardinal archbishop.[15] The Crowland Chronicles continuator offers a more positive account of what took place. He says that the delegation members asked Elizabeth 'in her kindness, to allow her son Richard, duke of York, to leave and come to the Tower for the comfort of his brother, the king. [And] She willingly agreed to the proposal.'[16]

Elizabeth's rapid decision on that point appears to be remarkably significant. After all, for her, young Richard was then the heir to the throne which was currently held by his childless elder brother, King Edward V. Thus until 16 June 1483 Elizabeth Widville had retained personal control of the heir to the English throne, even though she was residing in sanctuary, and did not control the person of the young king himself. Yet now she handed over the heir to the throne to Richard, Duke of Gloucester and others. Previously she had appeared to fear those men, because their assumption of governmental power just over six weeks previously had caused her to claim sanctuary. But her action on 16 June can only mean that then she no longer felt any fear in respect of transferring her youngest son, the heir to the throne, into the hands of the lord protector and his government.

The only other possible factor behind her decision is that either Elizabeth may already have heard the rumours which were circulating in London about what Bishop Stillington had told the royal council, or alternatively that Cardinal Bourchier told her, when he came to her in the sanctuary, that her royal marriage was now believed to be invalid, so that her children by the king were considered illegitimate with no further rights to the throne. Certainly she herself had been aware for years that she was balanced on a knife-edge in respect of the validity of her second marriage and the future of her royal children.[17] Thus for her it may now have become apparent that the worst had finally happened. But if she did find herself in that situation, provided the cardinal was able to offer her reasonable guarantees for her younger son's safety, she would have had no reason to keep him shut up with her in Westminster Abbey to ensure that she held the heir to the throne.

Whatever it was that brought about her decision, the result of it was that on that same day Richard, Duke of York left his mother and his sisters and departed from Westminster Abbey. Elizabeth handed the boy over to the cardinal, and he went to join his brother, King Edward V, at the King's Lodgings in the Tower of London. Presumably the journey back from Westminster to the Tower was again made by boat, so that the party must have entered the Tower via what later became known as 'Traitor's Gate'.[18]

How well young Richard actually knew his elder brother remains open to question. As we saw earlier, their period of residence at the Tower was probably the first time that the two boys had ever spent much time together. But it also seems that one of Richard's roles was to make his brother, the young king, feel better and more cheerful. Evidence in respect of this is to be found below, in chapter 17.

Why did Elizabeth Widville later hand over her daughters to Richard III?

Shortly afterwards – when the political situation had changed completely, because Edward V and his siblings had officially been adjudged to be illegitimate, and the Duke of Gloucester had been offered the English crown by the three estates of the Realm – the new government was no longer able to accord Elizabeth Widville the title of queen. For example, in March 1483/4, when Richard III was negotiating with Elizabeth, trying again to persuade her that she herself should leave the sanctuary at Westminster Abbey, together with her daughters, he called her 'dam Elizabeth Gray late calling her self Quene of England'.[19] Nevertheless, he promised her that he would secure suitable marriages for the daughters whom she had borne to Edward IV.

> Memorandum that I Richard by the grace of God king of England and of Fraunce and lord of Irland in the presens of you my lords spirituelle & temporelle and you Maire and Aldermen of my Cite of London promitte & swere *verbo Regio* & upon these holy evangelies of god by me personally touched that if the doghters of dam Elizabeth Gray late calling her self Quene of England that is to wit Elizabeth Cecille Anne Kateryn and Briggitte wolle come unto me out of Saintwarie of Westminstre and be guyded Ruled & demeaned after me than I shalle see that they shalbe in suertie of their lyffes and also not suffer any maner hurt by any maner persone or persones ... And that I shalle do marie sucche of theim as now bene mariable to gentilmen borne and everiche of theim geve in mariage lands & tenementes to the yerely valewe of CC marc for terme of their lyves and in like wise to the other doghters when they come to lawfulle Age of mariage if they lyff and suche gentilmen as shalle happe to marie with theim I shalle straitly charge from tyme to tyme loyngly to love & entreat theim as their wiffes & my kynneswomen As they wolle advoid and eschue my displeasure ... In witnesse wherof to this writing of my othe & promise aforsaid in your said presences made I have set my signemanuelle the first day of Marche the first yere of my Reigne [Monday 1 March 1483/4].[20]

Elizabeth's behaviour at that time once again appears to show that she fully trusted Richard III and felt absolutely no fear in respect of how he would treat her and her daughters. It is not entirely clear whether she herself then chose to leave the sanctuary at Westminster, but she certainly sent her daughters out to Richard, and probably she also left herself.[21]

And the subsequent evidence in respect of marriages seems to prove that she had been right to trust Richard III. For example, in 1484 he arranged a suitable marriage for her second surviving royal daughter,

Cecily. That girl then found herself married to Ralph Scrope, younger brother of Thomas, 6th Baron Scrope.[22] And in 1485, following the death of his own consort, Anne Neville, Richard III negotiated a second marriage for himself, with the Infanta Joana of Portugal. Significantly, his negotiations with the Portuguese court also included a good marriage project in respect of his eldest illegitimate niece, Elizabeth of York. Richard's plan was for her to marry a junior cadet member of the Portuguese royal family.[23] It is more or less certain that both of the projected Portuguese royal marriages would have taken place if the battle of Bosworth had never happened – or if it had been won by Richard III.

Why did Elizabeth Widville ask her eldest son to trust Richard III?

Further significant evidence as to how Elizabeth Widville felt about Richard III, and the promises she had received from him, is revealed by the fact that she also tried to persuade her eldest son, Thomas Grey, Marquess of Dorset – who had fled across the Channel after taking part in 'Buckingham's Rebellion' – to abandon the so-called 'Earl of Richmond' and return to England. 'By secret messengers [she] advised the marquise her soon, who was at Parys, to forsake erle Henry, and with all speede convenyent to returne into England, wher he showld be sure to be caulyd of the king unto highe promotion.'[24] Thus, in spite of the fact that her son, Sir Richard Grey, and her brother, Lord Rivers, had been executed, Elizabeth Widville does not seem to have believed that Richard III had in any way harmed her royal sons. Moreover, it seems she had no difficulty in persuading Thomas. He rapidly tried to return home from France. Unfortunately, however, he found himself prevented from doing so by 'the Earl of Richmond'.

One of the reasons why Elizabeth was willing to trust Richard III – and obviously did not fear him by the time when she wrote to her eldest son – may well have been that she had learnt, and understood, that the arrest of her brother Anthony, Lord Rivers and of her son Sir Richard Grey had not been thanks to the Duke of Gloucester (as he had then been called). Rather, those arrests had been brought about by his cousin, the Duke of Buckingham, who was a known enemy of the Widville family (see above, chapter 9). Of course Elizabeth also knew well that Buckingham had later changed sides, had staged a rebellion against Richard III, and had then been defeated and executed. She may also have been aware of the fact that Richard III had not been responsible in person for the executions of her brother and her second son after their arrests. The trial and execution of Earl Rivers and Sir Thomas Grey had actually been carried out by the Earl of Northumberland.[25]

11

WHY WERE THE 'PRINCES' DECLARED BASTARDS?

Why did Bishop Stillington come to London?
In May 1483 preparations were still being made for the coronation of the elder son of Edward IV and Elizabeth Widville, though by that month Edward V's coronation, which had originally been planned for 4 May by his mother, had been rescheduled for the Feast of the Nativity of St John the Baptist (Tuesday 24 June).[1] On Tuesday 13 May writs were issued summoning members of the first parliament in the new king's reign.[2] Then, a week later, on Tuesday 20 May, instructions were circulated to sheriffs telling them that all the young men who were eligible for receiving knighthoods at the coronation were to present themselves in London by 18 June.[3]

Government plans included the intention that the first parliament of Edward V should be opened on Wednesday 25 June. That was now seen as the day following the young king's forthcoming coronation. The fact that he would, by then, have been crowned King of England meant that on that day he would be able to formally open the first parliament of his reign at the Palace of Westminster. That was the reason why the summonses were sent out on 13 May to those who would constitute the new parliament. The dispatch of those summonses was an action which subsequently proved to be highly significant in one way.

And at the beginning of June, the young Edward V seems to have written fifty letters summoning men who were to receive knighthoods at his forthcoming coronation. One of these has survived.

Trusty and well-beloved, we greet you well; and by the advice of our dearest uncle, the Duke of Gloucester, Protector of this our royaume during our young age, an of the Lords of our Council, we write unto you at this time, willing and natheless charging you to prepare and furnish yourself to receive the noble order of knighthood at our coronation; which, by God's grace, we intend shall be solemnised the 22d day of this present month at our palace of Westminster, commanding you to be here at our Tower of London, four days before our said coronation, to have communication with commissioners concerning that matter; not failing hereof in any wise, as you intend to please us, and as ye will answer.

Given, &c. &c. the 5th day of June.

To Otes Gilbert, Squier.[4]

Thus it is apparent that his coronation planning was still in progress during the first week of June. Indeed, it was for that purpose that yet another royal council meeting was held on Monday 9 June. But significantly, that seems to have been the occasion on which Bishop Stillington of Bath and Wells addressed the royal council. Apparently he then expressed to the members his view that Edward V could not be crowned as King of England.

In 1460 Canon Robert Stillington had served in the government of the Lancastrian king Henry VI. But after the Earl of March was proclaimed King Edward IV in London, in March 1460/1, Canon Stillington entered his service in various ways. He had served Edward IV in government for a number of years, having been appointed keeper of the privy seal in the first year of that king's reign, on 28 July 1460 – just over a month after he had apparently served Edward IV in another significant way by carrying out the young king's secret marriage to the lovely Eleanor Talbot.[5]

Following Edward's subsequent public announcement of his second secret marriage with Elizabeth Widville, the king had promoted Canon Stillington to the next available English bishopric. That was the see of Bath and Wells, which became vacant when its existing bishop died in January 1464/5. Initially Edward IV's proposal in respect of appointing Stillington as the new Bishop of Bath and Wells had created a problem between the king and Pope Paul II, who had other plans for that appointment. However, the matter had finally been resolved, and on 30 October 1465 the pope issued a bull giving Stillington the bishopric.[6]

Presumably elevating Stillington to the rank of bishop was Edward's way of making sure that he did not raise any problems in respect of the Widville marriage, which had now been formally acknowledged by the king. Subsequently, on 20 June 1467, Bishop Stillington had been appointed by the king to replace Edward IV's cousin, Archbishop George Neville, who had then just been dismissed as the chancellor of England. Except for the months of the Lancastrian Readeption, in 1470–1, Bishop Stillington had then officially retained that post until December 1473. However, it seems that in the autumn of 1472 he had been unwell, and had asked the Bishop of Rochester (John Alcock) to take care of the great seal for him.[7]

After losing the official post of chancellor about a year later, he had not subsequently held any permanent government position. Thus, since 1473 he had basically not resided in London. It is true that Edward IV had imprisoned him there at one point – apparently in connection with the trial and execution of the Duke of Clarence. It seems that Edward – and Elizabeth Widville – then suspected that Stillington must have revealed to Clarence precisely the same evidence as that which, in 1483, the bishop presented to the royal council, in respect of the illegality of their royal marriage. However, the bishop had been granted a formal royal pardon on 20 June 1478.[8] After that he had never again been mentioned in Edward IV's patent rolls – except on one single occasion, in February 1480/1. Then his name had merely figured in the list of owners of some land which was rented by St Mary's Abbey in York.[9]

There is therefore no reason why Bishop Stillington would have been in London in April or May 1483, around the times of Edward IV's death and burial. But of course in mid-May, in the West Country, the bishop would have received one of those summonses to London which were then dispatched in the name of the new king, Edward V, to all those who would be members of the forthcoming parliament. Obviously Bishop Stillington would then have been summoned to attend the opening of that planned parliament as a member of the House of Lords.

Another significant point is the fact that, together with the Bishop of Durham, the Bishop of Bath and Wells traditionally carries out a special role at English coronations. At coronations those two bishops act as escorts to the new sovereign. Presumably, therefore, Stillington also received a summons to Westminster in respect of the planned coronation. His membership of the House of Lords and his required role at the forthcoming coronation would thus have comprised the two reasons why the bishop then made his way back to the capital. Probably he arrived there some time during the first week of June.

What was Stillington's position?

It seems that once his attention had been drawn to the forthcoming coronation – particularly in a situation in which the Widville family had now been removed from power – Bishop Stillington had reflected deeply. The final outcome was that he decided it was now time for him to reveal the truth. It is not clear whether he had ever done so before – though Edward IV and Elizabeth Widville seem to have suspected earlier that he might have discussed the marriage question with the Duke of Clarence. However, when Stillington got to London, he appears to have rapidly approached the new government.

The argument which the bishop presented to them in respect of Edward V's right to the throne must have been based upon the fact that, as he saw things (and he was an expert in canon law), that boy was illegitimate. His evidence in support of his statement was based upon the fact that he himself had secretly married Edward IV to Eleanor Talbot almost three years before Edward had secretly contracted a second secret marriage with Elizabeth Widville. What is more, significantly, Eleanor had still been alive at the time of the king's second secret marriage.[10] In other words, Edward had not then been free to marry Elizabeth. Therefore his contract with her was illegal.

There had already been speculations about the validity of Edward IV's Widville marriage for a number of years. Sir Thomas More's much later account (which contains errors) reports that Edward IV's mother may have questioned the matter in the autumn of 1464, when Edward made his Widville marriage public.[11] Mancini's more or less contemporary account tells us that George, Duke of Clarence had also questioned the validity of his brother's Widville marriage in 1464.[12] As for Elizabeth, she herself was well aware of the fact that not everyone accepted her as the royal consort. Indeed, Mancini says that she had feared 'that her offspring by the king would never come to the throne, unless the duke of Clarence were removed'.[13] Of course, that was what had led to the Duke of Clarence's execution in 1477/8. And as we have seen, apparently it had also led to Bishop Stillington's arrest at about that time.

It therefore appears that people in London must already have been aware that there were questions regarding the validity of Edward IV's marriage to Elizabeth Widville. And it seems that at the beginning of the second week in June 1483, rumours about what the bishop had just announced to the royal council must have been spread very rapidly in the capital city. Evidence in that respect survives in terms of a private letter. On the same day that the council met, Canon Simon Stallworth(e) – a priest in the service of the chancellor, Bishop Russell – found himself writing a letter to Sir William Stonor. In that letter Stallworth(e) mentioned to Sir William the fact that there was now 'gret besyness ageyns the Coronacione'.[14]

Obviously, Bishop Stillington's revelation in June 1483 did not relate in any way to the marriage issue itself. After all, the two key parties in that respect – Edward IV and Eleanor Talbot – were then both dead. As the Church traditionally sees things, a marriage only lasts for a lifetime. Hence, when one partner has died, the surviving partner has always been free to marry again. Moreover, the only people who would have had any right to raise the legal issue of having their marriage formally acknowledged were Edward or Eleanor. But of course, neither of them had ever taken any action in that respect – though the hearing of such marriage dispute cases in the English church courts was by no means unusual in the medieval period.[15]

The issue raised by the bishop in June 1483 did not concern the marriage itself. It was about the planned coronation of Edward V. Apparently Stillington was telling the royal council that preparations for that coronation (in which he had been expected to participate) could not go ahead, because young Edward was not the legitimate heir of his late father. In reality, that lad and all his siblings were merely royal bastards. Based on the evidence of Simon Stallworth(e)'s letter (see above) and other subsequent events, it seems that the bishop probably made this amazing statement to the meeting of the royal council which was held at the Palace of Westminster on Monday 9 June between 10 a.m. and 2 p.m. And the eventual outcome of

Stillington's announcement was precisely the consequence which Elizabeth Widville had feared ever since she herself had discovered that her marriage with Edward IV was questionable in terms of its legality.

In response to Stillington's revelation, Richard, Duke of Gloucester and the royal council did not take it upon themselves to form any decision as to what should be done. Ideally, Stillington's evidence should have been put to a parliament. But as we have seen, no parliament had yet been opened. Moreover, no formal opening of a parliament could immediately be set in motion, because as yet England had no crowned king. It was therefore necessary to find some other way of dealing with the political crisis which had now arisen.

The Duke of Gloucester evidently now felt anxious. Thus, on Tuesday 10 June he wrote to the mayor of York:

> Right trusty and welbelovyd, we grete you well, and as ye love the wele of us, and the wele and sortie of your oun self, we hertely pray you to come unto us in London in all the diligence ye can possible, aftir the sight herof, with as mony as ye can make defensibly arrayed, their to eide and assiste us ayanst the Quiene, hir blode adherents and affinitie, which have entended and daly doith intend, to murder and utterly destroy us and our cousin, the duc of Bukkyngham, and the old royall blode of this realme.[16]

Indeed, it seems that men-at-arms were summoned from the north and from Wales both by the Duke of Gloucester and by the Duke of Buckingham.[17]

Meanwhile, the people who had been summoned to the capital to form the first parliament of the new reign were assembled at the London Guildhall. There they constituted an unofficial parliament, referred to as the 'three estates of the realm'. Stillington presented his case to them, and the three estates formally decided that the children borne to Edward IV by Elizabeth Widville were all illegitimate and unable to claim any rights of inheritance.

Edward V was therefore set aside as 'the bastard king', probably on about Friday 20 June 1483 (see below, chapter 17 and appendix 1). In terms of the succession question which then arose, account also had to be taken of Edward IV's act of attainder against the Duke of Clarence, which had excluded that duke's two surviving children from legal rights to the throne. Based upon those two factors, the three estates of the realm formally offered the throne to Richard, Duke of Gloucester.

It appears that Gloucester then had to be persuaded to accept that offer. Even Shakespeare, in his play, written more than a century after the event, acknowledges that the Duke of Gloucester had *appeared* reluctant to accept the crown. In spite of the fact that Shakespeare employs the false allegation (put out in the reigns of Henry VII and Henry VIII) which claimed that Edward IV had been alleged to be married to the invented figure called 'Elizabeth Lucy', his Duke of Gloucester character is made to say

Alas! Why would you heap this care on me?
I am unfit for state and majesty:
I do beseech you, take it not amiss:
I cannot nor I will not yield to you.[18]

Actually it seems to have taken about five days to persuade the real Duke of Gloucester to accept the crown. Eventually, however, he was persuaded, and on Thursday 26 June he was proclaimed King of England at the Palace of Westminster as Richard III.

The decision which had been made by the three estates of the realm in June 1483 was subsequently ratified by a formal parliament, when one had been opened by the new king, Richard III, in 1484. The relevant act of parliament states very clearly that King Edward IV 'was and stoode marryed and trouth plight to oone Dame Elianor Butteler, doughter of the old Earl of Shrewesbury'. Thus his later 'pretensed marriage' with Elizabeth Grey (Widville) is said to have always been invalid. Of course one result of the decision of the three estates of the realm, later formalised as an act of parliament, was that, according to formal English law, neither of Edward IV's sons was a prince. This remained the case throughout the reign of Richard III – from the summer of 1483 until the summer of 1485.

Interestingly, the two families which were most intimately connected to the legal decision which had now been made both seem to have agreed with it. All living members of the royal house of York apparently did so, accepting Richard III as the legal king. As for Eleanor Talbot's closest surviving relatives, they also backed Richard III. For example, Eleanor's sister, the dowager Duchess of Norfolk, attended his coronation, and she seems to have had a good relationship with the new monarch.[19]

Eleanor Talbot's connection with Richard III's 'Catte'
- *whose father, Sir William Catesby, was her cousin by marriage, and served her in friendly and legal ways.*

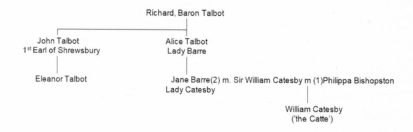

Another close relative of Eleanor Talbot was her cousin by marriage William Catesby – now known as 'the Cat'. He was a man who served Richard so faithfully that Henry VII promptly executed him after the battle of Bosworth. Interestingly, Henry VII also imprisoned Bishop Stillington. And of course he repealed and suppressed the 1484 act of parliament. For more evidence on that point, see chapters 3 and 20.

Even Elizabeth Widville said nothing against Richard III. An intelligent woman, she had long been aware of the fact that her royal marriage – and the future of her royal children – was questionable. Although she spent a significant amount of time in sanctuary at Westminster Abbey, after Richard III had ascended the throne Elizabeth actually wrote to her eldest son, urging him to come back to England and work with King Richard (see above, chapter 10). And significantly, although later she was briefly reinstated as dowager queen by Henry VII, eventually *that* king banished her to another abbey!

12

WHAT DID LORD HASTINGS DO?

After the passing of his friend King Edward IV in April 1483, William, Lord Hastings seems initially to have felt very strongly in favour of the late king's younger brother Richard, Duke of Gloucester, visualising him as the potential lord protector of England during the minority of the new king, Edward V. As we have seen, by about 13 April, Hastings had decided to inform Gloucester at Middleham that his brother the king had died, and to prompt him to begin to put himself forward as the potential lord protector on behalf of his nephew.

Yet, strangely, about two months later, on Friday 13 June, he reportedly found himself arrested and put to death by Gloucester. We will see shortly that the account which is traditionally given in that respect actually seems to be slightly erroneous on one point, and that although Hastings definitely was killed, he was probably not formally executed. Nevertheless, what happened to him on 13 June proves that in the course of the intervening eight weeks something very significant must have happened to part Hastings from the Duke of Gloucester politically. As we have already seen, the most significant event which occurred during that period had been a very recent one, namely the report made to the royal council by Bishop Stillington, probably on Monday 9 June, which questioned Edward V's right to the throne (and which gave rise to the important subsequent decisions taken on the basis of that information).

Born in about 1430, William, Lord Hastings became the brother-in-law of Richard Neville, Earl of Warwick, who had acted as guardian of the young Richard, Duke of Gloucester during his youth. Thus, while he had only been about a decade older than King Edward IV, Lord Hastings was, in effect, roughly a generation older than the Duke of Gloucester. Nevertheless, those two men must have known each other quite well. Indeed, in 1470–1 they had found themselves in close proximity to one another for about five months, when Lord Hastings had accompanied Edward IV and his brother Gloucester into exile in the Low Countries.

Hastings had been employed in various ways in respect of the Yorkist dynasty. In 1461 he had been appointed chamberlain of the royal household. Ten years later, when Edward IV resumed his kingship after the brief Lancastrian Readeption, Hastings was appointed lieutenant of Calais. Significantly, in that post he had replaced Anthony Widville. Thus the Calais appointment seems to have led to friction between Hastings and the Widvilles during the 1470s. His friction with Lord Rivers himself was obviously in respect of the Calais post. As for Elizabeth Widville, Hastings seems to have found himself at odds with her over the inheritance of certain lands.

Curiously, Elizabeth's eldest son, Thomas Grey, Marquess of Dorset was in a way related to Lord Hastings by marriage. Dorset's wife, Cecily Bonville, was Lord Hastings' stepdaughter, because Hastings had become her mother's second husband. Nevertheless, a very strong friction also emerged between Hastings and Dorset. In their case that friction was at a highly personal level, because each of the two men had become involved in a sexual relationship with a London woman called Elizabeth Lambert.

The woman in question is another splendid example of mythology in respect of fifteenth-century history as generally recounted. She is usually known by her first husband's surname, as 'Mistress Shore', in spite of the fact that actually her marriage with William Shore had been annulled by the Church. But unfortunately she has also long been referred to as '*Jane* Shore'. That name was only invented for her in the seventeenth century, because by then her real first name had been forgotten. Also, ironically, since the publication of Thomas More's account in the sixteenth century, it has popularly been assumed that, as More himself asserted, 'Mistress Shore' had been the mistress of King Edward IV. However, in reality not one single shred of contemporary evidence exists in support of that assertion.[1]

In April 1483, following the death of Edward IV, Hastings apparently spoke out strongly against the idea of Lord Rivers putting himself at the head of a large force to escort the new king from Ludlow to London. It seems that Hastings also argued for a formal minority in respect of the new young king, during which the boy's paternal uncle the Duke of Gloucester should act as protector of the realm. His proposal in that respect was based upon the thirteenth- and fourteenth-century English precedents in respect of the handling of government during the reigns of kings who were minors.

Although Gloucester and Hastings had apparently been on good terms with one another during the reign of Edward IV, there is no contemporary suggestion that in April 1483 they had actually formed a 'faction' opposed to the queen's family. Hastings had simply informed Gloucester of what had happened – and was happening – in the capital. Unlike the Duke of Buckingham, however, Hastings did not travel north in person to meet up with Gloucester.

Of course he must have met Gloucester when that royal duke arrived in London, together with the young King Edward V. And Hastings apparently remained on good terms with Gloucester throughout May and the first week of June – though, on a personal level, Hastings probably felt less close to the protector than he had been to the late King Edward IV. Also, it appears that although Lord Hastings was no friend of the Widville family, and definitely did not wish to see them take control of the country after the death of his friend King Edward IV, he was entirely happy for Edward V to be king of England, as long as that young lad's mother and her family were firmly kept in the background politically.

Thus, his response to the announcement made to the royal council by Bishop Stillington on 9 June must inevitably have been hostile. Since his personal wish was for the coronation of Edward V to go ahead, he would have wanted Stillington to be silenced, and for nothing to be done in respect of the information which that bishop had now formally put forward. Lord Hastings would not have approved of presenting the evidence in question to the three estates of the realm. And although, as a lord, he himself must have attended that meeting of the three estates at the London Guildhall, he would have felt very opposed to the decision that was arrived at on that occasion.

Presumably, based upon the discussion which must have taken place at the meeting of the three estates, Hastings also became aware of the fact that he was not alone in his opinion. Certain other lords must also have revealed the fact that they were disturbed by – and opposed to – the deposition of Edward V on grounds of his illegitimacy. The other opponents of the decision reached by the majority of the three estates included Archbishop Thomas Rotherham of York – who previously, in April, had been working with Elizabeth Widville – and also Bishop John Morton of Ely.

The account written in December 1483 by Domenico Mancini reveals that, following the Guildhall meeting of the three estates, Hastings, Rotherham and Morton were known to have met together in secret in one another's houses.[2] Since all three of them objected to the removal of Edward V from the throne, presumably their secret meetings had been for the planning of a campaign in the young king's defence. They must now have felt that they needed to oppose the lord protector and the government which he was leading.

As for the Duke of Gloucester, he must have been well aware of the fact that, while the majority of the three estates had come to the decision that the young King Edward V should be dethroned because he was illegitimate, some significant people were opposed to that decision. As a result, the lords who formed the royal council were now effectively split into two parties. The majority of them were in favour of the new decision. However, some of them were opposed to it. Because of that situation, Gloucester apparently decided to arrange for the two opposing factions to meet separately.

Two council meetings were therefore planned to be held simultaneously. One meeting took place at the Palace of Westminster. The other meeting was at the Tower of London.[3] These split council meetings in two separate venues segregated the minority of peers, who favoured retaining Edward V as king, from the majority of lords, who had accepted the evidence in respect of Edward IV's Talbot marriage, and who therefore believed that Edward V was illegitimate and had to be removed from the throne.

An account apparently penned by a Londoner in the 1480s reports that 'in the mene tyme ther was dyvers imagenyd the deyth of the Duke of Gloceter, and hit was asspiyd and the Lord Hastinges was takyn in the Towur and byhedyd forthwith, the xiij day of June Anno 1483.'[4] Although the writer of this statement cannot actually have been present at the Tower council meeting which ultimately resulted in the death of Lord Hastings, his account is interesting because it suggests that, at that Tower of London council meeting, Hastings must have been behaving with very obvious hostility. On the other hand, the continuator of the Crowland Chronicles simply stated that 'on 13 June, the sixth day of the week [Friday], when he came to the Council in the Tower, on the authority of the protector, Lord Hastings was beheaded.'[5]

Lord Hastings: a contemporary fifteenth-century caricature, depicting him as a pig.

Both of the above accounts state that Hastings was beheaded, and that has generally been interpreted as meaning that he was subjected to a formal execution. However, Mancini's account clearly describes the death of Hastings not as a formal execution but as a rapid killing by guards who were defending the Duke of Gloucester. His statement reads,

The protector cried out that a plot had been prepared against him, and they had come with concealed weapons, so that they could make the first attack. Then soldiers who had been stationed there by the lord, and the Duke of Buckingham, came running, and beheaded Hastings by sword under the name of treason. The others they arrested, whose lives were spared out of respect for religion and holy orders.[6]

Thus it seems that in actual fact Hastings and his allies had come to the council meeting with concealed weapons, and that they then openly displayed their hostility. Presumably Lord Hastings had then attacked the Duke of Gloucester, whose guards, defending Gloucester, cut off the head of Hastings in that very same room where the meeting was being held.

Mancini also states that at the same time Archbishop Rotherham and Bishop Morton were arrested. However, they were not killed. They were simply sent to prison in Welsh castles. It is interesting to note that, as a religious man, Gloucester's response seems to have been comparatively mild in respect of the two bishops. Actually, he would perhaps have found himself in a far better long-term situation had Morton, at least, been put to death together with his co-plotter Lord Hastings!

Morton's survival proved to be the cause of much later harm for Gloucester. As we shall see shortly, Morton subsequently conspired with the Duke of Buckingham (in whose custody he had been placed in Wales), thus leading Buckingham into rebellion later in 1483. Morton also worked with the self-styled 'Earl of Richmond', who seized the throne in 1485 as King Henry VII. And probably after the accession of Henry VII Morton was a key figure behind the political rewriting of history that then took place. For example, significantly, the young Thomas More found himself brought up, educated and informed in respect of the history of King Richard III by the then Cardinal Archbishop Morton. However, as Mancini's report shows, Richard, Duke of Gloucester was a man with strong respect for those who served in religious orders.

The situation in England had now become more disturbed politically. Local government records date the official end of the reign of King Edward V to Friday 20 June 1483 (see below, chapter 17). It was two days later, on Sunday 22 June, that Friar Ralph Shaa [Shaw], half-brother of Edmund Shaa, Lord Mayor of London, was asked to preach a sermon at Paul's Cross against 'bastard slips'. Friar Ralph took his basic text from chapter 4, verse 3 of the Book of Wisdom: '*Spuria vitulamina non dabunt radices altas, nec stabile firmamentum collocabunt.*' ['Bastard slips shall not strike deep root, nor take firm hold.'] Apparently all of this was being done as a consequence of the decision reached by the meeting of the three estates of the realm – and the problem which that had raised in terms of the future English regime.

However, it was only on Thursday 26 June, at his mother's London home (Baynard's Castle) that a formal petition was finally presented to the Duke of Gloucester, inviting him to assume the crown.[7] Subsequently the reign of Richard III was officially recorded as having commenced on that date.[8] The whole political situation was now completely unprecedented. Thus reappointments were rapidly made in the name of King Richard III of all those judges who had previously been appointed to the king's bench on 21 April 1483, in the name of 'King Edward V'.[9] That was followed by a number of other re-enactments of grants and appointments which previously had been made in the name of the 'bastard king'.

Yet, curiously, in spite of the very strange political situation in which the country now found itself, on Monday 30 June a private letter was written from London to Sir Robert Plumpton (who lived in Yorkshire).[10] The letter in question, which was written by Sir Robert's relative and servant Edward Plumpton, contained not one single reference to what had occurred politically in the capital city. Thus Edward Plumpton made no mention of the 'bastard king', of the revelation of Edward IV's bigamous Widville marriage, or of the offering of the crown to the Duke of Gloucester (now King Richard III). Evidently for the Plumptons – and possibly for most other families – personal matters seemed much more important than politics!

13

WHAT DOES THE CELY
NOTE MEAN?

Another private document, which has received a lot of attention from historians in respect of the meaning which they have alleged that it has, is an undated note.[1] On the evidence of its handwriting it is said to have been written by George Cely. George's family were middle-class Londoners. Some of their family papers (dating from 1472 to 1488) were subsequently used as evidence during a family dispute. As a result they are now preserved as part of The National Archives. The Cely note includes some strange symbols, and it is not clear what they might mean, though previous writers have all ignored that point, and have not referred to the inclusion of the symbols in question.

⊕   ♇

Ther ys grett Romber in the Reme/ the scottys has done grett

4

yn ynglond/ schamberlayne ys dessesset in trobell the chavnse

+   ß

ler ys dyssprowett and nott content/ the boshop of Ely is dede

++

yff the Kyng god ssaffe his lyffe were dessett/ the dewke of Glo

III

sett[er] wher in any parell/ yffe my lorde prynsse, wher God

ooo

defend, wher trobellett/ yf my lord of northehombyrlond

II

wher dede or grettly trobellytt/ yf my lorde haward wher

o

slayne

De movnsewr Sent Jonys/

Modernised slightly, the text of the note would read as follows:

> There is great rumour in the realm. The Scots has done great [*sic*] in England. Chamberlain is deceased in trouble. The chancellor is disproved [? *dyssprowett*] and not content. The bishop of Ely is dead.
>
> If the King, God save his life, were deceased, the Duke of Gloucester were in any peril, if my Lord Prince wh[ich] God defend were troubled, if my lord of Northumberland were dead or greatly troubled, if my lord Howard were slain.
>
> De Monsieur Saint John

The first part of the note appears to contain points which are presented as facts. As for the second part, that comprises what are clearly hypotheses and rumours. However, in reality the opening sentence makes it very clear that the whole note is actually 'rumour'. As for the initial statements which are presented as facts, in reality they are not compatible with one another in terms of dating. As a result, dates which have been proposed for the Cely note have simply been selected by focussing upon one of the so-called facts mentioned in the note, and ignoring all the others.

Working in that way, some past historians suggested that the undated note written by George Cely would probably have been written in August 1478. Their suggestion in that respect was based upon the fact that the note refers to the death of an unnamed Bishop of Ely. Bishop William Grey of that diocese is known to have died on 4 August 1478. In reality, however, it appears improbable that the Cely note could have been written quite as early as that, because it is penned on the reverse of another document which appears to date from the end of 1481 or the beginning of 1482.

More recently, other historians have suggested that the note in question must have been written between 13 and 26 June 1483. That claim was based on the mention in the note of the fact that 'Chamberlain is deceased in trouble'. While the note itself offers no name for the 'chamberlain' in question, the historians have assumed that the person referred to must have been Lord Hastings, who was chamberlain from 1461 to 1483.[2] As we have seen, Hastings was killed on 13 June 1483. However, he had also been in conflict earlier, with Elizabeth Widville, and because the Cely note contains 'rumours' it may not be referring to his actual demise.

One result of that new proposed date for the Cely note, of mid-late June 1483, was the hypothesis that when he wrote 'if the King, God save his life, were deceased', George Cely was expressing his fears in respect of the life of the young King Edward V. In reality, however, it remains clear that no precise date can be assigned to the note, so the king referred to in it could be Edward IV. But of course, it could not be Richard III, because the note refers clearly to 'the Duke of Gloucester'. Since it does not employ for him his later title of 'King Richard III' that means that it must have been written prior to 26 June 1483.

Curiously, no one has ever focussed upon the 'Chancellor' statement. That presumably refers to Archbishop Thomas Rotherham, who was dismissed from the chancellorship in May 1483. If the note does refer to Rotherham as chancellor that would mean that it must have been written prior to his dismissal on 13 May.

It also refers to 'my Lord Prince'. Those historians who assume that the king who is referred to in the note must have been Edward V, have therefore assumed that 'Lord Prince' means Richard of Shrewsbury, Duke of York. However, it is clear from the wording of the will drafted by Edward IV in 1475 (see above, chapters 4 and 5) that young Richard of Shrewsbury was not normally referred to as a 'Lord Prince'. Instead he was consistently referred to using his *ducal* title. The only person who definitely was referred to as a 'prince' was the young Prince of Wales (Edward V). And if the 'Lord Prince' mentioned in George Cely's note is the Prince of Wales (the future Edward V), then the obvious conclusion is that the king whose possible demise is mentioned in the note must have been Edward IV.

That would mean that the note must have been written earlier than the June 1483 date which has been put forward by some historians. If the king to whom it refers was Edward IV, the note must have been written before the public proclamation of his death, in April 1483. In that context the fact that the death of the king is not mentioned in the note as something which has actually taken place, but only as a possible future event, would be very appropriate. Likewise, if the 'king' of the note was Edward IV, then 'my Lord Prince' would refer to the Prince of Wales (the future Edward V), who was then definitely still living.

Armstrong tried to use the questionable evidence of the Cely note to conclude that Edward V's younger brother, Richard of Shrewsbury, might well have been dead by his proposed date for the writing of the note, namely 28 June 1483. He based his argument in that respect upon the fact that John, Lord Howard then found himself created Duke of Norfolk – a title previously held by Richard of Shrewsbury. However, the real evidence in respect of the grant to John Howard of that ducal title will be examined in detail shortly (see below, chapter 19). Meanwhile the only possible conclusion in respect of the Cely note is that no precise date can be assigned to it. However, it may have been written in about March 1482/3. As for its strange contents, that material seems to make very little sense. Therefore, in reality, the Cely note has very little value as historical evidence.

14

WOULD RICHARD III HAVE HAD THE BOYS KILLED?

Richard III (redrawn from the
Beauchamp Pageant).

As we have seen, on the afternoon of Sunday 4 May, Richard, Duke of
Gloucester, together with his cousin the Duke of Buckingham and his
nephew King Edward V, had arrived in London. Initially the young king
was lodged at the the Bishop of London's palace.[1] But apparently the
Duke of Gloucester did not stay with him there. Instead he seems to have
joined his mother at her official London residence, Baynard's Castle. That
residence was beside the river Thames. Thus it would have been just a

couple of minutes' walk to the south of the Bishop's Palace, which stood next to St Paul's Cathedral.

Evidence in support of Baynard's Castle as the chosen accommodation used by the Duke of Gloucester is the fact that, three days later, on Wednesday 7 May,

> the executors of Edward IV assembled at Baynard's Castle, the London house of Cecily, duchess of York, mother of the late king, and the archbishop [of Canterbury] then and there took over all Edward IV's seals, Great, Privy and Signet.[2]

Based on his published itinerary it seems that subsequently the Duke of Gloucester regularly joined the young king at the Tower of London to carry out his role as lord protector of the realm, and to do government work.[3] However, once again there is no evidence to prove that Gloucester was *residing* at the Tower with young Edward. It is possible that he may have been. But it is also possible that he continued to stay at his mother's abode. Certainly subsequent evidence reveals that he was at Baynard's Castle on other specific dates.

As we have seen, naturally, until the first week of June 1483, preparations continued to be made for the coronation of the son of Edward IV and Elizabeth Widville. However, it seems that on Monday 9 June Bishop Stillington of Bath and Wells had told the royal council that, in his view, Edward V could not be crowned because the boy was illegitimate. The Duke of Gloucester suddenly then found himself in a totally unexpected situation, which could well have felt rather disturbing for him. Previously it had seemed that everything had been sorted out. But now there were once again two conflicting parties in London. Hitherto, in April, the two conflicting parties had been the pro- and anti-Widvilles. Now they were those who accepted that Edward V was a bastard, and those who wished to dismiss or ignore the evidence in that respect.

Although members of the intended first parliament of Edward V had been summoned to the capital, there was, as yet, no crowned king available to open a formal parliament. However, as we have seen, in an attempt to resolve the new problem in a legal way, Gloucester, in his capacity as lord protector, had Bishop Stillington put his evidence to the closest available thing to a parliament, namely a meeting of the three estates of the realm, which was held at the London Guildhall. Then on Friday 13 June Gloucester had found himself forced into physical conflict with Lord Hastings and two other leading members of the party who opposed the decision which had been reached by the three estates. Hastings was killed in that conflict, and the two bishops were arrested. By mid-June the Duke of Gloucester felt himself obliged to request the support of northern troops.

A week later, on Sunday 22 June, based on the decision of the three estates, the Friar Ralph Shaa's sermons were given out at Paul's Cross by the mayor's half-brother. The sermons raised publicly the issue of the bastardy of Edward V and his siblings. They also put forward what the Bible said should be done in respect of bastardy.[4]

Later, in the reign of Henry VII, Vergil put forward a claim that the sermons had chiefly focussed on the bastardy myth in respect of *Edward IV.*[5] In reality, however, that was simply part of the new dynasty's political rewriting of history. There is actually no contemporary evidence to indicate that the sermon ever mentioned that myth. The key point in respect of lack of evidence is the fact that, while the government of Richard III subsequently regularly employed the term 'bastard king' to describe Edward V (see below, chapter 17), that term was never employed in respect of Edward IV. Richard III referred to Edward IV as 'oure derrest Brothere late king'.[6] Thus it seems that Edward IV was consistently acknowledged as a true king of England by Richard III's regime.[7]

Once again, the *real* issues raised by the preaching at Paul's Cross were the illegality of Edward IV's marriage to Elizabeth Widville, and the resultant bastardy of that couple's children – including Edward V. That action was, in a way, roughly the equivalent of modern publication of news in a paper, or the telling of the story on the radio or television or online, in that it brought the news to the wider attention of the residents of the capital.

The situation as it now stood was that

No one survived of the royal lineage save Richard, duke of Gloucester, who by law deserves the crown, and who, by his ability, can sustain its obligations. His previous career and blameless morals offered the surest pledge of a good government. Even though he refused such a burden, he might change his mind if asked to do so by the peers. On learning this, warned by the example of Hastings, and considering the agreement between the two dukes [Gloucester and Buckingham] – whose power it was hard and dangerous to resist because of their numerous soldiers – the lords thought about their own safety. They saw themselves surrounded, and in the hands of the dukes, so they resolved to declare Richard as king, and they begged him to take on the burden of that office. The next day [25 June 1483] at the house of Richard's mother (whither he had purposely gone, rather than to the Tower, where the king was kept) all the lords assembled. There, oaths of fidelity were taken and everything necessary was done.[8]

As was seen in the previous chapter, it had been ten days earlier, on Sunday 15 June, that the Duke of Gloucester had written to the mayor of York, requesting help. Presumably Buckingham's request for help from Wales had gone out at about the same time. But according to Mancini's account the two dukes are reported to have had 'numerous soldiers' just nine days later, on Tuesday 24 June. Would that have been feasible?

In an earlier study the present writer cited the fact that, two years later, on about 12 August 1485, John Howard, Duke of Norfolk, sent a letter to John Paston III, summoning him to the duke's array at Bury St Edmunds. That was part of Norfolk's preparations for the coming conflict (the battle of Bosworth – 22 August 1485).[9] Unfortunately, in that instance the duke's letter itself was not dated, though it does mention the Feast of the Assumption of the Blessed Virgin (15 August).[10] However, it sounds as though at least ten days were required on that occasion to assemble an army in East Anglia and then transport it to meet the king in Leicester. Yet the distances involved at that point would have been a good deal less than those involved in June 1483 for assembling soldiers in Yorkshire and then sending them to the Duke of Gloucester in London.

At all events, Richard, Duke of Gloucester now suddenly and unexpectedly found himself becoming King Richard III. We must note that there is not a shred of evidence to show that he had ever planned for that outcome, or desired it. Nevertheless, eventually he was apparently persuaded to accept the proposal that he should now take on the crown of England.

Even if he had stayed with young Edward and his brother at the King's Lodgings in the Tower on some occasions, it seems that he was now back at his mother's London castle. And in fact he may actually have been residing there ever since his arrival in London. As we have seen, 'on 25 June 1483 the duke of Buckingham accompanied by lords, knights and gentlemen together with the mayor, aldermen, and the chief commoners of the city waited on the Protector at Baynard's Castle, house of Cecily, duchess of York, to present a petition begging the Protector to assume the crown.'[11] It was also at Baynard's Castle that, two days later, on Friday 27 June 1483, the new sovereign appointed John, Bishop of Lincoln as his chancellor.[12] Thereafter Baynard's Castle seems to have remained Richard's main base and headquarters until the start of July.[13] This suggests that, in the difficult situation in which he had found himself, he had the support of his mother, and that ultimately Cecily Neville must have firmly backed her youngest son's accession to the throne. It also suggests that he himself now felt uncomfortable and embarrassed about being with the former 'King Edward V'.

Since he had the support of his mother, other members of his family and the three estates of the realm, and given that it had been formally decided that all the children of Edward IV and Elizabeth Widville were illegitimate and possessed no claim to the throne of England, the accession right of the Duke of Gloucester as King Richard III was beyond debate. Moreover, although a few nobles had questioned the deposition of Edward V, and had attempted to seize power in a council meeting at the Tower of London on 13 June, they seem to have acted violently, and had therefore been firmly dealt with by Richard's guards. Lord Hastings had been killed, and Archbishop Rotherham and Bishop Morton had been arrested. Thus when he formally accepted the English crown two weeks later, Richard III apparently had no one working against him. Even Elizabeth Widville and her family appeared obedient, in spite of the fact that she had now been deprived of the title of queen.

As we have seen (chapter 10), Richard subsequently continued negotiating with Elizabeth Widville in respect of her daughters by Edward IV, in order to get them out of sanctuary and arrange suitable marriages for them. It is therefore obvious that he felt no fear of, or threat from, those girls. After all, they were merely royal bastards.

Moreover, it indicates strongly that, on a purely personal level, he did care about them and their future.

There was also absolutely no reason why Richard should have felt any fear of, or threat from, the girls' brothers, Elizabeth Widville's two sons by Edward IV. They too had been officially declared to be bastards, and deprived of any claim to the crown of England. Moreover, they were already in Richard III's hands, so no one else then had control of them. In other words there was no logical reason why Richard should have feared his nephews.

And since he cared about their sisters and their future life, rationally he would surely have felt the same in respect of the boys. His conduct in respect of another nephew, Edward, Earl of Warwick, son of the Duke of Clarence, who had been excluded from his right to the throne by Edward IV, shows that Richard III trusted that nephew and wanted to prepare and train him for a future role as a key supporter of the Yorkist dynasty. Similarly, he prepared for his own recognised illegitimate son in a similar way. Therefore, why has it generally been considered likely that he would have decided to have the two sons of Edward IV put to death?

Moreover there is one other significant *lack* of evidence which, by its absence, strongly supports the hypothesis that Richard cannot have had the lads killed. As we shall see in chapter 23, many years later, when Henry VII felt himself and his dynasty potentially threatened by the 'princes' (who by that time had theoretically been restored to that legitimate royal status), it was *his* government which put out the story that they had both been killed. The aim behind that action was then to ensure that the two boys were generally believed to be dead. And obviously the motivation must have been the fact that both Henry VII and his government knew well that not everyone believed the boys to be dead.

The problem was that Henry VII had then recently had the stressful experience of dealing with 'Richard of England'/'Perkin Warbeck' – the youth who had claimed to be the younger of the two sons of Edward IV and Elizabeth Widville, and who had been widely accepted as such, both in foreign courts and in Yorkist circles in England. Obviously if Henry VII and his government could now succeed in persuading the general public that the sons of Edward IV had been killed in 1483, in future a claim like the one put forward by 'Richard of England' could never be repeated.

In other words, *publicising* the story of the death of the two boys was the obvious way of making sure that the two sons of Edward IV could never act as (or be used as) a threat to the reigning monarch. Therefore if Richard III had also feared that his nephews might act as (or be used as) a threat to him in his new post as king, undermining the security of his tenure of the English throne, obviously *his* logical response would have been to do precisely what Henry VII did later, and announce to the general public that both the boys were dead. Curiously, however, Richard III never did that. Even Polydore Vergil, writing for Henry VII, only asserted that Richard had *allowed* the story that his nephews were dead 'to go abrode'.[14] He does not claim that Richard himself ever issued a formal statement in respect of such a story.

15

DID 'EDWARD V' ATTEND RICHARD III'S CORONATION?

For more than two centuries now, there has been discussion and argument in respect of evidence which shows that items of clothing and other accoutrements were ordered in 1483 for the late Edward IV's elder son and namesake. Writing in 1768, Horace Walpole was the first historian to draw attention to this evidence, and he suggested that 'though Richard's son did not walk at his father's coronation, Edward the Fifth probably did'. He then quotes part of what he describes as the amazing entry in the coronation roll:

> To Lord Edward, son of late king Edward the Fourth, for his apparel and array, that is to say, a short gowne, made of two yards and three quarters of crymsy clothe of gold, lyned with two yards ¾ of blac velvet; a long gowne, made of vi yards D of crymsyn cloth of gold, lynned with six yards of grene damask; a shorte gowne, made of two yards ¾ of purpell velvett, lyned with two yards ¾ of green damask; a doublett and a stomacher made of two yards of blac satyn &c.[1]

The complete list of items ordered for young Edward is actually a good deal longer than the few lines which Walpole quoted.[2] However, he then says, 'Let no body tell me that these robes, this magnificence, these trappings for a cavalcade, were for the use of a prisoner.' Also, 'the absence from the accounts of any details concerning robes for the young Duke of York further implied to Walpole that the Duke was not in Richard's custody at the time of the coronation.'[3]

Horace Walpole.

Three-quarters of a century later, Caroline Halsted re-quoted the same text.[4] She also added additional information to the effect that the wardrobe account which contained the original entry was written on vellum, and covered the period from the death of Edward IV until February 1483/4, 'including the time of the intended coronation of Edward V, and the actual coronation of Richard III'. She reported that the vellum documents in question were bound up together with coronation rolls relating to Henry VII and Henry VIII, but said that those later documents were written, not on vellum, but on paper.

However, Halsted then proceeded to disagree with Walpole's earlier conclusion to the effect that the robes mentioned must have been ordered for the deposed Edward V to wear at the coronation of his uncle, King Richard III. Instead, Halsted argued that the robes must have been commissioned for Edward V to wear at his own coronation, at the time when that was still being planned. And as she herself acknowledged, Halsted's argument in that respect was not her own original conclusion, because it had actually first been put forward earlier, in 1770, by Revd Dr Milles.[5]

So who got things right? Should we go with Horace Walpole, or must we accept the interpretation of Milles and Halsted? It is impossible to produce a completely solid conclusion in respect of this debate. Presumably during the weeks of May 1483, suitable garments and other accoutrements definitely would have been ordered for

Edward V as part of the ongoing preparation for his own coronation at that stage. However, doubtless any robes ordered for him then would never have been assigned in the wardrobe accounts to 'Lord Edward, son of late king Edward the Fourth'. They would have been assigned to 'King Edward V'.

It must therefore be considered significant that the wording in the documents we have does not employ young Edward's royal title. Instead, the accounts really do refer to the boy as 'Lord Edward, son of late king Edward the Fourth'. Moreover, although they refer to him as a lord, these wardrobe accounts do not assign to young Edward the title of prince. That strongly suggests that the written evidence must date from June or July 1483, after the decision had been made that the children of Edward IV and Elizabeth Widville were bastards. Further interesting evidence in respect of how reference was made to Edward V after Richard III had become king will be presented later (see below, chapter 17).

Of course, the available evidence does not absolutely prove that young Edward actually did attend the coronation of his uncle, King Richard III. Nevertheless, that proposal, first put forward in the eighteenth century by Horace Walpole, does seem to be one possible explanation for the documentation in its surviving form.

It is also the case that, as Walpole noted, in the surviving accounts, no evidence exists to indicate that robes had also been ordered for Edward's younger brother, Richard of Shrewsbury. However, Walpole's deduction in respect of that point is simply one hypothesis. For example, it could equally well be the case that accounts in respect of the young Duke of York simply have not survived. Also, if the Edward accounts had related to his *own* planned coronation, there would have been no way in which robes would not also have been commissioned for his younger brother in respect of that event. Obviously, in May 1483, it was planned that Richard should attend the coronation of Edward V. That would have been one of the reasons why attempts were made to persuade his mother to send the boy out of the Westminster sanctuary.

If the robes commissioned for Edward were indeed for him to wear to the coronation of Richard III there are two possible reasons for the absence of accounts in respect of Richard of Shrewsbury. The first hypothesis would be that, as Walpole presumed, for some reason

Richard of Shrewsbury was not attending his uncle's coronation. However, once again, a second hypothesis would simply argue that Richard of Shrewsbury may also have been attending Richard III's coronation, but that for some reason the accounts in respect of his robes simply have not survived.

16

WHAT WAS THE DUKE OF BUCKINGHAM UP TO?

About two years younger than Richard, Duke of Gloucester (later Richard III), Henry Stafford, Duke of Buckingham was his third cousin once removed in terms of one line of their joint legitimate royal descent from King Edward III.

The closest legitimate royal relationship between Richard III and Henry, Duke of Buckingham

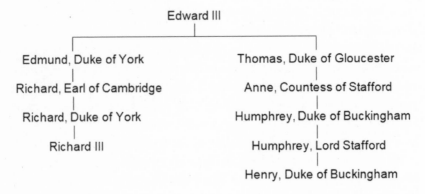

However, the two dukes were much more closely related in respect of their shared Neville ancestry (which also included descent from Edward III, but this time via the initially illegitimate Beauforts). In that line they were first cousins once removed.

Family Connections of Henry Stafford, Duke of Buckingham
first cousin once removed of Richard III and of Eleanor Talbot

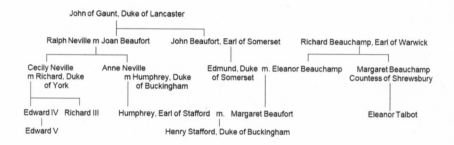

It is also interesting to note that, through his mother, Henry was the first cousin once removed of Eleanor Talbot, who was formally acknowledged in the summer of 1483 to have been Edward IV's legal consort.

Orphaned young Henry had been brought up as a royal ward. According to William Worcester, at the age of eleven, in February 1465/6, 'the king made Henry, duke of Buckingham, marry a sister of queen Elizabeth'.[1] Sadly William Worcester is not always to be trusted in the context of dates. In this instance the year he suggests must be incorrect, though the month may well be right. In reality, young Henry was married to Catherine Widville before Elizabeth's coronation, which took place in May 1465. So probably the wedding was celebrated a year earlier than Worcester suggests, in February 1464/5. Thus the young duke found himself attached to Elizabeth's younger sister, Catherine. He and his brother also became members of Elizabeth Widville's household in August 1465.[2] Nevertheless, as we have seen, Henry later despised the Widville family.

Rawcliffe argues that 'there is certainly no reason to believe that his subsequent hostility to the Wydevilles sprang from a sense of bitterness at being forced to marry beneath him ... He had a more genuine cause for complaint in his permanent exclusion from power and the business of government: his duties at court were purely ceremonial.'[3] One example of this was his appointment to act as High Steward of England in respect of the trial and execution of George, Duke of Clarence when Clarence's extermination was being instigated by Elizabeth Widville.

A report exists which offers an account of how, in 1483, the Duke of Buckingham sent to his cousin the Duke of Gloucester news of the death of the latter's elder brother King Edward IV. The original chronicle in question had been written by John Hardyng, a Northumbrian who had basically been pro-Lancastrian in political terms. However, Hardyng had died in 1465. It was during the reign of Henry VIII that Richard Grafton added that part of the text which covers later years. Grafton's addition includes the report of Buckingham's contact with the Duke of Gloucester. Obviously Grafton's text is not contemporary in respect of 1483. It claims that

> Henry the duke of Buckingham was the fyrste y^t sent to hym after his brothers deathe a trusty servaunt of his called Persall [= ?Persivall], to the cytee of Yorke, where the duke of Gloucetre kepte the kyng his brothers funeralles. This Persall came to Iohn Ward, a secret chaumberer to the duke of Gloucetre, desiryng that he in close and couert manier might speake with the duke his maistre: wherupõ in the deed of the nyght the duke sent for Persall, (all other beyng aduoyded,) whiche shewed to the duke of Gloucetre that the duke of Buckingham his maister in this newe worlde would take suche parte as he woulde, & woulde farther wayte vpon hym with a M. good fellowes yf need were.[4]

However, it sounds as though this sixteenth-century account is mistaken when it assumes that Gloucester *first* received news of the king's death from Buckingham. Since Buckingham's messenger only spoke to Gloucester when the latter had already gone from Middleham to the city of York – where he was already commemorating his brother's demise when Persall [= ?Persivall] arrived – presumably he must first have heard the news from Lord Hastings.

Although Rawcliffe's account offers significant information about the Duke of Buckingham in some respects, unfortunately, she chose to accept the traditional view of Richard, Duke of Gloucester (Richard III), quoting Thomas More as one of her sources. Like many other historians, she therefore speaks of Gloucester and Buckingham as having staged a *coup* in April 1483.[5] As we have seen, there is no true evidence for the use of that word. On the contrary, the two royal dukes found themselves trying to *prevent* a coup which was attempted by the Widvilles.

However, initially there appears to have been no problem between Gloucester and Earl Rivers, when the two of them met at Northampton. It was only once Buckingham also arrived there that the situation seems rapidly to have changed. Probably therefore it was Buckingham's animosity in respect of the Widville family which led to the arrest of Rivers and Sir Richard Grey on the following morning. Presumably overnight Buckingham had persuaded his cousin Gloucester not to trust them.

Once he had been officially accorded the role of protector, Gloucester seems to have felt that Buckingham had assisted him in coping with the genuine attempted coup of April 1483 – the one which had been undertaken by the Widvilles. On Thursday 15 May Gloucester appears to have acknowledged what he then saw as part of his debt to his cousin, the Duke of Buckingham, by giving him 'two vast grants of concentrated authority and patronage'.[6] On Friday 16 May there were further grants to the Duke of Buckingham.[7] Further (but undated) grants to Buckingham were issued about 20 or 21 May.[8] Yet more grants were made in his favour on Monday 26 May.[9]

The arrival of Bishop Robert Stillington, and his reporting to the royal council that Edward IV's true wife had been the Duke of Buckingham's cousin Eleanor Talbot, must have inspired Henry with the idea that his grateful relative the Duke of Gloucester – who was now being very kind to him and his ambitions – should become England's king. Thus it appears that he strenuously promoted the case for that solution. As we have seen, one of the results was the death of Lord Hastings, who felt strongly opposed to the removal of Edward V from the throne. Another outcome was the fact that Buckingham found himself given custody of Bishop John Morton of Ely. Subsequently that significantly seems to have altered Buckingham's political stance. Initially, however, before Bishop Morton began persuading him in a different direction, Henry also seems to have led the formal urging of Gloucester to accept the crown. In that respect he was finally successful, and the result was King Richard III's coronation.

King Richard III appointed Buckingham Chief Justice and Chamberlain of North and South Wales for life. He was also granted the Constableship, Stewardship and Receiver generalship of all the Crown lands in Wales.

Nor was this a matter of empty titles. Orders were sent out enabling him to take possession of castles and armaments throughout Wales. ... [Also] he was empowered to raise armed levies and keep back the King's revenues in Dorset, Somerset and the Marcher counties. These overwhelming marks of royal favour make it all the harder to understand Buckingham's sudden decision to join forces with his aunt [*sic*], Lady Margaret Beaufort, and a group of disgruntled Yorkists in a rebellion against the King.[10]

Actually, of course, Lady Margaret Beaufort was not the Duke of Buckingham's *aunt* – though, through his mother (who was also her namesake), he was indeed related to her.

Relationship of Henry Stafford, Duke of Buckingham and Margaret Beaufort, Countess of Richmond
first cousins once removed

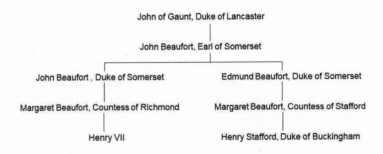

The other significant factor which now led Buckingham in a new political direction was probably his custodianship of Bishop John Morton. Unsurprisingly, a result of taking on that custodianship was that he then found himself in close contact with Morton. As a result it seems that, by September 1483, for some reason Buckingham had been persuaded to change his political position completely and to become opposed to his cousin King Richard III.

Meanwhile, Richard's coronation had taken place at Westminster on Sunday 6 July. Many had attended it, including Buckingham himself, Lady Margaret Beaufort, Eleanor Talbot's sister Elizabeth – and, as we saw above in chapter 15, maybe also the young ex-king

Edward V. A week after his coronation Richard went to stay at the royal manor of Greenwich, and a week after that he went to Windsor Castle. From Windsor he then set off on a tour of the realm.[11]

Initially he was accompanied by John Howard, who had now been created Duke of Norfolk. However, a crisis of some kind then seems to have arisen in London, and Richard sent Howard back to the capital to deal with the situation for him (see below, chapter 19). However, Buckingham appears to have stayed with the royal party until the beginning of August. He then took leave of the king and went westwards. Those two royal cousins were never to meet again.

On Wednesday 27 August, at Pontefract Castle, where he and his wife were then staying,[12] Richard III issued a signed warrant, conferring on Buckingham his share of the Bohun inheritance. On the following day he appointed Buckingham to take part, together with the Duke of Norfolk and others, in commissions of oyer and terminer in London, and in the counties of Surrey, Sussex, Kent, Middlesex, Oxford, Berkshire, Essex and Hertford.[13] The continuation of Richard's royal favour to the Duke of Buckingham until at least mid-September 1483[14] strongly suggests that the situation which John Howard had been sent to handle for the king in London, and which he dealt with from 25 July until 10 August, had not in any way been revealed to implicate Buckingham in political opposition. Thus if Buckingham was already conspiring against him in July or August, Richard III cannot yet have been aware of it.

Towards the end of August the king and queen went to York. There, on the Feast of the Nativity of the Blessed Virgin Mary (Monday 8 September), their son was formally invested as Prince of Wales.[15] On 21 September the king returned to Pontefract Castle, where he stayed until 8 October.[16] It was at about that time that he received news of risings which were now being staged against him in the south of England.[17] Those were the opening stages of an event which is generally known as 'Buckingham's Rebellion'.

Initially the aim of that movement is usually reported to have been to get rid of Richard III and restore the boy-king Edward V to the throne of England.[18] However, there is no solid evidence to show that the Duke of Buckingham – who had hitherto firmly backed the deposition of Edward V – ever supported the idea of that boy's restoration to the English throne. The problem is that, although the rebellion bears his name, he was by no means the only person involved in campaigning against Richard III in the late summer and early autumn of 1483. The rebellion apparently included 'many loyalists of Edward V',[19] among whom was the young ex-king's half-brother Thomas Grey, Marquess of Dorset.

Presumably those responsible for reasserting the claim of Edward V must have known – or at least assumed – that Edward V was still alive when they began their rebellion. That shows that apparently there was no widespread popular belief in August 1483 that the boy in question had then died, or been killed. However, it does not guarantee that those men in the south of England who were campaigning for his restoration to the throne possessed solid evidence in that respect.

Once the Duke of Buckingham became actively involved in the rebellion which bears his name, 'a rumour arose that King Edward [IV]'s sons, by some unknown manner of violent destruction, had met their fate.'[20] Since Buckingham was then living in Wales it is difficult to see how he could have received firm news in that respect from London at that point. However, it seems that the aim behind the spreading of that rumour was primarily to convert the focus of the rebellion from the attempted restoration of Edward V to support for the royal claim of the self-styled 'Earl of Richmond'. Maybe therefore it was Bishop Morton who proposed spreading the rumour in question. Significantly, he later appears to have been behind the spreading of other stories about the fate of Edward IV's sons (see below, chapter 23 *et seq.*). There is no evidence that the story which was put out in Wales and the west country in the late summer of 1483 was anything more than a rumour with a political objective.

The *Divisiekroniek*, an early sixteenth-century account which was written in the Low Countries in about 1517, suggested that the Duke of Buckingham himself was actually responsible for the fate of the two sons of Edward IV. The reasons for giving any attention to this source have been questioned by some historians. Nevertheless, its writer, Cornelius Aurelius, was born in about 1460. He would therefore have been in his early to mid twenties in 1483 – unlike Thomas More, who would only then have been five years old, but whose account in respect of the 'princes' generally seems to have been taken more seriously.

The account penned by Cornelius Aurelius first says that Buckingham was given overall responsibility for those sons of Edward IV by King Richard III. There is no precise documentary evidence to that effect surviving in England. It is true, however, that on Tuesday 15 July 1483 Richard III had appointed Buckingham as Lord High Constable of England.[21] That was a higher rank than that of Earl Marshal, which was given to John Howard, Duke of Norfolk, and it could possibly have included the assigning to Buckingham of a formal role in respect of the now officially bastard sons of Edward IV.

The *Divisiekroniek* then declares that

> the Duke of Buckingham killed these children hoping to become king himself and this for the reason that he had read a prophecy about a future King Henry of England who would be very great and powerful, and he believed himself to be this for he was called Henry. And some say also that this Henry Earl [*sic*] of Buckingham killed only one child and spared the other which he had lifted from the font and had him secretly abducted out of the country. This child was called Richard and after being in Portugal he came into France to King Louis the Eleventh and from there he secretly came to Brabant to Lady Margaret his aunt, King Edward's foresaid sister, the widow of Duke Charles of Burgundy.[22]

As for Richard III, when he heard the disturbing news that a rebellion was now in progress, once again he sent rapid instructions to the Duke of Norfolk to begin dealing with it. Thus the rebellion was quickly crushed, and the Duke of Buckingham was captured and then executed at Salisbury.

17

DID YOUNG EDWARD DIE
IN 1483?

The most likely fate of Edward V does appear to be that he died during the late summer of 1483. Certainly, after 1483 no one ever professed that they had seen him. However, there is no proof that he was *put to death*. No solid evidence exists to back that claim, and it appears more likely that he may have died from natural causes. If his death had not been natural, it could only have been brought about by one of the people who sought to control events at that period. And the lack of evidence in respect of the new monarch (Richard III) was examined earlier (see above, chapter 14).

Various other people are certainly known to have been active in respect of Edward V and his claim to the English throne in the second half of 1483. Sir John Fogge took that route as we saw earlier, in chapter 6. Fuller information will be offered shortly in that respect (see below, chapter 19). The conduct of such Edward V loyalists has usually been presented as part of the movement in opposition to Richard III which is known as 'Buckingham's Rebellion'. However, the supporters of Edward V were not directly associated with the Duke of Buckingham. They seem to have been men based in London and Kent. Initially some of them appear to have attempted to get hold of young Edward. Subsequently others fought in his favour – for his restoration to the throne.

However, the theoretical leader of the so-called 'Buckingham's Rebellion' was the Duke of Buckingham himself. And he seems to have consistently opposed Edward's tenure in the rank of king.

As we have seen, Buckingham was also accused in some more or less contemporary foreign quarters of having murdered Edward V. In that context the fact that Buckingham himself was later executed, and that no one seems subsequently to have been able to specify where young Edward might have been interred, might possibly be seen as significant. However, we have also seen that what actually happened was that a *rumour* was spread in respect of Edward's death – apparently by Buckingham and his supporters. They may have been inspired in that direction by Bishop Morton. Apparently the object of that rumour was to focus the aim of the rebellion on the claim to the throne of Henry, 'Earl of Richmond'.

Also, in respect of Edward V himself, contemporary evidence was presented earlier, in chapter 4, which suggests that he may have been a weak child in terms of his health. Likewise George Buck, who wrote his account of Richard III more than a century later, in the first half of the seventeenth century, also reported that Edward V was 'of a weake and sickly disposition'.[1] Buck was the descendant of people who, in the fifteenth century, had been active Yorkist supporters. His ancestor, John Buck, had been gravely wounded fighting for Richard III at Bosworth, and had subsequently been executed by Henry VII. Presumably therefore the description of Edward V which George Buck offered was based on information which had been handed down within his own family.

Overall, the idea that Edward died in the second half of 1483 would accord very well with Yorkist opinion of the 1490s. Apparently it was then generally accepted that Edward V was no longer living. Certainly no contester for the throne of Henry VII ever claimed to be him.[2]

First Death Evidence: Official Government Records Written from September 1483 to December 1484

Solid evidence definitely exists which indicates that by the autumn and winter of 1483 it was officially stated that Edward V had died. The first piece of evidence which I found in that respect is preserved among the medieval borough records of the town of Colchester, in a collection known as the Oath Book. This contains various records covering the period 1327–1564. An early twentieth-century published calendar version of the Oath Book clearly indicated that Edward V was believed to have died in 1483, since it referred to him as the 'late son of Edward IV'.[3] However, although that had been published in 1907, the significance of the Colchester evidence seems not really to have been noticed until I began drawing attention to it in 2004.[4]

The fifteenth-century Colchester borough records take the form of a year-by-year listing of the town's bailiffs and burgesses. Each annual list of officials is followed by a summary of the local documents relating to that year. The year headings naming the Colchester bailiffs are inscribed in red ink (see plate 9), while the lists of records following each of the yearly headings are inscribed in black ink. The records for each year are normally continuous and in the same hand, though occasionally one or two additions have been made, in different ink, at the end of a year's record, but before the heading for the following year.

The yearly headings focus chiefly upon the names of the two town bailiffs for the year in question. However, if a local bailiff or the reigning monarch died during a civic year, that death was recorded as part of the year's heading, and before the commencement of the list of local records for the year in question. That confirms that the year's records must regularly have been written up at the end of each civic year.

Obviously, 1483 was a rather unusual year, because there had been three reigning monarchs. Thus the Colchester town clerk, the lawyer John Hervy,[5] was obliged to offer a rather long heading in that instance, naming all three sovereigns. Hervy quoted specific dates for the ends of the reigns of both Edward IV and Edward V. In the case of Edward IV he said that the king's reign had ended on 8 April. As we saw earlier, the actual death date of Edward IV is confused.[6] The official announcement of his demise was given out on 9 April 1483 – the day following the one cited by Hervy. However, Mancini's contemporary report states that Edward died on 7 April – the day *preceding* the date cited by Hervy – while other contemporary sources cite slightly earlier death dates. Hervy presumably did his best to give the correct date, and significantly at least one other local official – employed not in the eastern counties but in the West Country – cited the same death date for Edward IV as Hervy.[7]

As for Edward V, we have seen that 26 June was the date on which Richard III was finally persuaded to accept the crown. However, the decision by the three estates of the realm that Edward V was not the legitimate sovereign must have been made earlier. That presumably explains why Hervy cites 20 June 1483 as marking the formal termination of the boy-king's reign. Significantly, the contemporary close rolls[8] also seem to confirm that 20 June was seen as the last official date of King Edward V's reign (see below, appendix 1). In other words it appears that in June 1483 England had the odd experience of living through a week with no official reigning monarch. On Friday 20 June Edward V had been officially ruled out. But repeated attempts then had to be made to persuade the reluctant Duke of Gloucester to accept the offer of the crown – which he only did on the following Thursday.

As we have already seen, each list of records for the borough of Colchester was written up retrospectively, at the end of each civic year. The civic years officially commenced on Michaelmas Day (29 September). The Colchester bailiffs were elected each year on the Monday following 8 September (the Feast of the Nativity of the Blessed Virgin Mary) and they then assumed the office to which they had been elected on the Monday following the Feast of St Michael.[9] In 1482 the election had taken place on Monday 9 September, and the bailiffs had taken office on Monday 30 September. At the end of that civic year the next Feast of St Michael fell on Monday 29 September 1483. John Hervy's 'three kings' note covering the year 1482–3 must have been therefore written up on, or shortly after, Monday 29 September 1483.

Hervy's full year heading for 1482–3 is illustrated in plate 9. In Latin it reads:

Tempore Iohannis Bisshop & Thome Cristemesse, Ballivorum ville Colcestrie a festo Sancti Michelis Archangeli Anno domini Edwardi quarti nuper Regis anglie, iam defuncti, vicesimo secundo, usque octavum diem Aprilis tunc primo sequentem, Anno regni Regis Edwardi ... [erasure of the term 'bastard'] *quinti nuper filii domini Edwardi quarti post conquestum primo, usque vicesimum diem Iunij tunc primo sequentem, Anno Regni Regis Ricardi tercij post conquestum primo incipiente, et abinde usque ad festum Sancti Micheli Archangeli extunc primo futuro quasi per unum Annum integrum.*[10]

The English translation of the heading is:

> In the time of John Bisshop and Thomas Cristemesse, Bailiffs
> of the town of Colchester from the feast of St Michael the
> Archangel in the 22nd year of the reign of the Lord Edward
> IV, late king of England, now deceased, up until the 8th day of
> April first following; [and] in the first year of the reign of the ...
> [erasure of the term 'bastard'] King Edward V, late son of the
> lord Edward IV after the Conquest, up to the 20th day of June
> then first following; [and] in the first year of the reign of Richard
> III after the Conquest, from the beginning, and thence until
> the first feast of St Michael the Archangel thereafter as for one
> complete year.[11]

As can clearly be seen, in the middle of this heading a term which
had been applied to Edward V had later been heavily erased, shaving
off some of the surface of the parchment. The obvious missing term
is a reference to Edward V's illegitimacy. By the autumn of 1483
the application to Edward V of the term 'bastard' was the official
government position and it would certainly have been required in an
official record. Subsequent erasure of such a term would then have
taken place after the accession of Henry VII, because he restored the
legitimacy of the children of Edward IV and Elizabeth Widville in
preparation for his own marriage with one of them. He is also known
to have visited Colchester.

In 2004, based on viewing the original document under ultraviolet
light, I suggested that the first erased letter might have been an
uppercase 'R'. Subsequently there had been a letter with a tail which
I suggested may have been a lower case 'p'. I therefore tentatively
proposed that two words – *Regis spurii* ('illegitimate King') – might
in this instance have formed the term which had later been erased.[12]
However, new evidence in respect of the terminology will be examined
in detail shortly (see below).

As for the *surviving* wording, that contains the key evidence
in respect of the probable demise of Edward V. Initially the Oath
Book year heading describes Edward IV both as *nuper Regis* (late
king) and as *iam defuncti* (now deceased). In the case of Edward V

the word *defuncti* (dead) is not included. However, the boy-king is described as *nuper filij Edwardi quarti* (late son of Edward IV). The logical interpretation of that phrase would be that Edward V was dead.

The Latin word *nuper* is actually an adverb which originally meant 'formerly' or 'recently'. However, it gradually acquired the English adjectival meaning 'late' (i.e. 'now deceased') when applied to a person. Specific evidence in respect of the evolution of use of *nuper* to mean 'late' (i.e. 'now deceased') is offered below, in Appendix 3. In the case of the 1482–3 year heading in the Colchester Oath Book the word 'late' is clearly the logical English translation. To have described Edward V as 'formerly the son of Edward IV' could only imply either that the identity of his father had somehow changed (which would be ridiculous), or that the boy himself was dead (i.e. 'late'). As for the English wording 'recently the son of Edward IV', that would sound odd. However, that too could only imply that the boy himself was no longer living.

In chapter 15, evidence was presented which appears to show how Edward V was referred to at a *personal* level once his uncle had become king. The wardrobe accounts refer to robes which had been commissioned for 'Lord Edward, son of late king Edward the Fourth'. In those accounts Edward V is not referred to either as 'late' or as a 'bastard'. There was no need for the use of either of those words in that context – though Edward's illegitimacy was presumably implied by the use of the title 'Lord' instead of his earlier title of 'Prince'.

However, other sources are available to confirm the fact that the terms 'late king' and 'bastard' – both of which originally figured in the Colchester Oath Book heading for the local records in respect of the year 1482–3 (though one of them was later erased) – definitely came to comprise the *bureaucratic* terminology which was employed to refer to Edward V *in official government documents* during the reign of Richard III. The introduction of both 'late' and 'bastard' took place before the end of 1483. However, the surviving documents also reveal that development of the precise terminology in respect of how Edward V was referred to by the new government took place gradually. They also show that the expressions used were not always identical.

The earliest document in the reign of Richard III which refers to Edward V records private gifts of 'Robert Holcombe, citizen and vintner of London'. This document is dated 5 July 1483 – only nine days after Richard III became England's king, and it shows no sign of any of the terminology which was employed later that year in the Colchester Oath Book. It simply refers back to an earlier document 'dated 2 June, 1 Edward V'.[13] In other words, at that very early stage in the reign of Richard III there was no application to the boy-king of the word 'bastard' and no indication that he was dead.

Interestingly, however, the second available source – which does confirm the Colchester Oath Book terminology – is a document which was probably written only about ten days after the Holcombe record. Unfortunately it bears no date. But it is recorded in a manuscript between two other documents which are dated 4 July 1483 and 18 July 1483. Thus it must have been written between those two dates – possibly on about 10 July. The document in question is a grant to Edward John, John Melyonek and twelve other men. It is written in English, and it refers to 'Edward Bastard late called king Edward the Vth'.[14] The wording 'late called king' obviously means that Edward had been removed from the throne, however 'late called' need not imply that he was dead at that point. In other words, when the document was written (between 4 and 18 July 1483), Edward V was presumably still alive. However, specific wording in respect of the term 'bastard' had then already been introduced.

A third piece of evidence also backs the Colchester Oath Book terminology. It comprises a royal grant made at Westminster, to William Daubeney. This document was written about two and a half months after the year heading in the Colchester Oath Book, on 16 December 1483. Daubeney had received appointment to the office of Searcher in the Port of London during the brief reign of the boy-king. The grant made to Daubeney by Richard III in December 1483 therefore had to refer to the young lad who had theoretically been the reigning monarch on 9 April 1483, but who had now been officially declared to be illegitimate, and who was probably also known now to have passed away.

As cited in the published *Calendar of Patent Rolls, 1476–1485*, Richard III's grant to Daubeney is said to allude to 'Edward V the bastard, late king'.[15] However, the original text of the document is in Latin, and refers to *Edwardi Bastardi nuper Regis Anglie quinti*.[16] That literally means 'Edward V, the Bastard, late King of England'. It is very interesting and informative to compare this reference in respect of Edward V with earlier government practice concerning allusions to the deposed King Henry VI. During Edward IV's first reign, no references to the deposed – but still living – King Henry VI had ever referred to *him* as 'late King of England'. However, that terminology was introduced in 1471, following Henry's demise. For example, on 18 August 1471, some two months after his death, King Henry VI was described by Edward IV as 'late king'.[17] Thus the logical interpretation of the employment of the term *Edwardi Bastardi nuper Regis Anglie quinti* in respect of Edward V in December 1483 must be that by that date he too was known to have died. And since, some two months earlier, he had been described in the Colchester Oath Book as '*nuper filij Edwardi quarti*', presumably he was also known to be dead by the end of September or beginning of October 1483.

When I first saw the Latin text of the royal grant to William Daubeney it raised in my mind the question of whether the September 1483 heading of the Colchester Oath Book might also originally have contained the Latin word *Bastardi*, rather than the term *Regis spurii* which I had previously proposed for the Colchester erasure. I therefore re-examined the Colchester Oath Book. As can be seen in plate 10, my recent re-examination of that original document – with the help of all possible lighting and magnification – at the Essex Record Office[18] showed that the long medieval letter 'ſ (s)' of *Bastardi* could conceivably account for what seems to be the end of a tail still surviving just above the letters of the word '*quarti*' in the line below. Also magnification revealed that the top of the long medieval letter 'ſ (s)' may also have survived. The top of the penultimate letter 'd' of *Bastardi* also seems to still be present immediately beneath a long 'ſ (s)' in the line above. It therefore now seems probable that my earlier proposed reconstruction was not correct, and that the Colchester text originally contained the word *Bastardi*, just like the text of William Daubeney's grant. Nevertheless, the Colchester year heading does differ slightly from the William Daubeney grant in terms of its use of the word *nuper*. As we have seen, the Colchester text reads *nuper filii* – 'late son', while the Daubeney grant reads *nuper Regis Anglie* – 'late King of England'.

A fourth piece of contemporary documentary evidence which supports the Colchester Oath Book in its references to Edward V is an indenture in respect of William Catesby, dated 1 December 1484. That refers back to an earlier document dated 13 June 1483 'first year of the reign of Edward bastard, late called king of England the fifth'.[19] In this case the original document was written not in Latin but in English.[20] And it employs very similar terminology to the earlier grant to Edward John and others, which was also written in English (see above). Thus it employs the term 'late called', which is not very informative in terms of its precise meaning. It therefore seems that texts written in Latin are more helpful in respect of *nuper*/'late' than texts written in English.

The evidence in respect of how Richard III's government referred to Edward V – and when – can now be summarised as follows:

4 July 1483
'Edward V'.[21]

c.10 July 1483
'Edward Bastard late called king Edward the Vth'.[22]
'... late called ...' probably means he was still alive.

c.29 September 1483
Regis Edwardi Bastardi quinti nuper filii domini Edwardi quarti
'the Bastard King Edward V, late son of the lord Edward IV'.[23]
It seems 'late son' can only mean that he was dead.

16 December 1483
Edwardi Bastardi nuper Regis Anglie quinti
'Edward V the Bastard, late King of England'.[24]
Compared to references to Henry VI, logically the use of the term '... late King of England' means that Edward V was dead.

1 December 1484
'Edward bastard late called kyng of Englond the v^the'.[25]
The term '... late called ...' does not necessarily imply that Edward was dead, but given the earlier evidence, presumably he was.

Second Death Evidence: Report Written in Beaugency (Orleans, France), December 1483

The apparent meaning of the formal entries regarding Edward V in the Colchester Oath Book and in other government documents is supported by a rumour which was recorded by Domenico Mancini. In 1483 that Roman friar had been sent to England by Archbishop Angelo Cato of Vienne to act as a kind of French diplomatic agent. Although Mancini appears not to have been able to communicate well in the English language, he had remained in England for some months collecting information. He then returned to the European mainland and submitted a report to Archbishop Cato, under the Latin title *De occupatione regni Anglie per Ricardum tercium* ('Richard III's take-over of the Kingdom of England').[26] His report, written in (or by) December 1483, contained the following statement in respect of Edward V:

> I saw not a few men distressed and weeping in memory of him after he was removed from people's sight, and the suspicion was that he had been carried off. But whether he had been carried off, and by what kind of death, I have not yet ascertained.[27]

This statement has often been taken to mean that Edward had been murdered. However, it can clearly be seen that Mancini states specifically that he has not found out for certain what had occurred. Moreover, he does not employ a Latin word such as *interfectus* (murdered) to describe what he thought had happened. Instead, he uses the word sublatus (carried off).

Mancini also wrote that Edward V was no longer in the public view (see above, introduction), and he named an individual who had offered him information in respect of young Edward. The man in question was Dr John Argentine. That source is very interesting, because Argentine was young Edward's physician (*medicus*). It is therefore a potentially very significant fact that he apparently visited Edward on a regular basis while the boy was residing in the Tower of London. Obviously the most normal reason why a patient receives frequent visits from his doctor is that the patient is unwell.

Dr John Argentine, Edward V's physician, redrawn from his funeral brass.

Dr Argentine told Mancini that Edward was making daily confessions because the boy 'thought his death was approaching'.[28] This phrase seems generally to have been taken to mean that Edward was expecting to be murdered. However, that is a very twisted view. It is important to remember that the source for this piece of information was young Edward's doctor who was then paying frequent visits to his young patient. The most obvious logical explanation of what he reported about Edward would therefore be that the young boy was seriously ill, and knew that he was dying. Possibly young Edward was repeating the experience of his elder sister, Mary of York. She had died, at about the same age, just over a year earlier.

Third Death Evidence: Family History Written in Cambridge c. 1510

A later record assigns a specific death date to Edward V. The document in question is the Anlaby Cartulary, the relevant folio of which (unlike the Colchester Oath Book and Domenico Mancini's report) is not strictly contemporary, because it was only put together in about 1510 (after the death of Henry VII). It attributes the death of Edward V to 22 June 1483.[29] The relevant folio of the Anlaby Cartulary has been carefully inspected by the present writer, and was shown to contain some errors.[30] However, it remains potentially interesting in that it is the only source which attempts to assign a specific date for Edward V's death. But since it contains other provable errors in respect of the dates it implies, it remains possible that it wrongly recorded the month in respect of Edward V. As the fourth piece of evidence will show, it could well be that Edward V actually died a month later, on 22 July 1483 – the day following the departure from London of his uncle King Richard III on his royal tour of the kingdom.

Fourth Death Evidence: Record of Papal Ceremonies, Written up in Rome, 1492

Pope Sixtus IV, who celebrated a Requiem Mass for King Edward in September 1483.

One near-contemporary fifteenth-century source does exist which appears to suggest 22 July 1483 as the likely death date for Edward V. It is the record of a papal Requiem Mass which was offered for the repose of the soul of an English king called Edward at the Sistine Chapel in Rome on Tuesday 23 September 1483. The document in question survives in a *Diary* written up by Iacopo Gherardi of Volterra, apostolic secretary and 'secret chamberlain' to Pope Sixtus IV, in the year 1492, after he had retired from his papal service. The text therefore dates from nine years after the event (the celebration of a papal Requiem Mass) which it records in respect of the English King Edward.

Gherardi's entry reads:

For King Edward of England a mass for the dead was celebrated today, 23 September, in the greater [= Sistine] chapel, with the pope and fathers present, Bishop Christopher of Modruss celebrated the divine service, but the pope performed the final part, after the offering of incense and the sprinkling of holy water, wearing not his pluvial [ordinary cope], but a purple *cappa* [more elaborate cope].[31]

The date on which the Requiem Mass was celebrated is extremely interesting. It has always been the tradition of the Catholic Church to celebrate prayers and Masses for the dead at specific intervals following, and related to, the date upon which the commemorated person died. The most common custom is to carry out such prayerful activities on the *anniversaries* of the death in question. The celebration of anniversary commemorations had already become common practice by the third century, when it was mentioned by Tertullian. In the fifteenth century, anniversary commemorations remained the norm. For example, Lady Eleanor Talbot is known to have arranged for annual memorial services for both of her parents on the precise anniversaries of their respective deaths.[32]

However, anniversary praying (known as 'Year's mind') was not the only possibility. Praying for the dead also focused in other ways upon the date of death. Another common practice was to celebrate 'month's mind'. This was done by focussing on both the date and the weekday on which the demise had occurred. For example, even though the precise date is not clearly recorded (see above), King Edward IV died around the end of the first week of April 1483. His relative and supporter John, Lord Howard (later Duke of Norfolk) had a Mass offered for the dead king's soul four weeks later, at the end of the first week of May.[33] Likewise the death of King Louis XI of France, which occurred on Saturday 30 August 1483, was commemorated in Rome by Pope Sixtus exactly two weeks (half a month) after that sovereign's demise, on Saturday 13 September.[34]

It seems possible that Edward V may have died on Tuesday 22 July 1483 (the fourth Tuesday of July) – just after Richard III's departure from London. If he did pass away on Tuesday 22 July, the celebration of a Requiem Mass for the repose of his soul in Rome on Tuesday 23 September (the fourth Tuesday of September) would have been very apposite. It would have marked the 'two-month's mind' of the boy's death.

Certainly the date of the Mass in the Sistine Chapel makes it improbable as a belated papal commemoration of the death of King Edward IV. Given that Edward IV had died around the end of the first week of April, if Pope Sixtus had chosen to commemorate *that* English king in September 1483 the date he would have chosen would probably have been towards the end of the first week of September. Alternatively he could have waited until the end of the first week of October, thereby commemorating the half-anniversary of Edward IV.

As we saw earlier, Richard III clearly received news at Reading on about 22 July, telling him that something important had happened in London. The new king then hastily sent John Howard, Duke of Norfolk back to the capital to take action there on his behalf. Those points might possibly be associated with the evidence for the potential death date of Edward V which has now been examined.

18

DID YOUNG RICHARD
SURVIVE BEYOND 1483?

While specific contemporary and near-contemporary evidence relating to the possible death of Edward V has now been examined, there is very little contemporary evidence to indicate that the same was believed in respect of his younger brother, Richard of Shrewsbury, Duke of York. It is true that the Crowland Chronicle Continuations (written after the seizure of the throne by Henry VII) reveal that, in connection with 'Buckingham's Rebellion', 'it was rumoured that, by some unknown violence, King Edward's sons had met the fate of death.'[1] However, as we have seen, the account in question is implying that the story was part of the propaganda associated with 'Buckingham's Rebellion'. It does not imply that the story was true, or even that it was widely believed.

It is also the case that, in his *Kalendar*, in respect of the civic year September 1483 to September 1484, Robert Ricart, Recorder of Bristol, added a marginal note saying that 'this yere the two sonnes of King E. were put to scylence in the Towre of London'.[2] But the words 'put to silence in the Tower of London' do not necessarily imply that the boys had been killed. The phrase could merely mean that Edward and Richard had been removed from contact with other people. Moreover, since he was living and working in a part of the country which experienced 'Buckingham's Rebellion', Ricart may simply have been promulgating the rumour mentioned in the Crowland Chronicle Continuations. Significantly, Ricart's entry for 1484 also records the execution of the Duke of Buckingham, and his report of that event was obviously entered earlier than his report of the rumour regarding the sons of Edward IV.

Some modern historians have asserted that by the autumn of 1483 both Edward V and his brother, Richard, 'were generally assumed to be dead'.[3] It has been claimed that evidence for young Richard's death exists in terms of the elevation of Lord Howard to the title of Duke of Norfolk on 28 June 1483. Since Richard had previously held the Norfolk ducal title, it is assumed that by that date he must have been dead. In reality, though, for about five years there had been questions in respect of the legality of the moves made by Edward IV (probably inspired by Elizabeth Widville) in order to ensure that, following his marriage to the Norfolk heiress Anne Mowbray, Richard of Shrewsbury would always retain the Norfolk title, even if Anne died childless – as she did on 19 November 1481. The conflict in that respect had caused problems between Elizabeth Widville and Lord Howard – who was a living potential Mowbray heir.

This means that when King Richard III bestowed the Norfolk title on one of the surviving cousins of the last Mowbray duke, he was simply giving legal acknowledgement to the well-known argument which claimed that after the death of Anne Mowbray young Richard of Shrewsbury could not retain a title which he had only acquired via his child bride. It seems clear that Edward IV's unusual legislation in respect of the Mowbray inheritance had widely been perceived at the time as unjust. There is no doubt whatever that another Mowbray cousin and potential heir, Lord Berkeley had taken exception to it.

Significantly, on Thursday 5 June 1483, less than a month before he was raised to the dukedom of Norfolk, 'my Lord [Howard] paied be his own handes to John Feeld, for to have owt sertayn wrytenges of lyvelode from my Lord Berkeley'.[4] In terms of their female-line descent from that family, Lord Berkeley and Lord Howard were the Mowbray co-heirs. Thus an agreement between them was needed if the Mowbray estates and titles were now to be divided amicably between them. Yet it is obvious that on 5 June, young Richard of Shrewsbury was not dead! On that date he had still been living in sanctuary at Westminster Abbey with his mother and sisters.

The evidence which shows that discussions were taking place between Lords Howard and Berkeley indicates that the subsequent partition of the Mowbray inheritance and Lord Howard's elevation to the dukedom of Norfolk were simply based on the dubious legality of the acts of Edward IV which had deprived both Howard and Berkeley of their legitimate shares of the Mowbray patrimony in favour of that king's own younger son. Also, Lord Berkeley is known to have formally petitioned for his share of the Mowbray inheritance – though the precise date of his petition is not known, and no evidence survives to show whether Lord Howard also made a petition.[5] Nevertheless, what was done for both of them by King Richard III was consistent with standard English practice in such situations. On Saturday 28 June 1483 John Howard was created Duke of Norfolk and Earl Marshal of England, while his cousin Lord Berkeley received another of the Mowbray titles, being created Earl of Nottingham.[6] The granting to them of those titles did not even depend on the fact that Richard of Shrewsbury had now been declared illegitimate – as the present writer once wrongly suggested![7] And it certainly did not mean that the boy was no longer alive. Thus the claim made by some modern historians that Richard III's grants on 28 June show that Richard of Shrewsbury was dead is ridiculous.

As for Richard of Shrewsbury, what really became of him remains far from clear. Certainly the suggestion that he was *known* to have died is completely unacceptable in view of the fact that some years later 'Richard of England *alias* Perkin Warbeck' was acknowledged by his supporters as Richard of Shrewsbury. The underpinning which that claimant received in the 1490s makes it absolutely clear that the death of the younger son of Edward IV and Elizabeth Widville had by no means been universally accepted at that time.

Domenico Mancini's source in respect of Edward V – Dr John Argentine – had apparently said nothing to Mancini about the health, let alone expectations of death, of Edward's younger brother, despite the fact that the two boys were then living together in the Tower of London. Of course, there is no indication that Dr Argentine was also the medical doctor of young Richard. But although Dr Argentine apparently offered Mancini no information about Richard, a later account by Jean de Molinet (1435–1507) suggests that at the time of Edward's putative illness, his younger brother had been in good health and had even done his best to help his melancholy and depressed elder brother by encouraging him to feel more cheerful and even to dance.[8] Although Molinet was a contemporary his text is not precisely so. It was written up about twenty years after 1483. Moreover, Molinet made obvious mistakes at times. For example, he gave the names of the two sons of Edward IV incorrectly.

Even so, Molinet was probably right when he asserted that Richard of Shrewsbury was a gleeful boy at the Tower of London, because a contemporary London account also exists which reports the exuberance of Richard of Shrewsbury in the summer of 1483. It is a letter, written by Canon Simon Stallworth(e) – a priest in the service of the chancellor, Bishop Russell – to Sir William Stonor on the 21 June, 1483. In his letter Stallworth(e) states:

> On Monday last was at Westm. gret plenty of harnest men: ther was the dylyveraunce of the Dewke of Yorke to my lord Cardenale, my lord Chaunceler, and other many lordes Temporale and with hym mette my lord of Bukyngham in the myddes of the hall of Westm.: my lord protectour recevynge hyme at the Starre Chamber Dore with many lovynge wordys and so departed with my lord Cardenale to the toure, wher he is, blessid be Jhesus, mery.[9]

It was also noted earlier (see above, chapter 2) that the Crowland Chronicle Continuations say that Richard, came 'to the Tower for the comfort of his brother, the king'.[10]

An imaginary nineteenth-century engraving, showing Elizabeth Widville handing over her younger son to Cardinal Bourchier, so that he could go and cheer up Edward V at the Tower.

One outcome of Richard's arrival to join his brother may have been the fact that both boys are reported by the Great Chronicle as having been frequently seen shooting together in the gardens of the Tower. Presumably they employed bows and arrows for their shooting. Indeed, Richard may have been known to have an interest in archery. On 30 January 1483, his father's distant cousin and supporter Lord Howard is recorded as having given 2s 6d 'to Poynes that dwellyd with my Lord of York'. Howard's purpose in giving Poynes that money was to enable him 'for to bye with a bowe'.[11] It seems that Lord Howard had been making a small gift to young Richard, who was named in Howard's household record of this payment. Maybe Lord Howard had been well aware of the fact that the young Duke of York – and Norfolk – enjoyed archery.

A young archer.

Subsequently, as we have seen, Lord Howard himself was created Duke of Norfolk by Richard III. And he then played another role which could be significant in respect of what happened to the two sons of Edward IV.

19

WHAT DID THE DUKE OF NORFOLK DO IN LATE JULY/ AUGUST 1483?

After Richard III had been crowned King of England, and had set off on his tour of parts of the realm,

> the two sons of King Edward [IV] remained in the Tower of London with a specially appointed guard. In order to release them from this kind of captivity people of the south and west of the kingdom began to murmur secretly, fomenting groups and meetings – many in private and some openly – especially those who, because they were afraid, were scattered through franchises and sanctuaries.[1]

Thus there was various secret planning in respect of attempts to get the two boys out of the Tower. The continuator of the Crowland Chronicle seems to have been accurate in his reference to the south of England. That would cover the movements in favour of Edward V in London and the county of Kent. However, his reference to the west presumably refers simply to 'Buckingham's Rebellion', and that never appears to have been focussed on the restoration of Edward V.

One specific plot in favour of the sons of Edward IV was reported by the French Bishop Thomas Basin. He seems to have written his account about six months after the actual event – early in 1484.[2] According to Basin the plot in question was staged by Londoners. However, it appears to have failed to gain widespread support.

Much later the sixteenth-century chronicler John Stow also reported an attempt to abduct Edward V and his brother from London. According to Stow's report, the plan was to ignite diversionary fires in the vicinity of the Tower.[3] Stow also said that the chief culprits were apprehended. He cites four names: Robert Russe, sergeant of London, William Davy, pardoner of Hounslow, John Smith, groom of King Edward IV's stirrup, and Stephen Ireland, wardrober of the Tower. No contemporary fifteenth-century evidence has been found in respect of those names. However, Stow also reports that the four men in question 'were tried at Westminster, condemned to death, drawn to Tower Hill and beheaded, and their heads were exhibited on London Bridge'.[4]

Thus one attempt to remove the sons of Edward IV from the Tower of London after their uncle had been crowned as king of England and had left the capital on his royal tour was reported by Basin, and a similar attempt was reported later by Stow. However, it is by no means clear whether the accounts of Basin and of Stow refer to *the same attempt*. In other words, it is perfectly possible that at least *two* endeavours were made to gain access to the sons of Edward IV. Indeed, further evidence suggests that there might possibly have been at least *three* such attempts. Moreover, although the manner in which Basin and Stow penned their reports suggests that the attempts to which those two sources refer must have failed, it is possible that the third attempt was successful, because, as we shall see, Richard III's government seems to have handled that issue very discreetly.

When Richard III set off on his royal tour, he rode first from Windsor to Reading. That was on Monday 21 July. Richard and his wife, Queen Anne Neville, then stayed at Reading until Wednesday 23 July.[5] From 24 to 26 July the couple were in Oxford.[6] When the king and queen first departed from Windsor Castle, John Howard – the newly created Duke of Norfolk – accompanied them. However, he only remained with the royal party as far as Caversham. There, presumably, they all visited the pilgrim shrine of Our Lady. But from Caversham John Howard suddenly rushed back to London.[7] It seems that Richard had requested him to carry out certain uniquely important functions there while the king continued his tour.

Sir John, Lord Howard, Duke of Norfolk. A nineteenth-century engraving based on a stained-glass window formerly at Stoke-by-Nayland.

John Howard got back to London very quickly. His private household accounts then record a payment of 4*d* which was made for him by his trusted servant Giles St Clare. The money in question is recorded as having been paid on the Duke of Norfolk's behalf 'for Seynt Anne, when he went to Crossbys place'.[8] The feast day of St Anne, which falls on 26 July, was the Name Day of the new queen, Anne Neville. It is therefore possible that the payment was for the celebration of a Mass which Howard had commissioned for Queen Anne. However, the precise significance of his payment is not specifically recorded, and may not matter.

What is important about the payment is that its surviving record reveals the fact that the Duke of Norfolk had made a visit to Crosby's Place at Bishopsgate on Saturday 26 July 1483. Crosby's Place was a *pied-à-terre* which had for some time been rented by the Duke of Gloucester. Although in recent years he had mainly served Edward IV in the north of England – and had chiefly been resident there – he was sometimes required to visit the capital. So he had needed an abode in the London area. And it seems that when, for whatever reason, Richard III had sent John Howard back to London, Howard then found himself required to perform some task for the king at Crosby's Place.[9]

On the day when the Duke of Norfolk paid his first recorded visit to Crosby's Place at Bishopsgate, Richard III was staying with his queen at the Palace of Woodstock.[10] But on the following Tuesday (29 July) they visited Minster Lovell.[11] There, Richard III issued a warrant to his Lord Chancellor:

> To the Right Reverend fader in god, our Right trusti and welbiloved the Bishop of Lincoln', our Chauncellr' of England.
>   By the King RR
> Right Reverend fader in god right trusti and welbeloved We grete you wele And where as we undrestand that certaine personnes (of such as of late had taken upon thaym the fact of an entreprise, as we doubte nat ye have herd) bee attached and in warde, we desir' and wol you that ye doo make our letters of commission to such personnes as by you and our counsaill shalbee advised forto sitte upon thaym, and to procede to the due execucion of our lawes in that behalve. Faille ye nat herof as our perfect trust is in you.
>   Yeven undre our signet at this Manoir of Mynster lovel the xxixth day Juyll.
>
> Herbert.[12]

The warrant says nothing specific about the precise nature of the 'entreprise' in question. Obviously what Richard III was referring to cannot have corresponded with the modern English definition of that word ('undertaking/venture'). Based on the meaning of the verb *entreprendre* in Old French, his use of the medieval English word 'entreprise' probably meant 'abduction'. Certainly it is clear from the letter that the 'entreprise' (abduction?) was seen by the king as a highly significant wrongdoing. It is also clear that 'certain persons' had been arrested ('attached and in warde'), and that they were now to be put on trial ('sitte upon thaym'). That trial was to be carried out by 'such persons' as the Lord Chancellor and the council instructed to 'sit upon them and proceed to the due execution of our laws'.

Of course, the precise motives behind the attempts made in July 1483 to access the sons of Edward IV in the Tower of London remain unknown. So too are the results, at least in respect of whether or not the boys were reached. Interestingly, however, there has been more mythology in that respect. For example, Pamela Tudor-Craig assumed that the attempt had simply been aimed at *butchering* the two boys.[13]

In reality, that seems highly unlikely. It is much more probable that the intention was to extract young Edward and Richard, and then make use of them for political purposes.

Also most writers seem to have assumed that the attempts to access the sons of Edward IV either failed or never progressed beyond plotting. For example, in respect of the following sentence which figures in the above letter written by Richard III:

certain persons ... of late had taken upon them the fact of an entreprise[14]

Alison Hanham avowed that this has no definite meaning. She asserted that

1) in the fifteenth century the word 'had' was a past subjunctive form of the verb 'have' – so that the medieval meaning of that word was 'would have'.
2) the word 'fact' then meant 'enterprise' or 'crime'.[15]

She did not explore the possible significant meaning of the word 'entreprise'. Based upon her own linguistic arguments, her conclusion was that only plotting had taken place. Nothing had ever actually been carried out in terms of an attempt to access the two boys. She also refers to the plot as having been aimed at murder, as Pamela Tudor-Craig had hypothesised.

But Hanham's claim in respect of the meaning of the medieval text is incorrect, as the following linguistic evidence will show:

1) In Middle English the plural preterite form of the subjunctive mood of a verb was normally identical to the plural preterite form of the indicative.[16] Thus the format of the word 'had' cannot, by itself, justify Hanham's conclusion that the subjunctive mood was intended. Indeed, if Richard really had intended the subjunctive mood, presumably he would have included the relevant condition which applied. But no such condition is included in his letter. Moreover, Richard's use of the words 'now late' clearly implies that something actually had taken place.[17] In other words the logical interpretation would be that Richard III's word 'had' is the

indicative preterite form of the verb, meaning precisely the same as
what 'had' means today.[18]

2) An examination of the *Oxford English Dictionary* suggests that in
the Middle Ages 'fact' normally meant 'deed' or 'action carried out'
(based, no doubt, on the word's Latin origin).[19]

In other words it seems that, when he wrote the letter, Richard III
was referring to a criminal entreprise (abduction?) *which had actually
taken place*. Presumably that is why he was asking the chancellor to
put those responsible for the 'entreprise' on trial.

Modern speculation also tends to play with the question of whether
the crime to which Richard III was referring was an unauthorised
attempt which had been made to extract Edward IV's daughters from
the sanctuary at Westminster, or an attempt to remove their two
brothers from the Tower of London.[20] As we have seen, the Crowland
Chronicle continuator says that there were plots to achieve both those
goals. He also states that

> when this became known the sacred church of the monks
> of Westminster and the whole neighbourhood took on the
> appearance of a castle and a fortress, and men of the greatest
> strictness were appointed as keepers there by King Richard.
> Over these men, as captain and chief was a certain John
> Nesfield esquire; he watched all entrances and exits of the
> monastery so that no one from outside could get in without his
> permission.[21]

John Nesfield, was probably one of Richard III's own servants,
from the north of England. He had recently been appointed a squire
of the body, and the king had granted him the office of constable
of Hertford Castle, together with the manor of Heytredesbury
[Haytesbury] in Wiltshire.[22] In the following spring (on 1 March
1483/4) Nesfield was appointed to further care for Elizabeth Widville,
and to ensure the payment of her pension.[23] Meanwhile, in late July
1483 it was presumably Nesfield who handled the situation in respect
of those members of Edward IV's family who were in sanctuary at
Westminster Abbey. There is no indication that John Howard was
acting in that respect.

However, when they received the king's instructions from Minster Lovell, Bishop John Russell and the council must presumably have appointed judges to 'sit upon' those who had been detained in connection with attempts to gain unauthorised possession of some or all of Edward IV's children. The trials could have been overseen by the Earl Marshal of England, John Howard, Duke of Norfolk. Thus it may be the case that the trial of at least some of those people was carried out in a fairly secret manner, at Crosby's Place, in the course of the following month, watched over by the Duke of Norfolk.

Crosby's Place, Bishopsgate.

Certainly, intriguing references to Crosby's Place continue in Howard's household accounts at the start of August 1483. There are further references to his personal presence there on 1 and 5 August. On Friday 1 August Giles St Clare paid 'for bere and alle, whan my Lord was at Crossbyes Place'.[24] On 5 August a small payment of 1*d* was made to someone called Burgesse to provide drink 'at Crossbyes Place'.[25] On 10 August St Clare paid 2*d* 'for nayles for makyng of the sege at Crosbyes Place'.[26] The Middle English word 'sege' (seat, throne, chair) obviously refers to the creation of some special piece of furniture. Possibly a formal seat had to be constructed so that the Duke of Norfolk could preside from it over a court hearing. On Monday 11 August the Duke of Norfolk departed from London and went home to Suffolk – to his manor of Stoke-by-Nayland. However, St Clare remained behind, and paid out a further 3*s* to Thorpe 'for straw leyde in Crosbys Place'.[27]

It is obvious from these records that some significant and highly unusual event had been taking place at Crosby's Place. The most likely explanation seems to be that John Howard, Duke of Norfolk – England's new Earl Marshal – had been dispatched back to London by the king himself to deal with a report which the king had received just after leaving London, telling him that a possibly successful attempt had been made to abduct the sons of Edward IV. Subsequently Howard may have been required to set up – and possibly supervise – a trial which was conducted privately at the new king's former London home, by a judge (or judges) formally appointed by the Lord Chancellor. It is more or less certain that such a trial would not have been against the culprits of the Basin plot or the Stow plot. After all, Stow reports that the men he refers to were tried openly at Westminster, not secretly at Bishopsgate.

However, based on the account given by the Crowland Chronicle continuator, we already know that there was plotting by more than one group in the summer of 1483, and that this plotting aimed at extracting the children of Edward IV from the Tower and from Westminster Abbey. That lends support to the hypothesis that Howard's task at Crosby's Place had been to handle an important trial. Certainly something significant, and mysterious, took place at Crosby's Place in July–August 1483. It is therefore possible that one of the attempts to extract the sons of Edward IV from the Tower of London may actually have succeeded. If so, some of the underlings who had played minor roles in the project for getting the two boys out of the Tower must have been caught. But probably the main instigators of the project had not been apprehended. It is difficult to suggest precisely who they may have been, and what they may have done. However, it is interesting to note that 'Richard of England' later reported that he had been got out of the Tower of London by a lord – though he mentions no name.

20

WOULD HENRY VII HAVE HAD THE BOYS KILLED?

The defeat and death of Richard III at the battle of Bosworth, followed by the usurpation of the English throne by Henry VII, changed the political situation in England completely. As we saw in chapter 11, after he had seized the throne, Henry hastened to execute William Catesby, Richard III's 'Catte', the stepson of one of Eleanor Talbot's first cousins. He also re-imprisoned Bishop Stillington of Bath and Wells,[1] who had announced to the royal council that he had secretly married Eleanor to King Edward IV before that king's subsequent secret marriage to Elizabeth Widville. The motivation behind both of those actions was Henry's concern in respect of King Edward IV and his marriage issue. And the reason why he felt concerned on that front was based upon the fact that he was already planning a political union for himself, by means of which he proposed to attempt to win over Yorkists to his side. The bride Henry had in mind was Edward IV's eldest child by Elizabeth Widville, her namesake, Elizabeth of York. Fortunately for Henry (possibly thanks in part to the marriage rumours which had been spread in England by his supporters), Elizabeth of York's planned marriage with a Portuguese prince, which her uncle Richard III had been negotiating for her, had not yet been concluded.

Henry VII was well aware of the fact that his own claim to the English throne was weak. His project of marrying the eldest surviving daughter of Edward IV meant that he would be able to promote the claim that his consort – and the mother of his future dynasty – was the heiress of the house of York. However, two important actions were required first. Unless they were taken, the situation which was then current precluded any possibility of him making such a claim in respect of his intended bride. The first of the two key issues was that the woman who had been known in the reign of Richard III as 'Lady Grey' now had to be formally acknowledged as the dowager queen of England. In other words, Henry VII had to reinstate Elizabeth Widville in her role as the former wife (now the widow) of King Edward IV – which he did (for a reference in this respect, see below, appendix 3). The second key point was the removal of the act of parliament which had established that Elizabeth's children by Edward were bastards. Unless that was removed – thus restoring the legitimacy of those children – Henry VII's intended bride was illegitimate and had no possible claim to the English crown.

Henry VII.

In his first parliament, Henry VII therefore organised a bizarre and unique procedure. He ordered that the 1484 act of parliament should be repealed. Normally when an act of parliament was repealed the text of the original act was quoted in full. At the very least, it was summarised in terms of its content. However, Henry VII would not allow either of those things to be done in this case. Instead he firmly prevented the words of the 1484 act from being quoted. He only permitted the first thirteen words of that act to be cited. Significantly, those few words revealed absolutely nothing of what the act had contained. Moreover, he firmly commanded that all copies of the 1484 act should be destroyed 'upon Peine of ymprisonment, ... so that all thinges said and remembered in the said Bill and Acte maie be for ever out of remembraunce and also forgott'.[2]

Henry VII's objective was obviously that Eleanor Talbot, and her marriage with Edward IV, should be completely expunged from history. Eleanor's sister Elizabeth Talbot, dowager Duchess of Norfolk appears to have been well aware of the fact that her dead sister was now being written out of history, because in 1495, when she was updating Eleanor's patronage of Corpus Christi College, Cambridge, she provided in the documentation a great deal of family information relating to Eleanor. This appears to have been an attempt on her part to ensure that, in some ways, at least, her beloved sister should not be entirely forgotten.[3] But for Henry VII, writing Eleanor out of history seemed to be the only sure way in which he could reinstate Elizabeth Widville as Edward IV's consort. That move would also result in the restoration to legitimate royal status of his own intended bride, Elizabeth of York, who could then be presented to the nation as the Yorkist heiress.

Unfortunately, of course, there was always a danger that, even when the 1484 act of parliament had been repealed, and all accessible copies of it had been destroyed, living people might still remember what kind of case had been put forward in respect of Edward IV, his marriages and his offspring. For example, many Londoners must have heard about the sermons which had been preached at St Paul's Cross in the summer of 1483. It was the fear that Eleanor Talbot and her cause might possibly still be remembered by the populace of England which inspired leading members of Henry VII's government to invent a fairy story for him in respect of the Edward IV marriage dispute. They did that by fabricating a woman's name. According to their newly created myth, the claim which had been put forward in 1483 in respect of Edward IV had been that the late king's legal marriage was with a woman called 'Elizabeth Lucy'. That was obviously intended to confuse anyone who might retain a vague memory of what had been proved in 1483 and 1484, and to ensure that all their brains would gradually mislay the name of Eleanor.

All the actions of Henry VII and his government in respect of the 1484 act of parliament did indeed effectively reinstate Elizabeth of York as a legitimate English princess. In addition, they also gave

Henry VII the advantage of being able to present Richard III to the world as a usurper. In reality, of course, that had not been the case. But for Henry it constituted helpful propaganda. Another outcome was that, for about two years, Elizabeth Widville found herself back at court. There she was once again formally recognised as the legal consort of the late king, Edward IV. She was also now recognised as the mother of the new queen consort. Hopefully she was additionally in the process of becoming the grandmother of a new royal dynasty.

Curiously, however, Henry VII's tenacious destruction of the 1484 act of parliament did not merely restore his intended consort, Elizabeth of York, to legitimate royal status. One unfortunate but inevitable side effect of Henry's repeal was that it also restored the rights to the throne of all his bride's sisters – not to mention the rights of both of her brothers! In other words, if either Edward V or Richard of Shrewsbury was alive in 1486–7, as the now reinstated legitimate son of a former king, the claim of the boy in question in respect of the sovereignty of England had once again become impeccable. Moreover, such a claim on the part of either of those boys would have been far stronger than the feeble claim of their new brother-in-law, King Henry VII. The fact that in those days masculinity gave precedence in respect of all rights of inheritance also meant that the claim of either or both of those boys would have been far stronger than the claim of Henry VII's bride. In other words, after the 1485 repeal of the 1484 act of parliament a surviving son of Edward IV (if there was one) would have had the strongest possible legal claim to the status of heir of the house of York. That was a status to which Elizabeth of York would have had no right if either of her brothers had still been provably in existence.

Elizabeth of York, consort of Henry VII, and the alleged Yorkist heiress.

One intriguing consequence of this is that after 1485 Henry VII's motivation for ending the lives of his brothers-in-law (the elder of whom would by then have been aged at least fifteen – and able to reign in his own right) would have been extremely strong. Indeed, it would have been far more compelling than Richard III's alleged earlier – but non-existent – motivation in that respect. The situation in which he had found himself in June 1483 meant that as far as Richard III had been concerned his two nephews represented absolutely no threat to him, or to his tenure of the English crown, because they had already been legally excluded from the succession.

On the other hand it is very clear that for Henry VII the sons of Edward IV represented a very strong potential threat now that their legitimacy had been re-established. The most significant proof in respect of this statement lies in the fact that he definitely did put to death 'Richard of England'/'Perkin Warbeck', who had advanced a powerful (and to some people, very convincing) claim to be the younger of those two 'princes'.

Earlier, in 1487, Henry VII had been forced to confront another claim to the English throne, made on the part of an earlier Yorkist pretender. At least one of Henry VII's servants subsequently suggested that the earlier pretender had also claimed to be the second of Elizabeth Widville's sons by Edward IV. That claim was made by Bernard André who wrote his account from about 1500 onwards. Thus he penned his assertion some thirteen or more years after the real claim of the actual pretender whom he was describing – and also after the more recent claim of the second Yorkist pretender, who definitely had claimed to be Elizabeth's second son by Edward IV – Richard of Shrewsbury, Duke of York.[4]

It is therefore more or less certain that, when he was writing his account, André was confused, and got things wrong. In reality the first pretender – who used the royal appellation of 'King Edward VI' – was definitely claiming to be the son of George, Duke of Clarence. Indeed, he may actually have been that Yorkist prince whose name he employed. Nevertheless, his presence on the political scene seems to have made Henry VII decide that maybe it would be wise for him to get rid of Elizabeth Widville. His mother-in-law therefore found herself disgraced. Deprived of her dower lands, and left with only a very small pension, she retreated to Bermondsey Abbey.

It is very interesting to note that, in spite of the fact that he had become her son-in-law, Henry VII treated Elizabeth in a much more dominant way than Richard III had ever done. It is also interesting to note that, at the same time as his dismissal from his royal court of Elizabeth Widville, Henry VII was behaving very firmly in his handling of one of her sons. His brother-in-law Thomas Grey, Marquess of Dorset, found himself imprisoned by Henry in the Tower of London in 1487. Of course, that son of Elizabeth was not of royal birth. If he had been, one could assert that Henry VII had created yet another 'prince in the Tower'!

Also, as we have seen, Henry definitely executed 'Richard of England'/'Perkin Warbeck' – who claimed to be the younger of Edward IV's two sons – in 1499. If Henry was mistaken in respect of the identity he attributed to that pretender, and if the pretender was telling the truth, then obviously it would then have been Henry VII who killed the younger of the so-called 'princes in the Tower'.

In addition, he also executed another 'prince in the Tower' – the prisoner he himself had placed there, who was believed to be the son of George, Duke of Clarence – and who, on that basis, would have possessed a much stronger *Lancastrian* claim to the throne than Henry VII. That was because the Duke of Clarence had been formally recognised by Henry VI, in 1470, as the next Lancastrian heir after himself and his own alleged son, Edward of Westminster, Prince of Wales.

In other words, proof exists that Henry VII definitely put to death two so-called 'princes' who were imprisoned in the Tower! One of the two was a young man whom Henry himself formally recognised as an English prince. The other was a young man whose identity Henry himself denied, but whose own claim was that he was an English prince – and the younger son of Edward IV and Elizabeth Widville.

In addition, other members of the royal house of York – the sons of Elizabeth Duchess of Suffolk, sister of Edward IV and Richard III – would also probably have been put to death by Henry VII if they had not escaped out of their homeland. Indeed, later one of them was extradited and put to death by Henry VIII. Thus there is firm evidence to show that the first two kings of the new dynasty did precisely the kind of thing which Richard III has long been accused of doing. However, in the case of Richard III there is no evidence to show that he put any royal relatives to death, other than the Duke of Buckingham, who had led a public rebellion against him. And Buckingham was not held for years in prison, but executed as soon as he had been defeated and captured.

So what did Henry VII believe in respect of the so-called 'princes in the Tower'? Did he believe that they were dead? Did he believe that Richard III had killed them? Or did he find them still living in the Tower of London when he took possession of it? It is hard to say. Undoubtedly he later put out the story that Richard III had organised their murder, as we shall see in chapter 23. However, that was done nineteen years after the alleged event. Why did it take him so long?

Obviously Henry was well aware of the fact that in the autumn of 1483, during 'Buckingham's Rebellion', the news had been promoted, 'possibly by Bishop Morton and his agents',[5] that the sons of Edward IV were dead. But he also knew well that the purpose which lay behind the spreading of that story was to draw those who felt opposed to the sovereignty of Richard III in the direction of *his own* support. As we have seen, initially the 1483 rebellion is said to have aimed for the restoration of Edward V to the throne. However, Henry's supporters needed to dispose of Edward V in order to win more backing for Henry, and the feeble – and originally lying – claim which he was putting forward for the English crown.[6] In other words Henry VII must always have been well aware that the story which had been told in the late summer and autumn of 1483 was merely propaganda aimed at winning support for him, and that there had never been any evidence to show that it was true.

He must also have known that a number of people in England believed that at least one of the sons of Edward IV was still alive. If that had not been the case, who would have given their support to 'Richard of England'? And if Henry VII had possessed any evidence in 1493 which could prove that both of Edward IV's sons were then dead, surely he would have used it as part of his campaign against the second Yorkist pretender. However, he never did that.

It therefore seems likely that Henry himself never had any precise knowledge in respect of what had happened to the two boys. Doubtless when he first seized the throne he sought them and tried to find out what had happened. That is probably why he rapidly sent for all the Yorkist princes and princesses whom Richard III had established at Sheriff Hutton Castle in Yorkshire. But all that emerged seems to have been that Edward IV's sons had never been sent to Sheriff Hutton by Richard III. Thus they had not been living there with their sisters and their Clarence cousins. Beyond that, it seems likely that Henry VII never found out what had really happened to the two boys.

21

WHAT MYTHS ARE TOLD ABOUT 'RICHARD OF ENGLAND'?

In respect of the second Yorkist contester for the ousting of Henry VII – the young man who claimed to be the younger of the two so-called 'princes in the Tower' – various stories are told. These include the claim that Henry VII knew, and revealed, his true identity. Certainly Henry assigned to him the name of 'Perkin Warbeck'. However, no solid evidence exists to prove that point, even though, when he was tortured and killed, the claimant himself was made to accept it.

It has been claimed by one modern writer that the young contester 'remained in *Malines* [*Mechelen*] until the summer of 1495'.[1] However, that seems to be incorrect, and to ignore surviving source material from the Low Countries, which shows that 'Richard of England' was on the move just after Easter (Sunday 19 April) 1495. For example, Aurelius reports,

> In the year 1495 on Monday after the octave of Easter [Monday 27 April 1495, or Monday 4 May 1495?],[2] late in the evening, Richard, the son of King Edward, who is called 'The White Rose' arrived at the town of Haarlem. There he stayed for a while with the Knights of the Order of St John[3] to wait for his people and other military equipment, because he wanted to go to England to reclaim his fatherly inheritance and the crown, which belonged to him by right.[4]

Also a document dating from about 18 April 1495 has recently been rediscovered in the Dutch National Archives which requests the welcoming of 'the Duke of York' (*Hertoghe van Juorck*) to Leiden.[5] That may well have referred to his journey to Haarlem.

Among the stories told about him are the very strong claims which have been made in respect of some so-called coins in his name. One set of specimens, made of silver, is said to have been issued for him by his supporters. Another type of coin, made of base metal, is said to have been produced at the town in the Low Countries from which he was alleged by Henry VII to have come, and it is said to confirm that his true identity was 'Perkin'. Unfortunately, however, both of those stories seem merely to be further examples of mythology.

History of Coins

For more than two thousand years, one of the normal outcomes of the tenure of sovereignty has indeed been the issuing of coins. That practice probably began in Lydia, towards the end of the seventh century BC. It was then promoted and developed by the Achaemenid dynasty of shahs in Iran (Persia).

A silver coin issued by the Achaemenid dynasty in Iran *c.* 400 BC, from the author's collection.

Where monarchs were involved, it rapidly became the norm for an image of the reigning monarch to be stamped into the metal. Later, other royal symbols, names, and titles were usually included. Finally its production date was added to a coin. In England, however, that development only occurred in the sixteenth century.

It is also clearly the case that the political significance of the issue of coins did often make claimants to a throne try to issue coins in their name. For example, claimants to the Roman Empire did so. And later, in England, the Empress Matilda, daughter of Henry I and mother of Henry II, is known to have issued coins in her name in the 1140s, when she was fighting her cousin Stephen for the crown. Later, after the 1688 revolution, King James VII and II continued to issue coins in Ireland despite having been robbed of his thrones by his own daughter and his nephew and son-in-law. Subsequently coins were also prepared in the name of his son and heir, 'James VIII and III' (the 'Old Pretender'). And ironically the 'Old Pretender' is another claimant to the English throne whose true identity was questioned by his opponents![6] Later, in the nineteenth century, coins were issued in the names of the dethroned Legitimist Bourbon king 'Henri V' of France, and of Carlist pretenders to the Spanish throne.

A silver penny of Richard III and a silver four penny piece ('groat') of his ancestor, Edward III, from the author's collection, showing how the symbolic images of monarchs on English coins were not really portraits in the fifteenth century.

Were there coins of Edward V?

As we have seen, in fifteenth-century England no date was normally included on coins. And although an image of the monarch was represented on the front (obverse) of the coin, it was not a real portrait. A forward-facing crowned bust which was first introduced in the reign of King Edward I simply continued in use more or less unchanged until the reign of Henry VII. Moreover, the basic design of all English silver coins remained unchanged throughout that period. As a result all the English monarchs from Edward I to Henry VII look more or less identical on their coins. Around their royal images the name and titles of the monarch were inscribed in Latin. However no royal numeral was ever employed on medieval English coins. It can therefore sometimes be rather difficult to determine which 'Henry' or 'Edward' it was for whom a particular coin was issued.

One result of that problem which is relevant in respect of the present study is the fact that it is very difficult to discover whether any coins were ever issued in England for the young King Edward V during his brief reign. Presumably coins would have been produced at the English mints in April and May 1483. But of course they would simply have borne the same royal image and royal name, and had the same design, as the coins which had been issued in earlier months on behalf of the boy-king's father.

Were there coins of 'Edward VI'?

Curiously, however, it does seem that coins were issued in Ireland, in 1486–7, on behalf of the first Yorkist pretender to the throne which was then occupied by Henry VII, namely 'King Edward VI'. The evidence in that respect depends upon the fact that in the last months of his reign Edward IV appears to have been planning to update the design of the Irish coinage. His surviving indenture on that subject is not precisely dated. However, it was probably issued at about the same time as the appointment of Thomas Galmole as master of the Irish mints, which occurred on 7 March 1482/3.[7] The indenture in question made provision for the issue of new Irish coins, which would bear on their reverse the medieval Irish coat of arms. That comprised three open crowns (the harp was only introduced as the symbol of Ireland later, in the sixteenth century, by King Henry VIII). Nevertheless, in spite of the fact that such plans had been made, it appears that the death of King Edward IV shortly afterwards meant that the proposed new coins were never actually issued on his behalf, or in his name.[8]

The medieval arms of Ireland, redrawn from a manuscript commissioned by King Edward IV.

In Ireland, as in England, it appears to be impossible to distinguish coins which were minted during the brief reign of Edward IV's eldest son, the boy-king Edward V. But when Richard III accepted the crown, initially he continued to produce Irish coins of Edward IV's earlier 'rose on cross' reverse design – though of course the royal name which they bore was now changed to RICARDVS. However, after a short time Richard III began having groats and half groats produced in the new 'three crowns' reverse design which had been planned earlier by his brother. It therefore appears to be the case that the minting of coins of that design was actually introduced by King Richard III. Later, after August 1485, minting of the new 'three crowns' coins was continued by Henry VII, though of course the royal name on the obverse inscription was then changed to HENRICVS.

However, curiously, some 'three crowns' coins were produced bearing the name 'EDWARDVS'. Since coins of that design had not been produced either for Edward IV, or for Edward V, it seems that the examples in question must have been produced for the Dublin-crowned Yorkist boy-king, who assumed the royal name and number of 'Edward VI'. One further piece of evidence supports that belief. Every 'three crowns' coin displays the royal arms (France quartering England) on its obverse. However, in the case of a few coins bearing the name EDWARDVS those royal arms are flanked on either side by tiny shields bearing the personal arms of the Earl of Kildare. He was the chief Irish supporter of 'King Edward VI'.[9] Thus it does seem that Irish coins were issued in the name of the first Yorkist pretender, 'King Edward VI'.

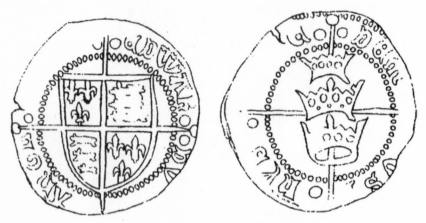

A 'Three Crowns' Irish groat bearing the name of Edward ('King Edward VI').

Coins of 'Richard of England/Richard IV'?

Later, it has been alleged, a silver coin was also produced on behalf of the second Yorkist pretender, 'Richard of England'. Various claims have been made in respect of where the alleged coin was produced. However, all the existing examples of it are to be found in England. Ann Wroe's book *Perkin: A story of deception* includes an illustration of what Wroe describes as 'a silver *gros* coin of Richard IV'.[10] For one example of the so-called 'coin' in question, see plate 31 of the present book. However, the 'coin' does not carry the name 'Richard'. (It also does not carry the numeral 'IV' – but, as we have already seen, no medieval English coins ever bore the sovereign's numeral.)

What Wroe depicted – and what are illustrated here in plate 31 – are actually extremely rare silver pieces bearing the date 1494. They are often described as 'groats' – though their weight of 60.3 grains (3.91 grams) actually makes them heavier than either the contemporary English groat or the Irish coin of the same name. They were also somewhat heavier than the silver *double patard* issued by Charles the Bold, Duke of Burgundy.

Curiously, they approximate very closely to the weight of the English groat prior to Edward IV's unpopular coinage reforms of

1464.[11] In fact their bullion value would have made them equivalent to just over *five* English silver pennies in 1494, had they ever actually been used as currency. However, unlike the EDWARDVS 'three crowns' coins produced in Dublin, it seems highly unlikely that the so-called 'groat' bearing the date of 1494 was ever really intended to serve as currency. Although some surviving examples do show signs of wear, they seem rather to have been intended as medallic, commemorative pieces of some kind. It would probably therefore be more accurate to refer to them as 'medallions'.

As can be seen in plate 31, the obverse of the 1494 medallion bears the royal arms (France quartering England). The shield is surmounted by a royal crown, which is closed with arches. Also there are a crowned lis and a crowned rose to the right and left of the shield. As for the obverse inscription, that reads

[leopard] DOMINE SALVUM FAC REGEM.

Which means 'Lord save the King'.

The reverse of the medallion bears a lis, a leopard and a rose, all beneath a closed crown, together with the inscription

[leopard] MANI TECKEL PHARES 1494.

Key features of the iconography will be considered in greater detail shortly.

We have already noted that the introduction of regular dating on English coins is a phenomenon of the sixteenth century. Thus the fact that a date appears on the 1494 medallion makes it highly unusual in English terms. Curiously, however, in France – a country with which King Henry VII had close personal connections – the date in Arabic numerals had first been added to a coin just three years earlier (in 1491).[12] As for the intriguing reverse inscription of the 1494 medallion, that is a quotation from the Book of Daniel, chapter 5, verse 25 (as it figures in the Latin *Vulgate* version of the Bible). It is the threatening 'writing on the wall' which is said to have appeared at Belshazar's feast, to warn a king of his approaching doom.

Overall, the inscription on this medallion has usually been interpreted as comprising first a prayer for the legitimate king of

England (the second Yorkist pretender, 'King Richard IV'), and second a warning to the usurping Henry VII that his days were numbered.[13] However, in reality there is nothing on the medallion – either in terms of inscriptions or symbols – which firmly links it to 'Richard IV'. In fact, the attribution of these medallions to 'Richard IV' appears simply to be based upon the year date of 1494 which they bear.

Yet, curiously, certain features of the design of the medallion actually seem to link it more closely to Henry VII, and his claim to be the Lancastrian heir to the English throne. For example, no coins issued under the house of York display a closed crown – though it is true that the royal seal of 'King Richard IV' reportedly bore a closed crown (see above, chapter 5, and plate 8). Yorkist kings certainly seem to have sometimes used closed crowns. However, that feature was only first depicted on the English silver coinage by King Henry VII in about February 1488.[14] As for the medallion's juxtaposed use of a fleur-de-lis and a leopard, those symbols had figured prominently upon the Lancastrian dynasty's French coinage. For example, a lis and a leopard flanking a Latin cross adorned the reverse of both the *salut d'or* and the *grand blanc aux écus* of Henry V and Henry VI. However, there is no evidence for the use of those juxtaposed symbols on any Yorkist silver coins.[15]

Yet, as we have seen, the 1494 medallion combines those two symbols with a rose. Roses had not figured on any English coins until they were introduced by Edward IV. However, by 1494, the rose was no longer an exclusively Yorkist emblem, because it had clearly also been adopted by Henry VII. As the roses on the 1494 medallion bear no sign of their colour, it is impossible to be certain whether it is the Yorkist white rose that is intended, or the new red rose symbol of Henry VII. However, one of the roses is crowned, and the crowned rose image certainly seems to have been introduced by Henry VII.[16] Moreover, neither of the depicted roses is associated with the Yorkist sunburst. On balance it therefore seems more likely that the red rose of Henry VII is intended.

In the light of that evidence, it is not surprising to discover that the crown over the royal arms on the obverse of the 1494 medallion appears to be identical to the closed crown worn by Henry VII as depicted on some of his English groats. In a paper offered to the 1986 International Numismatic Congress in London, Marion Archibald (then curator at the British Museum) demonstrated conclusively 'that some of the punches used to create the dies from which [the 1494 pieces] were struck were identical with some on dies for groats of Henry VII ... This showed that, special pleading apart, the pieces in question were made in the same place as the groats of Henry VII, namely the Royal Mint in the Tower of London and that they were therefore official Tudor tokens.'[17]

Thus it appears to be the case that it must have been Henry VII himself who commanded the manufacture of the 1494 medallion, which was then struck for him at the Tower mint. In other words the medallion was presumably manufactured as a token backing Henry's attempt to oust the second Yorkist pretender, 'King Richard IV'. The inscription which reads *Domine salvum fac regem* would therefore constitute a prayer *for* Henry VII, not a prayer against him. In other words, it appears to be true that the 1494 medallion is linked in a way with the campaign of 'Richard IV'. However, it was produced by his opponents, not by his supporters.

Later, in the nineteenth century, another claim was made that a coin had been produced which was associated with 'Richard IV'. Once again, however, the example was not a true coin. This time it was a jetton or counter. *Jettons* (jetons), tokens or reckoning counters, are coin-like objects, made of base metal and used in calculations. The suggestion was made that this particular example must have been minted when 'Richard IV' had already been defeated. He was then a prisoner in the hands of Henry VII, still alive, but now known as 'Perkin Warbeck'.

The claim in respect of this alleged jetton was published in 1860 by Longpérier.[18] He illustrated a drawing (not a photograph) of a jetton which he presented as part of a well-known series of base metal jettons or tokens, production of which began in Tournai in about 1475 and continued throughout the sixteenth century. Specifically Longpérier's example, as depicted by him, appears to be one of what Mitchiner later defined as a series of jettons bearing the 'three circles' badge of Tournai.[19]

The genuine jettons of the series defined by Mitchiner include frequent minor variations in the details of their design. Also, examples of jettons belonging to the 'three circles' group were certainly shipped to, and used in, England. For example, my own coin collection contains two 'three circles' jettons, though neither of them bears the alleged *Vive Perkin* inscription cited by Longpérier. One of them was excavated in Cambridgeshire. It might therefore be tempting to imagine that the alleged *Vive Perkin* jetton design may have been specially introduced 'tongue in cheek', to fulfil an English export order. Unfortunately, however, evidence in support of the actual production of the alleged jetton described and published by Longpérier is entirely lacking. For example, England's Small Finds Register produces no evidence that *Vive Perkin* jettons have ever been discovered in England.

As described and illustrated by Longpérier, the *Vive Perkin* jetton depicts on its obverse a cross fleury with flowers in its angles, all enclosed in a quatrefoil, accompanied by the French inscription

VIVE PERKIN IETOIS DE TOURNAI

This could be taken to mean either 'Long live Perkin; I was from Tournai', or 'Long live Perkin; Tournai jetton'. However, the form *ietois* for 'jetton' seems to be otherwise completely unknown. On the reverse Longpérier depicts three circles, each containing a small flower of four petals, with fleurs-de-lis between the circles. The reverse is said to be inscribed in Latin

O MATER DEI MEMENTO MEI

'O Mother of God, remember me.' Longpérier states that this was the motto of King Louis XI of France, and certainly it is an inscription which appears on many of the early Tournai jettons. For the drawn image of this alleged 'Perkin' jetton as published by Longpérier, see plate 32.

There can be no question that very similar Tournai tokens really do exist. One is illustrated in plate 33. However, all the genuine examples have different obverse inscriptions from the one claimed by Longpérier. The key feature of his alleged inscription is obviously the inclusion of the words *Vive Perkin*. If authentic, the piece of numismatic irony which was published by Longpérier would presumably have been inspired by the fact that, according to Henry

VII, the second Yorkist pretender was really called Perkin Warbeck and came from Tournai.

Sadly, however, the major difficulty in respect of the *Vive Perkin* Tournai jetton is the question of whether such a thing ever really existed. Longpérier did not illustrate it by photograph, so there is no solid proof that he really had one. As for Mitchiner's more recent detailed list of medieval jettons, that does not include Longpérier's alleged example. And although the present writer has hunted very hard for one, he has completely failed to find a single specimen of the 'Perkin' jetton. It therefore seems probable that Longpérier must have been handling a very worn example of a fifteenth-century Tournai jetton, the inscription of which had been hard for him to read. Moreover, there are many genuine examples which bear inscriptions consisting wholly or in part of nonsensical strings of letters which never made any sense.[20]

Among the jettons listed by Mitchener, one of the closest to Longpérier's alleged *Vive Perkin* specimen is Mitchener's number 753a (p. 243), which bears the inscriptions *Vive le roi* and *Se [sic] sois de Tournai*. One possibility, therefore, is that the obverse inscription which was reported by Longpérier as reading

VIVE PERKIN IETOIS DE TOURNAI

was in reality a worn inscription which had originally read

VIVE LE ROI IE SOIS DE TOURNAI

Meaning 'Long live the king; I am from Tournai'. That inscription would make sense, and all of its component parts are actually to be found on authentic Tournai jettons. On the other hand no known jetton bears an inscription which includes the reported words *Perkin* and *ietois*.[21] It therefore seems likely that Longpérier's alleged *Vive Perkin* jetton never really existed.

Sadly, Longpérier's would not be the only false claim which has been put forward in respect of an alleged coin of 'King Richard IV'. Another case also occurred in the nineteenth century – and has also proved to be illusory. In 1889 Longstaffe published an article claiming that he had discovered a 'Richard IV' groat. But his claim ultimately proved to be false. What he actually had was an altered groat of Henry VII.[22]

In other words, no real evidence exists to prove that there were ever any coins issued on behalf of 'King Richard IV'. In the case of the 1494 medallion, nothing but its date appears to connect it with the second Yorkist pretender. Moreover, although the medallion may, in a way, have been connected with him, it now seems more likely to have been produced by his opponents than by his supporters. As for the supposed *Vive Perkin* Tournai jetton, probably that never really existed.

22

WHAT MYTHS ARE TOLD ABOUT 'RICHARD OF EASTWELL'?

Record of the burial of Rychard Plantagenet at Eastwell on 22 December 1550.

The church records of the parish of Eastwell in Kent, which were written (copied from an earlier manuscript) in about 1598, record that on Monday 22 December 1550 a man named as 'Rychard Plantagenet was buryed' there.[1] Nothing is known for certain in respect of who 'Rychard Plantagenet' was. However, a story is recorded in a letter written on 1 September 1733 by a clergyman living not far away at Wye. In that letter, local, orally transmitted stories about the man in question are reported, which assert that he had worked locally as a bricklayer, but that, in his youth, he had reportedly been taken to Leicestershire in August 1485, just before the battle of Bosworth, and presented to King Richard III, who 'told him he was his son'.[2]

Subsequently, myths grew up in respect of precisely where at Eastwell 'Rychard Plantagenet' had been buried. As is standard with burial data of that period, his burial site was not noted in the records of 1598. Nor was it mentioned in the 1733 report. Probably in reality he had simply been buried in the graveyard, and his grave was never marked, because whoever he was, he had clearly been living in a low social status as a bricklayer, and was therefore not well off.

Sadly, however, a stone monument which survives in the ruins of Eastwell church later came to be popularly identified as his burial site (plate 35).[3] The monument in question has on top of it a slab which once depicted a husband and wife and children in costumes of the 1480s. Since 'Rychard Plantagenet' is not recorded as ever having had a wife or children, and since he did not die in the 1480s, that evidence seems to prove that the tomb is not his. As a result, despite the popular mythology in respect of that monument, 'archaeologists of the present day confidently declare that the tomb is not that of Plantagenet'.[4]

The upper surface of the tomb which is erroneously assigned to 'Rychard Plantagenet', showing that it dates from the 1480s and bore brasses commemorating a husband, wife and children. Reproduced from *Archaeologia Cantiana*, 59, 1946.

New mythology developed in respect of 'Rychard Plantagenet' comparatively recently. As we have seen, eighteenth-century accounts suggested that he had been a bastard son of King Richard III. That story may or may not be true. However, there is certainly no genuine contemporary evidence in that respect. What is more, genuine contemporary evidence certainly does survive which shows clearly that Richard III recognised his known illegitimate children publicly, and made arrangements for them in respect of their futures.

However, earlier in the present century David Baldwin put forward the suggestion that in reality 'Rychard Plantagenet' may have been Richard of Shrewsbury, the younger son of King Edward IV. As was proposed earlier, in chapter 17 of this present study, Edward IV's elder son, Edward V, the bastard king, probably died from natural causes shortly after he had been excluded from the throne on the grounds of his father's bigamy. Baldwin agrees with the theory that Edward probably died naturally, and he believes that thereafter Edward's younger brother, Richard, was reunited with his mother. Baldwin suggests that young Richard then lived with Elizabeth Widville under the supervision of two trusted courtiers (John Nesfield and James Tyrell).

Of course during the reign of Richard III, Richard of Shrewsbury would always have been a bastard, and as we have seen, at that time his mother was referred to as 'Lady Grey'. However, Baldwin makes the error of referring to young Richard as a 'prince', and of referring to Elizabeth Widville as a 'queen'. That shows that he did not really understand the true nature of Richard III's kingship and the reasons behind it.

He also accepts a story which was put out by Richard III's enemies. It was an allegation that, following the death of his wife, Anne of Warwick, King Richard planned to marry his bastard niece, Elizabeth of York. Obviously the planning of such a marriage would have been ludicrous. As we have seen in 1483 the three estates of the realm had decided that Edward IV's marriage with Elizabeth Widville was bigamous and therefore invalid. It was then publicly stated that the children of the Widville marriage were all bastards. Moreover, in 1484 those decisions had been formalised in an act of parliament. Nothing was ever done during Richard III's reign to reverse that legislation – which was why Henry VII found himself obliged to take such firm action in that respect in November 1485, in order to proceed with his own planned marriage with Elizabeth of York. It is therefore completely illogical to suggest that Richard III would ever have considered marrying one of his elder brother's illegitimate daughters.[5]

Indeed, contemporary sources show very clearly that, while the marriage story was put about in certain quarters in 1484/5, it greatly upset King Richard III.[6] As we have seen, in reality he was then planning Portuguese royal marriages both for himself and for his eldest illegitimate niece. Indeed it was probably Richard III's plans in that respect which caused supporters of the 'Earl of Richmond' (later Henry VII) to propagate the marriage myth in respect of the king.

The 'Earl of Richmond' had already voiced his *own* hopes of marrying Elizabeth of York. Thus he and his supporters would have been very concerned to hear that Richard III was now planning a Portuguese royal marriage for Elizabeth. That probably explains why the myth was put out which alleged that Richard himself was planning to marry his own bastard niece. The objective behind the spreading of that story would presumably have been to try to cause problems for the king in respect of his ongoing Portuguese royal marriage negotiations.

True contemporary evidence shows very clearly that the distressed King Richard III hastened to put out public statements denying the rumour that he himself planned to marry Elizabeth of York. On Wednesday 30 March 1485 (the day before Maundy Thursday) at the Priory of the Knights of St John at Clerkenwell, in the presence of the lord mayor and other significant London citizens, Richard III denied any plans for a marriage between himself and his niece. He also ordered the mayor to arrest and punish anyone who was caught spreading that story.[7] A week later, after Easter, on Tuesday 5 April, the king sent similar instructions to the city of York.[8]

Baldwin's acceptance of the notion that Richard III was planning to marry his bastard niece is therefore clearly contradicted by all the surviving contemporary source material. Unfortunately, however, his misunderstanding of the bastardy issue in respect of the children of Edward IV and Elizabeth Widville then also leads Baldwin to make another mistake. Based on the eighteenth-century story in respect of 'Rychard Plantagenet', Baldwin states that the 'Rychard' in question – whom he believes was really Richard of Shrewsbury – was transported to Lutterworth in Leicestershire, and that from there he was taken to see the king at the Bosworth battlefield on the day before the battle. His suggestion in respect of that alleged meeting is that Richard III may then have been considering naming the boy (the surviving son of Edward IV) as his heir.

This will not do for two reasons. First, as we have seen, Richard III's kingship depended upon the bastardy of Edward V, Richard of Shrewsbury and their sisters. Second, Richard had two other acknowledged nephews who were definitely not bastards, and who could potentially have been his heirs. The first of them was the eldest son of his middle sister, the Duchess of Suffolk – namely John de la Pole, Earl of Lincoln – and the second was the boy who was thought to be the son and heir of his middle brother, the Duke of Clarence – namely the theoretical Edward, Earl of Warwick. Since his accession to the throne in the summer of 1483, Richard III had been working with both of those nephews. It is true that, legally, the Earl of Warwick was excluded from the succession to the throne by Edward IV's 1477/8 act of attainder against his father. However, that could have been repealed if Richard III so wished.

Subsequently Baldwin suggests that, following Richard III's defeat and death at Bosworth, young 'Rychard' was rescued by Francis, Viscount Lovell, who then took him to the safe sanctuary of St John's Abbey in Colchester. Unfortunately Baldwin's account also contains errors in respect of Colchester. For example, he states that the then Abbot of Colchester, Walter Stansted, *'was not a noted Yorkist'*.[9] Yet once again, on the basis of the genuine contemporary evidence, that statement appears to be incorrect, as the present writer's previously published work has indicated.[10]

The important Benedictine Abbey of St John's was a mitred abbey with impressive rights of chartered sanctuary, identical to those enjoyed by Westminster Abbey.[11] Also the abbot of Colchester had a seat in Parliament. When the long abbacy of Abbot Ardeley ended with his death in 1464, he was succeeded by John Canon (1464-68), who was a Howard *protégé*.[12] In theory the choir monks of the abbey had freedom to elect their father abbot, but evidently in this instance John Howard had exerted some influence in the matter, since he himself recorded that he had secured Canon's election as abbot.

When Abbot Canon died after only four years of office it seems probable that Howard would also have sought to influence the choice of his successor. No direct evidence survives of Howard's involvement in the election of 1468, which brought to power Walter Stansted (1468–97).[13] However, Abbot Stansted gave Lord Howard sanctuary at his abbey during the Lancastrian Readeption, and the abbot seems not to have attended the

Lancastrian Parliament of 1470–71. If he was known as a Howard nominee, the Earl of Warwick may have wished to avoid summoning him.[14] It does seem likely that Stansted shared Howard's political loyalties.

After the battle of Bosworth, the abbot received Yorkist fugitives at the abbey, most notably Francis, Lord Lovell.[15] The abbey may subsequently have been implicated in the Yorkist risings which focussed on 'Lambert Simnel' and 'Perkin Warbeck'. Later, it received indirect bequests from Cecily Neville, dowager Duchess of York.[16] Interestingly, when Abbot Stansted died no election was permitted. Instead, the new abbot was directly appointed by the Bishop of London. This procedure was unusual, and may represent an attempt on the part of King Henry VII (through the bishop) to bring the abbey to heel. Another innovation at that time was the fact that Henry VII had subsequently to be paid in order to secure restoration of the abbey's temporalities![17]

Baldwin does accept that Yorkists saw St John's Abbey in Colchester as a very safe place of sanctuary. He then invents a theory which suggests that 'King Richard may have thought Lutterworth too precarious a refuge for his nephew if Henry Tudor gained the victory, and ordered Lovel and the Staffords to deliver the boy into the safer hands of Abbot Stansted in the event of his defeat or death'.[18] But as Baldwin himself admits, there is not a shred of evidence to prove that. Nor is there a shred of evidence to prove *his* theory that 'Rychard Plantagenet' was Richard of Shrewsbury – or ever claimed that identity.

Nevertheless, despite the fact that it has now been shown that a lot of mythology exists regarding 'Rychard Plantagenet' of Eastwell, the notion that he might have been Richard of Shrewsbury is worth considering. The significant points in support of that notion are:

1. The geographical location of Eastwell – just a few kilometres north of Ashford and Repton, in Kent.
2. The fact that the attempted abduction of the two sons of Edward IV from London in July 1483 appears to have been led by men from Kent.
3. One of the Kentish men involved in the abduction attempt was probably Sir John Fogge of Ashford and Repton.
4. Sir John Fogge's wife was Elizabeth Widville's first cousin and lady-in-waiting Alice Lady Fogge (*née* Haute), whom Richard of Shrewsbury must have known very well, because she figured in his mother's household while he was growing up there.

In other words, it is possible that Richard of Shrewsbury actually was abducted from London in July 1483 and was taken to Kent, where he was placed in the care of his mother's cousin at the Repton manor house. It is also possible that he then lived the rest of his life secretly in that vicinity, ultimately dying and being buried in the churchyard at Eastwell in 1550, aged seventy-seven. If so, it is not likely that Richard III ever discovered his whereabouts, or had him brought to Leicestershire just before the battle of Bosworth. Nevertheless, if 'Rychard Plantagenet' of Eastwell really was Richard of Shrewsbury, he himself must presumably have been well aware of the fact that Richard III had recognised him as a royal bastard. So he may have described himself in that way!

23

WHEN WAS THE STORY OF THE MURDER OF THE 'PRINCES IN THE TOWER' PUT OUT?

An imaginary nineteenth-century engraving, showing the alleged murder of the 'princes in the Tower'.

Contemporary late fifteenth-century sources in respect of the fate of the 'princes' are conflicting, and very much lacking in detail. Some people assumed they were alive, others assumed they were dead.

Some people thought then (or think today) that they were concealed somewhere in England (or one of them was), others thought then (or think today) that they (or one of them) had been taken out of the country. Some believed that the Duke of Buckingham was responsible for their fate, whatever it had been. Other assumed that the reigning monarch (Richard III) must have been responsible.

There was never universal belief that both of Edward IV's sons had experienced the same outcome. As we have seen clearly, no one ever came forward claiming to be the living Edward V. It therefore seems to have been generally accepted that he was dead. Indeed, it appears that the pope himself must have heard that Edward V had died, and accepted that. Celebrating a Requiem Mass for someone who is not dead is – and always was – sinful. So the pope would not have done it if he had not felt certain.

Of course a great deal of rumour in respect of contemporary events in England was circulating in the second half of the 1480s. For example a chronicle written in the Low Countries by Adrien De But, Prior of the Cistercian Abbey of the Dunes at Koksijde, reveals that on 5 October 1485, when Bishop John Morton stayed at De But's abbey on his way back to England from Rome (travelling via Calais), he received the news that his recently enthroned master, King Henry VII – though De But prefers to call him 'the Earl of Richmond' – had just died of plague:

> 5th October, the Reverend Father in Christ, the Bishop of Ely, returning from our most holy Pope Innocent VIII, making his trip back to England via the Dunes monastery (when he reached Calais), heard of the death of the Earl of Richmond, who was recently made king.[1]

There does seem to have been plague in England, but obviously the story of Henry VII's death later proved to be false. However, the telling of it underlines the fact that Henry VII was then a very new king, who had seized power by armed rebellion. In 1485 and 1486 no one simply assumed that his reign would go on for years. Thus De But's account also indicates that, both in England and abroad, people were then speculating as to when, how and possibly by whom Henry VII would himself be ousted.

False stories were by no means unusual. As we have seen, another story, produced early in the sixteenth-century by Bernard André, also seems to have contained a mistake. André stated that the 1487 pretender to the English throne had initially claimed to be Richard, the younger of the two sons of Edward IV. Yet the actual surviving evidence clearly shows that the pretender in question used the royal name of 'King Edward VI'.[2] Thus he cannot have claimed to be Richard of Shrewsbury. Yet, even though André's account was inaccurate, it has a certain value in respect of the so-called 'princes'. It shows that, in the late 1480s and the 1490s, many people must have believed that at least the younger of Edward IV's two sons by Elizabeth Widville might still be alive.

Curiously, although Henry VII's government referred to Richard III as 'in dede and not of right King of England',[3] thereby systematically characterising him as a 'usurper' who had seized the crown,[4] and although Henry's parliament of 1485 attainted 'the late Duke of Gloucester, calling himself Richard the Third',[5] at that stage no one ever specifically accused Richard of having killed his nephews.

It is true that the condemnation of Richard III and his supporters which was enacted in Henry VII's first parliament stated that the new king was

> not oblivious or unmindful of the unnatural, wicked and great perjuries, treasons, homicides and murders, in shedding infants' blood, with many other wrongs, odious offences and abominations against God and man, and in particular against our said sovereign lord, committed and done by Richard, late duke of Gloucester, calling and naming himself, by usurpation, King Richard III.[6]

However, that inexplicit reproof merely includes the vague term 'shedding infants' blood' in the midst of a total of eight ambiguously asserted misdemeanours.

Also, while the statement cites the name of the ousted monarch first, it then goes on to list the names of twenty-eight of his supporters, who are also condemned for the same imprecise offences, which are said to have had the future Henry VII as their prime target. The list of other culprits begins with John Howard, Duke of Norfolk. It also includes Richard Ratcliffe, Robert Brackenbury and William Catesby. In other words it is clear that no specific accusation was being personally directed at Richard III on this occasion. It is also clear that Richard was not explicitly being accused of having murdered the sons of Edward IV. Moreover, since any (or all) of the twenty-nine named men might have been being accused of 'shedding infants' blood', it appears that the allegedly reluctant Robert Brackenbury (who was later categorically stated by Thomas More to have *refused* to kill the sons of Edward IV in the Tower of London – see below, chapter 25), may also have been thought, in 1485, to have been responsible for having harmed some children. But of course there had allegedly been more than a score of other wrongdoers in that imprecise and vague respect.

Moreover, since the 'odious offences and abominations' were said to have been directed 'against God' as well as against human beings, it is also possibly significant that in the Middle Ages the devil and his devotees were believed to murder children. Thus the words that were employed by the government of Henry VII on this occasion could merely have been part of a wider attempt by the new regime to blacken the reputations of the former king and his supporters who had recently been killed at the battle of Bosworth, or executed after the battle.

It was only in 1502, when nineteen years had elapsed after the supposed date of the alleged killing of Edward IV's two sons, that Henry VII's government finally produced a serious account of how Richard III was said to have had his nephews put to death. That was after 'Richard of England' had claimed the throne as the surviving Richard of Shrewsbury. And *his* claim was one of the motives which led Henry's government to put forward *their* new claim in respect of Richard III. Their other motives will be explored in the next chapter.

As for Thomas More, he was the man who subsequently wrote the account of the purported (but unproven) killing which is now usually cited (see below, chapter 25). However, he wrote that about thirty years after the reputed event. More himself had been a mere boy of five in 1483, when the drama which he later reported in such detail was supposed to have occurred. In reality, his source for the story as he later wrote it must have been Cardinal Archbishop John Morton. In 1490, at the age of about thirteen, the young Thomas More had been placed by his father in the Lambeth household of Archbishop (later Cardinal) Morton.[7]

Although More's account certainly helped in the blackening of Richard III, its source was even more significant in another way for England's new ruling dynasty. In 1502 the initiation of the story which More later included in his text meant that although previously there had been three Yorkist pretenders – at least one of whom had claimed to be the younger son of Edward IV – in future no one would be able to claim to be a living son of Edward IV. From 1502 onwards the official version of their life story stated clearly that both Edward V and Richard of Shrewsbury were deceased, having been murdered nineteen years earlier, in 1483.

24

HOW AND WHY WAS THE STORY PROMULGATED?

TIMESCALE
Names and titles which are disputable are marked in inverted commas.

1483
July/Aug. ?Abduction of the two boys from London;
?Death of Edward V (?natural causes);
?Rescue of Richard of Shrewsbury;
?Alleged murder of the 'princes'.

1485 Usurpation of Henry VII.

1486-7 'John (*BLANK*)/Lambert Simnel/Edward, Earl of Warwick/King Edward VI' claims the throne.

1488 Marriage proposed between Arthur, Prince of Wales and a legitimate Lancastrian princess, the Infanta Catherine of Aragon.

1489-90 Attempt made to extract the 'Earl of Warwick' from the Tower.[1] The Abbot of Abingdon is indicted for treason.

1491 'Richard of England/Perkin Warbeck/King Richard IV' arrives in Ireland.

1493 Edmund de la Pole, the senior living male member of the house of York as recognised by Henry VII, is demoted by the king from the title 'Duke of Suffolk' to 'Earl of Suffolk'.

1494–5	'Richard of England/Perkin Warbeck/King Richard IV' claims the throne.
1497	Proxy betrothal of Prince Arthur and Catherine of Aragon.
1498–9	Ralph Wilford claims to be the Earl of Warwick, who has escaped from the Tower. He is captured and executed.
1499	
19 May	Arthur, Prince of Wales married by proxy to the Infanta Catherine of Aragon, but her parents will not send her to England while the 'Earl of Warwick' remains alive.[2]
23 Nov.	'Perkin Warbeck' (prisoner in the Tower) executed.
28 Nov.	'Earl of Warwick' (prisoner in the Tower) executed.
1499/1500	
Jan.	The Spanish ambassador in England informs his sovereigns that Henry VII's dynasty is now safe on the English throne.
1501	
July/Aug.	Edmund de la Pole and his younger brother, Richard (Yorkist heirs) flee from England to the Habsburgs.
Nov.	Arthur, Prince of Wales receives his wife, the Infanta Catherine of Aragon.
1502	
6 May	Sir James Tyrell executed for supporting Edmund de la Pole. It is then claimed that he also confessed that he had murdered the sons of Edward IV in 1483 – but there is no real evidence that he ever made that confession.

Most people who have an interest in fifteenth-century history are well aware of the fact that two Yorkist pretenders contested Henry VII's right to the English throne. As we have seen, the first, in 1486–7, was a young lad who claimed to be the son of George, Duke of Clarence. He was crowned in Dublin as 'King Edward VI', but Henry VII's

government gave out that he was an imposter and that his rea.
was either 'John [*BLANK*]', or 'Lambert Simnel'.³ The second Yorki.
pretender, in the mid-1490s, claimed to be the younger of the two
sons of Edward IV and Elizabeth Widville, and presented his own
name as 'Richard of England', or 'Richard IV'. Once again Henry
VII's government said he was an imposter and that his real name was
'Peter (or Perkin, or Pierre) Warbeck (or de Werbecque)'.

However, not so many people seem to be aware of the fact that
there was also a third pretender. In 1498/9 he repeated the first
pretender's claim, stating that he was Edward, Earl of Warwick and
had escaped from the Tower of London. The late fifteenth-/early
sixteenth-century Great Chronicle dates his voicing of that claim
between 8 and 24 February 1498/9.

> In this passing of tyme In the bordurs of Norffolk and Suffolk
> was a newe maumet [*puppet*] arerid which namyd hym sylf
> to be the fforenamid earle of warwyk, The which by sly &
> coverty meanys essayed to wyn to hym soom adherentis, But
> all In vayn, In conclusion he was browgth before therle of
> Oxynfford, To whom at length he confessed that he was born
> In london, and that he was sone unto a Cordyner dwelling at
> the blak Bulle In Bysshoppsgate street, afftir which confession
> he was sent up the the kyng & ffrom hym to prison, and upon
> that areygnyd & convict of treason, and ffynally upon shrove
> tuysday [12 February 1498/9] hangid at Seynt Thomas watering⁴
> In his shirt, where he soo hyng styll tyll the Satyrday ffoluyng
> [16 February], and then ffor noyaunce of the way passers he was
> takyn doun & buried, being of the age of xix yeris or xxᵗⁱ.⁵

Polydore Vergil also recorded the case of this third pretender.

> There was [a] certain Augustinian monk named Patrick,⁶ who,
> I suppose, *for the purpose of making the earl [of Warwick]
> unpopular*, began to suborn a disciple of his (whose name, as far
> as I know, is not recorded) and drum into his ears that he could
> easily gain the throne, if he would agree to follow his advice. The
> student not only did not refuse, but asked [*sic*] again and again
> asked him to be quick in putting his design in to practice. For

what man is there who fears the law or danger to the extent that he refuses to do or suffer anything in the world for the sake of gaining a crown? Therefore the monk shared his plan and both of them went boldly to Kent, a county on other occasions not deaf to innovations. There the young man first revealed to some the secret that he was Edward of Warwick, lately escaped from the Tower of London by Patrick's help and art. Then he openly proclaimed this and begged all men's help. But the sedition lost its leadership before they could bring it to fruition, when teacher and pupil were both enchained, the latter put to death, and the former consigned to eternal darkness of prison because he was a monk. For among the English the clergy are held in such respect that a priest condemned of treason, like ordained priests guilty of other crimes, is spared his life.[7]

It is interesting to see that Vergil states that the reason behind the plot involving this third pretender had been to make the Earl of Warwick *unpopular*. The significance of that suggestion will be explored further presently.

The accounts of the Great Chronicle and of Vergil differ in their assertions regarding the geographic location in which the third pretender first put forth his claim. The Great Chronicle says it was on the Norfolk–Suffolk border, whereas Vergil says it was in Kent. The fact that the Great Chronicle also states that the Earl of Oxford received the pretender as a prisoner seems to make its alleged location the more likely of the two, because the Earls of Oxford were based in East Anglia.

Also, no surviving *contemporary* account records the real name of the third pretender. However, it appears that it must have been noted at the time, because about a century later, like the Great Chronicle, Francis Bacon described him as the son of a cordwainer. Bacon then states that his real name had been Ralph Wilford.[8] And although the surname Wilford had apparently originated in Nottinghamshire, in the sixteenth century there were indeed Wilfords living in London, in the general vicinity allocated to the third pretender's father by the Great Chronicle.[9]

As the present writer suggested in an earlier study, based on Vergil's claim that the aim behind this third pretender was to bring down the

Earl of Warwick, it seems probable 'that those who wished to bring about the deaths of Henry VII's Earl of Warwick and of "Richard of England" thought that by producing a third (and obviously false) Yorkist pretender they could first, further undermine the claim of "Richard", and second, bring about the executions of all three Yorkist claimants'.[10] In other words, it may have been Henry VII's own government which had deliberately inspired the training of Ralph, and the putting forward of the royal identity claim which he then made. The reasoning behind such action on the part of the government would have been that, by producing a third, and obviously false, claimant to the throne, not only could *he* be put to death, but also, as part of the follow-up, excuses could be found to justify the executions of the young man imprisoned in the Tower as the Earl of Warwick, together with that other Tower prisoner, 'Richard of England/Perkin Warbeck'.

At that point, Henry VII was struggling very hard to convince King Ferdinand of Aragon and his wife, Queen Isabel of Castile, that a planned marriage between his own eldest son and heir, Arthur, Prince of Wales, and their young daughter, the Infanta Catherine of Aragon, should be finalised. However, it seems that Ferdinand and Isabel had been very worried by the obvious evidence to the effect that Henry VII's claim to the English throne was contested. The Spanish monarchs were well aware of the claims made by the three Yorkist pretenders. They also knew the situation in respect of other, undoubtedly genuine Yorkist claimants to the English throne, namely the 'last white roses', Edmund and Richard de la Pole. Those two were the sons of Elizabeth of York senior, Duchess of Suffolk – the aunt of Henry VII's consort who bore the same name. Thus they were living nephews of both Edward IV and Richard III. Given all those Yorkist claims, Ferdinand and Isabel believed that the future of Henry VII's new English royal dynasty remained very uncertain. Therefore they felt reluctant to send their daughter to England while Henry still held a living prisoner known as the 'Earl of Warwick' in the Tower of London.[11]

However, the executions of Ralph Wilford, of Henry VII's 'Earl of Warwick', and of 'Richard of England/Perkin Warbeck', made the situation of Henry VII and his family appear more secure. In January 1499/1500 the Spanish ambassador in England sent his monarchs a positive report to the effect that not 'a drop of doubtful Royal blood' was now threatening Henry VII and his son and heir.[12] Thus the planned union of Prince Arthur and the Infanta Catherine of Aragon finally went ahead the following year.

Meanwhile, to strengthen his position even further, Henry VII attempted to deal with the de la Pole issue. One consequence of that was the execution of Sir James Tyrell. He 'was executed on May 6 1502, for his involvement in the conspiracy of Edmund de la Pole against Henry VII'.[13] Moreover, another benefit was derived from Tyrell's execution by Henry VII and his government. That was their announcement of a claim that, prior to his execution, Tyrell had made a secret confession, admitting that, years before, he had murdered the two sons of Edward IV on the orders of King Richard III. And of course, Tyrell's alleged confession was later reported by Sir Thomas More.

> Very truth is it and well known that at such time as Sir James Tyrell was in the Tower for treason committed against the most famous prince, King Henry the Seventh, both Dighton [see below, chapter 25] and he were examined and confessed the murder [of the sons of Edward IV] in the manner above written, but whither the bodies were removed they could nothing tell.[14]

More's account sounds very positive. But in reality not one single shred of genuine documentary evidence exists in respect of James Tyrell's alleged confession. And it is obvious that actually the story recounted by Thomas More was only originated by Henry VII's government nineteen years after the alleged killing was supposed to have taken place. As we have seen, the account was first put out then in order to help secure the future of the new ruling dynasty in terms of a politically important planned royal marriage.

In spite of the fact that a claim had now been made to the effect that solid evidence existed to prove that the sons of Edward IV had been put to death, sadly no dead bodies could be produced, and no burial site could be identified. Thus, as More's later written version clearly shows, the account was forced to include the allegation that after the murder, and the initial burial of the remains at the Tower of London, the corpses had subsequently been exhumed and secretly removed to some other location. Obviously that point will be very important when we come to consider the alleged identity of the bones which were discovered at the Tower of London in 1674 (see below, chapter 26 *et seq.*).

25

HOW ARE THE BOYS SAID TO HAVE BEEN KILLED?

Various stories about how Edward IV's sons had been put to death were told. The Great Chronicle of London, which seems to have been completed in about 1512, and may possibly have been written by Robert Fabyan, cites three different rumours to the effect that the two boys may have been smothered in their feather beds, or possibly they were drowned in malmsey wine (just as their uncle George Duke of Clarence is also said to have been put to death), or maybe they were poisoned.[1] Much later a sixteenth-century French writer, Martin du Bellay (1495–1559), claimed that Richard III had given out the news that his nephews had been accidentally lost, 'having fallen from the bridge which leads into the Tower'.[2]

As for what is generally seen as the 'official' story of their alleged murder, that was most fully reported some thirty years after the event

Thomas More.

was supposed to have taken place by Sir Thomas More. He begins by suggesting that Richard III's motive for the killing was 'forasmuch as his mind gave him that, his nephews living, men would not reckon that he could have right to the realm, he thought therefore without delay to rid them, as though the killing of his kinsmen could amend his cause and make him a kindly king'.[3]

As has already been shown, that suggestion is nonsense. The two boys had officially been ruled to be bastards by the three estates of the realm, based upon the evidence in respect of their father's bigamy which had been presented by Bishop Stillington. It was purely on that basis that the throne had then been formally offered to Richard III as the legitimate sovereign. In other words Richard's claim to the throne was in no way impeded by the survival of his two nephews. They had officially been defined as illegitimate, so that, alive or dead, they possessed no right to the kingship.

In reality the effect of the bastardy ruling must also have been generally accepted. That is the only possible explanation for the fact that Henry VII subsequently found himself forced to deal with the legislation in question by repealing and destroying it in 1485, and by publicly restoring Elizabeth Widville to queenly status as dowager. As we have seen, it was only by acting in that way that Henry was able to proceed with his projected marriage to Elizabeth of York and his presentation of her to the nation as the Yorkist heiress.

Nevertheless, More's pretence that the bastardy claim was of no significance had been preceded by Polydore Vergil's account in that

Polydore Vergil.

respect. Vergil had asserted that 'there is a common report that king Edwards children were in that sermon caulyd basterdes, and not king Edward, *which is voyd of all truth*'.[4] So More was simply following the new ruling dynasty's political rewriting of history in that respect.

Following his ludicrous suggestion in respect of Richard III's supposed motive, More's full account of the crime which that king was alleged to have set in motion continues as follows:

> He sent one John Green,[5] whom he specially trusted, unto Sir Robert Brackenbury, Constable of the Tower with a letter and credence also that the same Sir Robert should in any wise put the two children to death. This John Green did his errand unto Brackenbury, kneeling before Our Lady in the Tower, who plainly answered that he would never put them to death, to die therefor.[6]

Brackenbury was a northerner. He had been a neighbour of the Duke of Gloucester when Richard had been living at Barnard Castle in Durham. Previously his family had been in the service of Richard's father-in-law and cousin, the late Richard Neville, Earl of Warwick. Brackenbury had become a close associate of the young Duke of Gloucester, and subsequently it was Richard who had appointed him as Constable of the Tower of London approximately three weeks before Green's mission (see below in respect of the date of Green's mission), on Thursday 17 July 1483.[7] More's account implies that Brackenbury did not always obey orders. Reportedly in this instance he expected to be punished for his refusal of the alleged royal command by being put to death himself. But in reality, of course, Richard III did not kill him. Brackenbury continued loyally serving Richard until August 1485, when he died at the king's side at the battle of Bosworth.

Thomas More claims that John Green took Brackenbury's response back to his sovereign, who was then located in Warwick. In More's own words, 'John Green, returning, recounted the same to King Richard at Warwick.'[8] On the basis of that location it appears that More must have been claiming that Richard III sent the order to Sir Robert Brackenbury, in London, some time during the second week of August 1483.[9]

At Warwick Castle, Richard III is said to have received Green's report,

> wherewith he took such displeasure and thought that the same night he said unto a secret page of his: 'Ah, whom shall a man trust? Those that I have brought up myself, those that I had went would most surely serve me—even those fail me and at my command will do nothing for me'.
>
> 'Sir', quod his page, 'there lieth one on your pallet without,[10] that, I dare well say, to do your grace pleasure, the thing were right hard that he would refuse', meaning this by [= by this] Sir James Tyrell, which was a man of right goodly personage and for nature's gifts worthy to have served a much better prince, if he had well served God and by grace obtained as much truth and good will as he had strength and wit. The man had an high heart and sore longed upward, not rising yet so fast as he had hoped, being hindered and kept under by means of Sir Richard Radcliff and Sir William Catesby, which longing for no more partners of the prince's favor, and namely not for him whose pride they wist would bear no peer, kept him by secret drifts out of all secret trust. Which thing this page well had marked and known. Wherefore this occasion offered, of very special friendship he took his time to put him forward and by such wise do him good, that all the enemies he had except the devil could never have done him so much hurt.[11]

Thus it was reportedly Richard III's unnamed page who proposed Sir James Tyrell as a more trustworthy potential royal murderer. As recounted by More, it appears as though Richard himself might never have thought of approaching Tyrell.

Since, according to More's account, the murders in question were apparently required to be kept secret (though, once again, that is a point which contradicts Thomas More's proposed *motive* – see above), it seems odd that Richard reportedly entrusted the task to a man whom he was alleged not to know very well in terms of service. Moreover, the fact that the patent rolls reveal that James Tyrell had been in the service of Edward IV, and was also subsequently appointed to posts by Richard III,[12] appears to contradict More's account once again in that respect.

More also alleges that Richard's conversation with his page took place while the king was using the toilet – which More describes as a very suitable royal seat for the conversation in question!

> For upon this page's words King Richard arose (for this communication had he sitting at the draught,[13] a convenient carpet for such a council) and came out into the pallet chamber, on which he found in bed Sir James and Sir Thomas Tyrell,[14] of person like and brethren of blood, but nothing of kin in conditions. Then said the king merrily to them: 'What, sirs, be ye in bed so soon ?' and calling up Sir James brake to him secretly his mind in this mischievous matter, in which he found him nothing strange. Wherefore on the morrow he sent him to Brackenbury with a letter by which he was commanded to deliver Sir James all the keys of the Tower for one night, to the end he might there accomplish the king's pleasure in such thing as he had given him commandment. After which letter delivered and the keys received, Sir James appointed the night next ensuing to destroy them, devising before and preparing the means.[15]

More also speaks of how the sons of Edward IV were supposed to have been feeling at the time. Apparently, according to his version of events, Edward V did not regret losing the crown so long as his life was spared. He is reported to have expressed his thoughts in those respects to the messenger who had conveyed to him the news that he had lost the throne.

> The prince, as soon as the protector left that name [= stopped using the title 'protector'] and took himself as king, had it showed unto him that he should not reign, but his uncle should have the crown. At which word the prince, sore abashed, began to sigh and said: 'Alas! I would my uncle would let me have my life yet, though I lose my kingdom'. Then he that told him the tale used him with good words and put him in the best comfort he could.[16]

More also claims that both the boys then became more or less prisoners.

> Forthwith was the prince and his brother both shut up and all other removed from them, only one called Black Will or William Slaughter except, set to serve them and see them sure. After which time the prince never tied his points nor ought rought of himself, but with that young babe his brother linger in thought and heaviness till this traitorous death delivered them of that wretchedness. [17]

In other words, it seems More claims that Edward V became so depressed that he no longer bothered to dress properly or take care of himself.

As for the actual killing, More asserts that took place as follows:

> Sir James Tyrell devised that they should be murdered in their beds, to the execution whereof he appointed Miles Forest,[18] one of the four that kept them, a fellow fleshed in murder before time. To him he joined one John Dighton,[19] his own horse-keeper, a big, broad, square, strong knave. Then, all the other being removed from them, this Miles Forest and John Dighton about midnight (the sely children lying in their beds) came into the chamber and suddenly lapped them up among the clothes – so bewrapped them and entangled them, keeping down by force the featherbed and pillows hard unto their mouths, that within a while, smored [= smothered] and stifled, their breath failing, they gave up to God their innocent souls into the joys of heaven, leaving to the tormentors their bodies dead in the bed.[20]

Thomas More's account that the two boys were smothered to death using pillows is the account which has subsequently been widely accepted as true.

Later a claim was made that fabric had been discovered with the bones which were found at the Tower of London in the seventeenth century (see below, chapter 26). It is therefore interesting to note that Thomas More's murder story relates that the boys' bodies were buried *naked*:

After that the wretches perceived, first by the struggling with the pains of death, and after long lying still, to be thoroughly dead, they laid their bodies naked out upon the bed and fetched Sir James to see them. Which, upon the sight of them, caused those murderers to bury them at the stair foot, meetly deep in the ground, under a great heap of stones. [21]

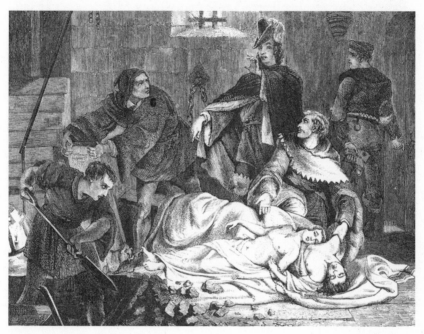

The alleged first burial.

Then rode Sir James in great haste to King Richard and showed him all the manner of the murder, who gave him great thanks and, as some say, there made him knight. But he allowed not, as I have heard, the burying in so vile a corner, saying that he would have them buried in a better place because they were a king's sons. Lo, the honorable courage of a king! Whereupon they say that a priest of Sir Robert Brackenbury took up the bodies again and secretly interred them in such place as, by the occasion of his death which only knew it, could never since come to light. Very truth is it and well known that at such time as Sir James Tyrell was in the Tower for treason committed against the most famous prince, King Henry the Seventh, both Dighton and he were examined and confessed the murder in manner above written, but whither the bodies were removed they could nothing tell.[22]

Obviously Henry VII never knew where the alleged dead bodies might be found, because, in spite of his strong desire to inspire the belief that the sons of Edward IV were both dead, he always failed to produce their remains. Presumably that is why More's account (and presumably also More's sources) insisted that although the murderers had confessed the killing, they could not reveal where the bodies had finally been buried because someone else had subsequently moved them. Moreover, it is amazing that, while it had reportedly taken no less than two or three men to bury the bodies initially (interring them deeply at the foot of some stairs), apparently they were then exhumed and removed by one single priest, acting alone and in secret!

26

WHAT BONES WERE FOUND AT THE TOWER OF LONDON, AND WHEN?

As we have seen, according to Sir Thomas More's very full – but dubious – account of the alleged murder of Edward V and Richard, Duke of York (as published in 1557 by William Rastell), when Sir James Tyrell was shown the boys' dead bodies he 'caused those murderers to bury them at the stair foot meetly deep in the ground, under a great heap of stones'.[1] However, that proved not to be the final fate of the dead remains. More then goes on to say (presumably sarcastically) that, because he had the honourable characteristics which are expected of a reigning sovereign, Richard III objected to the unsuitable kind of burial which had been given to the carcasses of his murdered nephews

> in so vile a corner, saying that he would have them buried in a better place because they were a king's sons. Lo, the honourable courage [= nature] of a king! Whereupon they say that a priest of Sir Robert Brackenbury took up the bodies again and secretly interred them in such a place as, by the occasion of his death which only knew it, could never since come to light.[2]

Of course, More's account is dubious in respect of the alleged murders. However, it also raises a very significant question in respect of what was then supposed to have been done with the dead bodies. Although More says that they were initially buried at the foot of some stairs, he then claims that the two boys were exhumed and reburied in another, unrecorded but suitable location. Logically, what was then regarded as a suitable location for interment would presumably have been a religious site. Intriguingly, however, earlier versions of More's text (published by Richard Grafton in 1543 and 1548) had alleged a different outcome. Those versions asserted that the unnamed priest put the bodies in a lead-weighted coffin which was then cast into 'Black depes' of the River Thames.[3]

Nevertheless, the logical conclusion based upon all three versions of More's posthumously published text is that, as a result of their reburial in 1483, the remains of Edward V and Richard, Duke of York could not possibly be found lying in a secular location at the Tower of London. Any bones found in such a location at the Tower would therefore have to belong to other people. Given that fact, it is curious that in 1674, when bones were found beneath a staircase at the Tower of London, they were assumed to belong to the sons of Edward IV, and were subsequently reburied in the Henry VII Chapel at Westminster under that alleged identity.

Nearly 200 years after the Princes' disappearance, the bones of two[4] children were found during demolition work within the Inmost Ward of the Tower of London. Accepted as the Princes' bones they were placed in an urn in Westminster Abbey.[5] ...[Yet] these were not the first bones, nor the last, to be found within the Tower of London. Their uniqueness is a product of the urn and our own perceptions. Thus one possible line of investigation should ask why *these bones* were accepted and put in a place of prominent display, while others were not.[6]

Indeed, the truth is that sets of bones have reportedly been found at the Tower of London on several different occasions. Moreover, some of the other sets of bones were also tentatively identified as the sons of Edward IV at the time when they were found.

The first recorded sets of bones seem to have been found in about 1610. George Buck's *History of Richard III*, first published in 1646, reports vaguely that 'certaine bones like to the bones of a Child being found lately in a high desolate Turret, [are] supposed to be the bones of one of these Princes, [though] others are of opinion it was the carcass of an Ape kept in the Tower'.[7] George Buck's friend and antiquarian colleague Ralphe Brooke had also published a brief statement about the discovery of bones in 1622. He then stated that although previously the burial place of the sons of Edward IV had been unknown, recently at the Tower, 'their dead carcases were there found, under a heape of stones and rubbish.'[8]

Much more specifically, a handwritten note, dated 17 August 1647 and signed 'Jo. Webb', states that

> when ye Lo: Grey of Wilton and Sir Walter Raleigh were prisoners in ye Tower, the wall of ye passage to ye King's Lodgings then sounding hollow, was taken down and at ye place marked A was found a little roome about 7 or 8 ft square, wherein there stood a Table and uppon it ye bones of two children supposed of 6 or 8 yeares of age, which by ye aforesaid nobles and all present were credibly believed to bee ye carcasses of Edward ye 5th and his brother the then Duke of York.[9]

For Webb's plan of the location of room 'A', see below, Appendix 2, Tanner's page 26. Jo. Webb can be identified as John Webb (1611–72). He served as deputy to Inigo Jones, who was Surveyor of the King's Works from 1615 to 1643.

Sir Walter Raleigh had found himself imprisoned in the Tower of London on three occasions: in 1592; in the period 1603–16; and in 1618. As for Lord Grey, he was brought as a prisoner to the Tower in July 1603. He remained there for the rest of his life, dying at the Tower on 9 July 1614. It therefore seems that the reported discovery of these bones in the concealed room 'A' must have taken place at some point during the eleven years 1603–14.

However, a later account, published in 1680, claimed that the discovery in question had actually taken place earlier, 'in Queen Elizabeth's time'.[10] That same report also asserted that the bones which had comprised the earlier discovery were also the ones which were (re)discovered in 1674. Actually it is not known what was done with the bones which comprised the earlier discovery. However, they do seem to have been found in a location which may not have been a huge distance away from where the later bones were found buried in 1674. Could it therefore be that the *c.* 1610(?) bones were simply buried somewhere in the Tower – possibly under a staircase – and were found again during rebuilding work about sixty-four years later? Probably not, because reportedly the bones found in 1674 were buried very deeply (see below).

The later seventeenth-century-discovery bones were found just outside the White Tower on Friday 17 July 1674 – though a nineteenth-century brass plaque at the Tower of London (plate 30) misleads visitors by suggesting erroneously that the remains were found *inside* the White Tower![11] More will be said about these remains shortly. However, they were not the final discovery. Many more bones were found in the Tower moat in the nineteenth century, and

> in 1977, archaeologists unearthed a youthful Iron Age skeleton ['young male between 13 and 16 years of age'] from the southeast corner of the old Inmost Ward [of the Tower of London], beneath the site of the medieval palace buildings and the earliest levels of Roman occupation.[12]

In respect of the bones which were found just outside the White Tower on Friday 17 July 1674, the following roughly contemporary reports of the discovery survive:

> *Die Veneris* July 17 Anno 1674 in digging some foundacons in ye Tower, were discoverd ye bodies of Edw 5 and his Brother murdred 1483. I my selfe handled ye Bones Especially ye Kings Skull. Ye other wch was lesser was Broken in ye digging. Johan Gybbon, Blewmantle.[13]

> A° 1674. In digging down a pair of stone staires leading from the Kings Lodgings to the chappel in the white tower ther were found bones of two striplings in (as it seemed) a wooden chest wch upon the presumptions that they were the bones of this king [Edward V] and his brother Rich: D. of York, were by the command of K. Charles the 2nd put into a marble Vrn and deposited amongst the R; Family in H: 7th Chappel in Westminster at my importunity. Jo. Knight.[14]

Christopher Wren, whose father (Sir Christopher) created the Westminster urn in which the bones were reinterred, wrote in 1750 that the bones had been discovered 'about ten feet deep in the ground … as the workmen were taking away the stairs, which led from the royal lodgings into the Chapel of the White-tower'.[15] He must have received that information from his father, because the 1678 Latin inscription on the Westminster urn also says that the bones had been found 'buried deep'. However, the inscription (the official translation of which is below) certainly does contain some errors:

> Here lie the relics of Edward V, King of England, and Richard, Duke of York. *These brothers being confined in the Tower of London, and there stifled with pillows, were privately and meanly buried, by the order of their perfidious uncle Richard the Usurper*; whose bones, long enquired after and wished for, after 191 years in the rubbish of the stairs (those lately leading to the Chapel of the White Tower) were on the 17th day of July 1674, by undoubted proofs discovered, being buried deep in that place. Charles II, a most compassionate prince, pitying their severe fate, ordered these unhappy Princes to be laid amongst the monuments of their predecessors, 1678, in the 30th year of his reign.[16]

The *known* errors in this appalling inscription have been italicised by the present writer. Richard III was definitely not perfidious, he was a deeply religious man. Also he was definitely not a usurper (see above, chapter 11). As for the claims made regarding the identity of the bones and the deaths of the boys, as has already been shown, these claims are merely allegations, based upon no contemporary fifteenth-century evidence.

There is also no modern scientific evidence to back the claims made. In other words, we do not know for certain that the bones found were remains of *two* young people. Interestingly, until recently it was generally believed that the Clarence Vault at Tewkesbury also contained the bones of two individuals (see plate 11). However, when the present writer had those remains re-examined in 2013, they proved to comprise parts of at least three and possibly four skeletons.[17] As for the bones in the Westminster urn, we also do not know for certain that they are *male*. We do not know that they belong to individuals who were related to one another (see below, chapters 27 and 28). We also do not know the period in which they lived and died.

However, in that context, the fact that the bones were reportedly found deep beneath a medieval staircase is interesting. That could well mean that the bodies had been placed where they were found in 1674 *long before* the medieval stairs were built. In other words, like the remains found at the Tower more recently, in 1977, the bones discovered in 1674 could well be pre-medieval (possibly Roman or Iron Age) skeletons. Only carbon dating of the bones would now be able to clarify that point. Carbon dating is not entirely to be trusted in respect of very *precise* accuracy. However, it should certainly be able to reveal whether or not the Tower bones date from the second quarter of the second millennium of the Christian era (AD 1251–1500).

One hundred and sixty years after the publication of Christopher Wren's account, in 1910, a claim was made that another contemporary, late seventeenth-century, hand-written report had been discovered, which described the 'small bones, of lads in their teens, and [claimed that] there were pieces of rag and velvet about them'.[18] However, it has subsequently proved impossible to confirm that such a source genuinely exists. Moreover, it conflicts with Thomas More's earlier report that the remains of Edward IV's two sons were interred naked. For various reasons the claim about fabric having been found with the bones in 1674 can therefore probably be disregarded.

27

WHAT DID THE 1933 URN OPENING REVEAL?

The urn designed for King Charles II by Sir Christopher Wren and used for the reburial of bones found at the Tower in the Henry VII Chapel at Westminster. An early eighteenth-century engraving, published by Francis Sandford.

Following the reburial of the bones, which had been found at the Tower of London in 1674, in Henry VII's Chapel, in 1678, they simply remained there in their marble urn – originally topped with palm branches (symbols of martyrs) – for two and a half centuries. Then, however,

> permission was sought and granted in 1933 for the urn to be opened and its contents examined by the most up-to-date methods known to science at that time. Dr William Wright, Dean of the London Hospital Medical College and President of the Anatomical Society, and Mr Lawrence Tanner, Keeper of the Muniments at Westminster Abbey, were given charge of the examination, while Dr. George Northcroft, late President of the Dental Association and British Society of Orthodontists, made a detailed examination of the teeth in order to try to establish the ages of the children.[1]

One amazing outcome of the 1933 examination and the conclusions drawn from it was contained in a speech made shortly afterwards by the then Dean of Westminster, Dr Foxley Norris, at the Society of Antiquaries. The Dean

> commented upon the startling fact that the tear ducts of the skulls were vastly enlarged, the suggestion being that the boys had undergone such a harrowing experience that they actually wore a groove in the bone by constant weeping! Dr Barton states that each tear duct must have long since perished, but the bony canal through which it passed from the eye into the nasal cavity could not possibly, under any circumstances, be affected. It would take, states Dr Barton, far more years than each child had lived to produce such a result.
>
> I mentioned these tear ducts to Professor Wright, but the only explanation he could give for the Dean's statement was that a casual remark made to Mr Tanner about the position and size of the lower orifice of the lachrymal duct had been passed on to the Dean and misunderstood. All is mystery. Those casually mentioned ducts grew in some peculiar manner in the Abbey until the Dean produced the complete tale before the Society of Antiquaries.
>
> And that is how traditions are made!'[2]

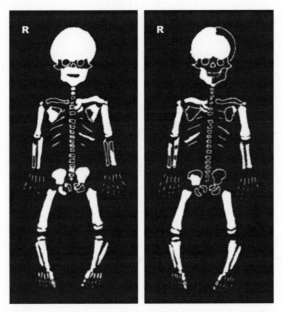

The human bones found in the urn in 1933, depicted as comprising parts of two children. (Redrawn from images published by Molleson in 1987.)

The report in respect of the 1933 examination as subsequently published by Lawrence Tanner is reproduced in full in Appendix 2 (see below). Tanner's firm conclusion was that the bones in the urn belonged to two *boys* of the correct ages to correspond with the sons of Edward IV. He felt that the evidence also confirmed the theory that both of those boys had died violent deaths in about the late summer of 1483. However, actually there were – and are – a number of important remaining questions in respect of the bones in the urn.

The four main questions are as follows:

1. What was the number of living creatures whose bones were present?
2. What was the gender of the human bones?
3. What was the age at death of the humans?
4. What was the date of death of the humans?

Those four questions will all be dealt with now, both in respect of the evidence presented by Tanner in 1933, and in respect of other evidence which has been put forward subsequently.

1. *What was the number of living creatures whose bones were present?*

Tanner states in the conclusion to his report that the bones in the urn 'have been definitely proved to be those of two children'.[3] However, that is not true. Tanner's earlier statement was that, when the urn was opened, and the bones exposed, 'it was at once apparent that they belonged to two human beings, for a fairly complete skull and a portion of another lay upon the top'. Unfortunately, however, that argument sounds identical to a view which was formerly held in respect of the remains in the Clarence Vault at Tewkesbury. There, too, substantial remains of two skulls were obviously present (see plate 11). However, in the case of the Tewkesbury remains the re-examination organised by the present writer in 2013 then proved that in reality parts of *three* skulls were present, though the very small parts of the third skull had not previously been obvious to non-experts.[4] A similar modern re-examination of the human bones in the Westminster urn could now establish clearly whether those bones belong to two individuals.

Moreover, Tanner's report itself clearly acknowledges that other, non-human bones were also found lying in the urn. As Wright wrote in the second part of the report, 'a large variety of other bones such as those of fish, duck, chicken, rabbit, sheep, pig, and ox' were also present.[5] Interestingly, human bones were found mixed with animal bones in English Iron Age graves in some more recent archaeological explorations. For example, at one grave in Dorset 'the researchers found the skeletal remains of a woman placed carefully atop a mound of animal bones'.[6] Might that suggest that what was found at the Tower of London in 1674 was a pre-Roman burial?

Pre-Roman human and animal remains which were found buried together.

Incidentally, Tanner also reported that Wright had found something which he claimed was 'a blood stain ... probably caused by suffocation'. However, as we shall see presently, that claim in respect of the stain appears to be improbable, and has subsequently been disputed. The bones as found in the urn in 1933 were mixed with various other items which could possibly have caused some staining,

2. *What was the gender of the human bones?*

In respect of the gender issue, Professor Wright seems to have made no formal statement in his part of the 1933 report (though he clearly assumed throughout the examination that the two skulls both belonged to boys).

The gender issue in respect of the urn bones was later taken up much more specifically by Dr Theya Molleson. On 29 June 1985, at a symposium entitled 'The Fate of the Princes', held by the Richard III Society at the Glazier's Hall, London:

Dr. Theya Molleson, of the Department of Anthropology, British Museum of Natural History, gave an illustrated talk on 'the evidence of human skeletal remains, both general and particular': in effect, the bones of the Princes. By studying the X-rays of the bones [= 'skiagrams' as published by Tanner], in the light of the report issued by Dr. Wright and Mr Tanner, and by comparison with the remains of Anne Mowbray and other examples from mediaeval times, Dr. Molleson showed how, from close-up examination of unerupted teeth in the jawbones, as well as of bones in the skulls, a reasonably accurate estimate could be made of the age and the sex of the skeletons. She concluded that the younger one, although more advanced in skeletal and dental development than the older one, was that of a nine or ten year old, and the older that of a thirteen or fourteen year old. Both were, according to the size and position of the teeth, boys. Once again, no estimate as to the possible cause of death, or of the date when they died; even of the century they died in, and no more positive identification other than their being possibly male, was given.[7]

Moreover, Dr Molleson's conclusions on that occasion in respect of gender, based upon dental evidence, has also since been queried.

The crowns of the teeth are generally larger in boys than in girls and the most important tooth for sex determination is the lower permanent canine tooth. This tooth survives unerupted in the jaw of the younger child, and if the published X-ray [= 'skiagram'] is to scale, as it is less than 7mm in diameter (contrary to Dr. Molleson's conclusions) there is the possibility that the owner of the skull was female. This possibility is further enhanced by the absence of a wisdom tooth in the jaw of the older child, which might tend to show that it was the skull of a female, since these teeth are more frequently absent in females than in males.[8]

Later, in an article which she published in 1987, Dr Molleson agreed that 'sex determination of juvenile skeletons is notoriously unreliable.' But she said that 'the teeth are the only area that offers a method of sexing with any degree of confidence.' In respect of the gender of the urn bones, her final conclusion in that article was simply that

> suggestions that the two skeletons are of boys are not contradicted by the rubicon put forward by Hunt and Gleiser,* that 'if dental age and skeletal age correspond the skeleton is that of a boy but should the age from the bones have been in advance from that of the teeth it is more likely to be female'. In neither case is the skeletal development, as distinct from size, ahead of the dental.[9]

However, it certainly does not sound as though the gender of the bones should be considered 100 per cent confirmed. Nevertheless, that issue could also be settled nowadays, by a re-examination of the bones. A modern examination could definitely resolve the gender issue, because it would now be possible to explore the DNA of the bones to see whether Y chromosomes are present.

3. *What was the age at death of the humans?*
In respect of the two sons of Edward IV, evidence in respect of their ages in the late summer of 1483 would be as follows:

Edward V – born: 2(?) November 1470, died: *c.*1483?
Therefore his age, if he died in July/August 1483 would have been approaching thirteen.

Richard of Shrewsbury – born: 17 August 1473 – died: unknown. Therefore his age, if he died in July/August 1483 would have been more or less precisely ten.

Tanner and Wright concluded in their 1933 report of the examination of the bones in the urn that they were of the correct ages to be the remains of Edward IV's two sons. Tanner stated that his colleague Professor Wright had been able to show that the older human bones in the urn belonged to an individual 'between the ages of twelve and thirteen'.[10] That certainly would appear to correspond with the age of Edward V. Tanner also stated that Wright had shown that the younger bones belonged to someone 'about mid-way between nine and eleven'.[11] That appears to correspond with the age of Richard of Shrewsbury.

However, questions have subsequently been raised about the estimated ages of the human bones in the urn. It has been proposed that actually the comparison between the lengths of the bones assigned to the two individuals implies an age difference of between eighteen and twenty-four months.[12] That is less than the age difference of about thirty-six months which was proposed by Professor William Wright in 1933. Thus it raises a question as to whether the remains really are of the correct age to belong to their alleged owners, the sons of Edward IV.

In a lecture given to the Richard III Society in 1963, Dr Richard Lyne-Pirkis argued that there can be a significant difference between the apparent age of bones examined by X-ray and the real age of the bones in question.

He concluded that not enough is known about diet and its effect on teeth and bones in the fifteenth century accurately to pinpoint the ages of the skeletons within four years either way; that heredity must be taken into account (i.e. if their father was Edward IV, whose height was over 6 ft) they might well be taller than average, while the apparent osteitis in the jawbone of the elder might well have slowed down his growth, and the supposition that the stain on the jawbone of one child was due to suffocation was untenable because of the presence in the urn of three rust nails, which could have caused the discolouration.[13]

Subsequently arguments have also been produced – and questions have been raised – in respect of the dental evidence published by Tanner. That will all be examined in detail in the next chapter.

As for Dr Molleson's evidence in respect of the age of the bones in the urn, in her 1987 article she offered two possible answers for the remains attributed to the elder child, and two possible answers for those attributed to the younger one, by employing two different methods of evaluation.

> The teeth of the older child from The Tower, as described by Tanner and Wright, yield a maturity score of 97.0, giving a dental age of 14.4 and a chronological age between 12.9 and over 16 years. The teeth of the younger child yield a maturity score of 87.0, giving a dental age of 9.6 and a likely chronological age between 8.6 and 10.7 years. For the older child to have been 12.9 years at death he would have been quite precocious dentally. Precocious dental development is unlikely in individuals with hypodontia, which predisposes to delay in development of the teeth.* It is possible for the older child to have been 15 years and seven or eight months at death. He would have been below the average for his age, but this retardation might he expected in an individual with hypodontia.
>
> Another, more traditional, method or dental age assessment also relies on the evaluation of the developmental stage of each tooth as seen in radiographs.** By this method the older child was between 10.6 and 12.7 years, the younger [between] 6.3 and 9.3 years.[14]

It therefore appears that the precise ages at death of both of the alleged two children whose bones are said to be in the Westminster urn actually remain unclear. Moreover, if they really were the two sons of Edward IV, and if they both died (or were killed) at the same time, Molleson also concludes that their deaths may have taken place about a year later than is usually claimed, in 1484.[15]

4. *What was the date of death of the humans?*

No evidence in this respect was (or could be) offered in 1933. Indeed, no claims were made on that point, either in 1933 or subsequently.

Thus the only claim which can be made for certain is that the human beings whose bones are preserved in the Westminster urn must have died some time before about 1650. In other words they *could* be medieval. However, they could equally well be Anglo-Saxon, Roman or pre-Roman.

Of course, in the present day and age, a re-examination of the bones in the urn, accompanied by carbon dating, would now certainly be able to suggest to which century and historic era the remains belong.

In other words, re-examination of the bones in the urn today would definitely be able to resolve three of the four questions. It could establish how many people are represented by the remains (as was achieved by the present writer in respect of the Clarence Vault bones at Tewkesbury). A modern re-examination could also determine the gender of the individuals. As we have seen, it could also date them fairly precisely.

Moreover, in addition the mtDNA of the human remains could hopefully now be established to see whether it corresponds to the haplogroup subgroup which will be revealed shortly (see below, chapter 29 and plate 27). That would either confirm or disprove the alleged identity of the bones in the urn.

In 1980 (when less scientific evidence was available to clarify the issue of identity) 'the Richard III Society made a further application to the Dean and Chapter of Westminster to allow the urn to be reopened for a more up-to-date examination'.[16] The request was then refused. But hopefully if a request was repeated now it would be seriously considered like the 1933 call. It appears that the 1980 refusal was based purely upon the suggestion that the remains should be allowed to rest in peace. Firstly that conflicts with the earlier granting of permission for their examination in 1933, when the precedent was set. After all, the 1933 permission was obviously granted in order to try to help to clarify the identity of the remains. However, as we have seen, that investigation was by no means conclusive. Its alleged findings are actually deeply flawed. Secondly, there is no Christian religious issue in respect of the handling of bones. After all, the Old Testament dismisses the lasting significance of physical remains, reporting that 'the dust returns to the earth as it was, and the spirit returns to God who gave it,' and that 'dead bodies shall be food for the birds of the air and for the beasts of the earth.'[17] Likewise, in the New Testament, St Paul makes clear when he speaks of resurrection of the dead in chapter 15 of his first letter to the Corinthians that

> what you sow [i.e. bury] is not the body which is to be, but a bare kernel ... There are celestial bodies and there are terrestrial bodies ... What is sown is perishable, what is raised is imperishable. It is sown in dishonour, it is raised in glory.[18]

28

HYPODONTIA?

As we have seen, easily recognisable portions of two skulls were found in 1674 at the Tower of London and reburied in the marble urn in the Henry VII chapel. In the present study the elder of those two skulls will be identified as 'Tower of London 1' – abbreviated hereinafter as 'TL1'. The younger skull will be referred to as 'Tower of London 2' ('TL2').

In respect of TL1, Professor Wright stated in Tanner's report that 'both jaws ... were present in their entirety, [but] they contained no teeth'. As for TL2, 'only the right half of the lower jaw of the younger child ... was present'. But 'fortunately the empty sockets of the teeth in all cases were in good condition, so, that it was not difficult to determine the state of development of the missing teeth'.[1]

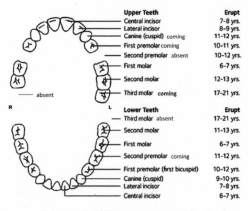

The evidence in respect of the teeth of TL1 as presented by Professor Wright in 1933.

The evidence presented by Professor Wright in respect of the teeth of TL1 can be seen in Appendix 2, on page 17 of Tanner's report, and a plan of them is illustrated here (see above). Most of the adult teeth would have been present during the life of the young person in question. However, some were still in the process of coming, and others were absent.

In his report Professor Wright made no reference to 'hypodontia' or the congenital absence of teeth. However, he does briefly refer to 'the absence of the upper second premolars in Edward [*sic* – TL1] and of the lower second deciduous molar in Richard [*sic* – TL2]'[2] as one possible piece of evidence which could suggest that the owners of the two skulls were related to each other.

Later, after the remains of Anne Mowbray, Duchess of York and Norfolk, (plate 5) – who was both the child wife of Richard of Shrewsbury, and his second cousin once removed – were accidentally found in London in 1964, claims in respect of the significance of hypodontia in connection with TL1 and TL2 were put forward much more strongly. For example, that was done in the televised 'Trial of Richard III' which was broadcast on Channel Four in 1984. One of the prosecution witnesses on that occasion was Dr Jean Ross. As questioned by the prosecution barrister, Mr Russell, she presented evidence as follows:

MR RUSSELL: Now in relation to blood relationship, your second conclusion. I think there was a missing tooth and upper pre-molar in Edward's jaw bone.
DR ROSS: On both sides.
MR RUSSELL: And a missing milk tooth in Richard's lower jaw bone. When we say missing, never there at all.
DR ROSS: Never there at all.
MR RUSSELL: Is that unusual?
DR ROSS: Very unusual for these particular teeth.
MR RUSSELL: And in addition what did that indicate to you?
DR ROSS: A similar anomaly, if I may call it that, in the two boys would indicate that they were possibly blood relations.
MR RUSSELL: And I think there were missing teeth also in another young woman who died about that time aged eight and a half. In fact Richard's wife Anne Mowbray.

DR ROSS: That is right.

MR RUSSELL: Was she a distant relation?

DR ROSS: Yes she was.

MR RUSSELL: She had missing teeth as well?

DR ROSS: She had very unusual missing teeth. Similar to those of Edward.

MR RUSSELL: So it would appear to be a family trait.

DR ROSS: That is right.[3]

Thus the hypothesis was put forward that TL1 and TL2 must have been related to each other, and also that both of them must have been related to Anne Mowbray, and that their shared hypodontia was evidence to that effect.

If it had been the case that Edward V, Richard of Shrewsbury and his wife Anne Mowbray shared congenital absence of teeth because of their common bloodline, the chief bloodline in question would have been their shared descent from the Neville family. That represented their closest common relationship.

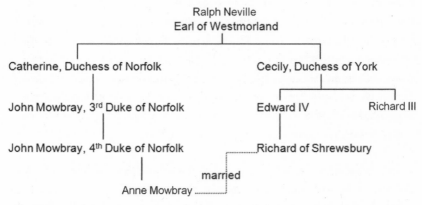

The blood relationship between Richard of Shrewsbury and his wife, Anne Mowbray.

That point was published earlier by Dr Molleson in 1987. However, in some ways the family tree she produced (figure 2, p. 259 of her article) was rather misleading. For example it implies that Anne Mowbray also had Neville descent via her mother, Elizabeth Talbot, Duchess of Norfolk. Molleson's family tree shows Elizabeth's father as John Talbot (which is correct). However, John's wife is shown as

Maud Neville/Furnival. It is true that Maud Neville was John Talbot's first wife. However, she was not the mother of his daughter Elizabeth. The mother of Elizabeth Talbot was John's second wife, Margaret Beauchamp. In other words, on her mother's side Anne Mowbray had no Neville ancestry.

Molleson also reported that

> the permanent dentitions of the older child and of Anne Mowbray are incomplete (Fig. 3). The prevalence of missing permanent teeth in a British sample is 3.1% in boys and 5.7% in girls.* The frequency of upper molar agenesis in the same sample was 0.8%. This is the same frequency (0.86%) as was found in the medieval Winchester sample, so it is unlikely that the population frequency for hypodontia as a whole was very different for an English population of the past.
>
> Brook* has recently reported that agenesis occurs more often among first degree relatives of an individual with hypodontia than in the population as a whole. Females are more likely to be affected than males. This suggests a considerable inherited component in the aetiology. In Brook's study, 30% of first degree relatives of an individual with hypodontia of 1-5 teeth also had hypodontia, and 47% of relatives with hypodontia of six or more teeth. Thus if an individual has hypodontia, a relative is eight times as likely also to have hypodontia as the general population; that is, at least one in three relatives also has hypodontia.[4]

That is an interesting point. It means that if the hypodontia of the TL1 skull really is evidence in respect of Edward V, all his close relatives would have been eight times more likely to have hypodontia than the general population.

As the above family tree (The blood relationship between Richard of Shrewsbury and his wife, Anne Mowbray) clearly shows, Richard of Shrewsbury (and also his brother, Edward V, of course) was much more closely related to his uncle, King Richard III, than to his second cousin (and bride), Anne Mowbray. A better way of confirming the alleged identity of TL1 and TL2 as the skulls of Edward IV's sons would therefore seem to be to show that their hypodontia was shared by Richard III. Curiously, however, as the present writer has pointed out recently,[5] it seems that, in reality Richard III did not have hypodontia (see plate 16).

At the same time, other evidence produced by the present writer seems to suggest that Anne Mowbray may not actually have inherited her hypodontia via her father, from her Neville great-grandmother. Instead, she may have inherited hypodontia from her mother. When Anne's body was examined in 1965, a report on her teeth was published in the *British Dental Journal*.[6] That report states that Anne's skull showed that she had

> congenital absence of upper and lower permanent second molars on the left. There is no sign of these tooth germs or of any relevant disturbance of the bone structure, so that it is clear that the teeth could never have been present. There is no indication of third molars and it is rather probable that these also would have been lacking.[7]

Significantly, Anne's mother, Elizabeth Talbot, Duchess of Norfolk, was the daughter of John Talbot, 1st Earl of Shrewsbury. Anne's maternal grandfather had been killed in France, in 1453, at the battle of Castillon. His body was initially left lying on the battlefield, and was probably robbed of its arms and robes. Later it was hard to identify.

In the end it had been thanks to the old earl's missing left molar that his disfigured remains were recognised. As reported at the time by Mathieu d'Escouchy, the earl's herald was requested to identify his master's body. Strangely, what he then did was to open the mouth of the corpse and put his fingers inside it. He then located a place on the left side of the mouth, where there was a molar missing. It was based on that discovery that the herald then announced that he had found and recognised Lord Shrewsbury's corpse.[8] Of course, based simply on that account it is not certain that John Talbot suffered from hypodontia. But it is possible that he did, particularly since his missing molar was such a well-known feature as far as his herald was concerned. Sadly, although Lord Shrewsbury's remains were re-examined in 1874, at that stage no one addressed the issue of exploring his possible hypodontia. And the only photograph taken of the earl's skull on that occasion reveals nothing useful in respect of his dentition, because it focuses chiefly on his death wound – on the back of his head.[9]

Nevertheless, the present writer has found other potential evidence in respect of hypodontia within the Talbot family in the fifteenth century. Anne Mowbray's mother was the younger sister of Eleanor Talbot – that very important lady who in 1483 was adjudged the rightful queen consort of King Edward IV. Eleanor therefore became the key figure in respect of the judgement of bastardy which was made in respect of Edward IV's Widville offspring. Eleanor and her relationship with Edward IV were also the chief reasons why the English throne was then offered to Richard, Duke of Gloucester (Richard III).

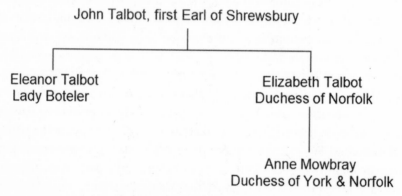

John Talbot, first Earl of Shrewsbury

Eleanor Talbot
Lady Boteler

Elizabeth Talbot
Duchess of Norfolk

Anne Mowbray
Duchess of York & Norfolk

Anne Mowbray's significant Talbot connections in respect of hypodontia.

Eleanor Talbot was buried by her sister at the Carmelite Priory in Norwich, to which she had been linked (as a laywoman) in her closing years. In the 1950s a female skeleton was discovered by archaeologists in a wooden coffin on the Carmelite Priory site. Recent re-examination of that site seems to now indicate that the lady in question was found buried within the priory church. The present writer had those bones examined in 1996 by consultant osteologist Mr W. J. White. His examination confirmed that she was of the right age and social status to have been Eleanor Talbot, and subsequent re-examinations by other experts have confirmed the evidence in respect of age and social status which was produced by Bill White.[10] The present writer has also shown that the lady in question appears to have resembled surviving portraits of some of Eleanor's closest relatives. Recent carbon dating of the bones showed that, assuming she continued the Talbot family consumption of seafood,[11] the woman in question may well have died at about the right time.[12] Meanwhile, short of absolutely positive identification (which it would be very difficult to achieve) it does seem that the Norwich remains, known as 'CF2', may indeed be those of Eleanor Talbot. For her possible appearance, based on a facial reconstruction of the Norwich skull and portraits of close relatives, see plate 6.

It is therefore very interesting that CF2 showed signs of hypodontia. In her case that meant the absence of the left upper second premolar (see plate 17). That point was first reported by Christine Meadway, BDS, who conducted a dental examination of CF2 for the present writer in July 1998. More recently the CF2 skull has been re-examined by several other experts, all of whom have confirmed Christine Meadway's conclusion. Some of them have also suggested that the right upper second premolar may also have been congenitally absent – though that side of the skull has suffered some damage, so the evidence in that respect is not absolutely certain.

Although the congenital absence of the left upper second premolar is less rare than the pattern of congenital absence of the left molars which was discovered in Anne Mowbray's skull, the dental evidence, together with other evidence such as the place of discovery, the age at death and the evidence of social status, does tend to support the contention that the CF2 remains may be those of Anne Mowbray's aunt, Eleanor Talbot. That also supports the possibility that Anne's hypodontia might have been inherited from the Talbot family of the young girl's mother.

It therefore cannot be stated as a fact that Anne Mowbray's congenitally missing teeth prove that she was related to TL1 and 2 – and that therefore those remains must belong to Anne's second cousins, the two sons of Edward IV. Yet previously that claim was put forward by some dental experts. Moreover, if congenitally missing teeth really had been a Neville inheritance, it now seems rather odd that Richard III apparently showed no sign of it.

29

CAN DNA NOW REVEAL THE TRUTH?

'DNA' stands for '*Deoxyribo*N*ucleic Acid*'. It is composed of four nitrogenous bases – adenine, cytosine, guanine and thymine – which are normally referred to by their initial letters: A, C, G, and T. All living things have two kinds of DNA. Their major component is nuclear DNA, residing in the cell nucleus. But they also have mitochondrial DNA (mtDNA). That is the DNA of tiny structures called the mitochondria, which reside outside the cell nucleus in the surrounding cushion of cytoplasm.

Unfortunately, because nuclear DNA is inherited 50 per cent from each parent, its composition can change greatly over a number of generations. The only element of nuclear DNA which can normally be used in a historical context is the Y chromosome, because that is transmitted, usually unchanged, in the male line only – from father to son. Even so, there is a problem in respect of the possible historic evidence of the Y chromosome, as we shall see shortly. On the other hand all mitochondrial DNA is inherited by children of both sexes exclusively from their mothers. As a result, like the Y chromosome, it too is normally inherited unchanged. Its composition only alters very slowly, making mtDNA by far the most useful DNA component in a historical context.

As many people with an interest in fifteenth-century history will already know, in 2004, as a result of genealogical research, I found Joy Brown (Ibsen), a living all-female-line descendant of Anne of York, Duchess of Exeter. Anne of York was the eldest sister of Edward

IV and Richard III. My purpose in seeking Joy had been to find a living sample source for mtDNA which could help to establish the identity of some bones found in Belgium which it was then thought might possibly belong to the youngest sister of the same two kings, Margaret of York, Duchess of Burgundy.

Joy Ibsen and her great … aunt, Margaret of York, Duchess of Burgundy.

Unfortunately, in the end Joy's mtDNA proved not to match that of the Belgian bones, thus indicating that Margaret of York's remains have not yet been rediscovered. That was very disappointing both for Joy and me – and disappointing for the town of Mechelen in Belgium. Nevertheless, the publication of Joy's mtDNA sequence – which would also have been that of Richard III – was one of my key contributions to the eventual rediscovery of that king's lost remains in 2012.[1]

Meanwhile, however, I had also been seeking other DNA information in respect of the medieval royal family of England. Since the two kinds of DNA information which are most useful in a historical context are mtDNA (which is inherited, normally unchanged, in all-female lines of descent) and Y chromosomes (which are inherited in all-male lines of descent), I also sought the Y chromosome of fourteenth- and fifteenth-century kings of England. But that revealed a problem. Unfortunately the men whom one finds named as fathers in documentary records are not always the genuine *biological* fathers of the boys listed as their sons. Thus the living male members of the family which I highlighted as comprising theoretical illegitimate male-line descendants of King Edward III ultimately proved to have Y chromosomes which did not match that of King Richard III. Moreover, some living male members of the family in question proved to have different Y chromosomes than their cousins! It seems that, in spite of sharing a family surname, the living alleged descendants are not all genuinely related in terms of their male line of descent.[2]

At the same time, I was also seeking the mtDNA of the so-called 'princes in the Tower'. At that time it seemed to me to be impossible to find any living all-female line descendants of their mother, Elizabeth Widville, or of her sisters. However, I traced some close historic female-line relatives who would have shared the mtDNA of Elizabeth Widville and all her children.

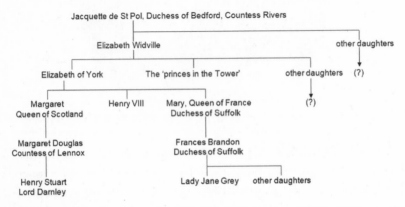

The author's early research on the bloodlines bearing the mtDNA of the so-called 'princes in the Tower'.

One important fact which emerged was that Henry VIII and his two sisters would all have shared the mtDNA of their maternal uncles, the so-called 'princes in the Tower'. That was significant, because at Bury St Edmunds (where she lies buried) some hair belonging to Henry VIII's younger sister, Mary, Queen of France and Duchess of Suffolk, is on display in Moyse's Hall Museum, in an eighteenth-century locket (see plate 22).

Mary, Queen of France and Duchess of Suffolk (1496–1533) was the younger of the two daughters of Henry VII and his wife, Elizabeth of York. And of course, Mary would have inherited her mtDNA from her mother. Since she was a daughter of Elizabeth of York, she would also have shared her mtDNA with her mother's missing brothers – and her own maternal uncles – Edward V and Richard of Shrewsbury, Duke of York. All of them would have inherited the mtDNA of

Elizabeth Widville, who, in turn, had inherited her mtDNA from her mother, Jacquette de St Pol, Duchess of Bedford,[3] and the latter's female-line ancestry.

Earlier sources for the mtDNA.
The female line ancestry of Elizabeth Widville.

Imperatrice d'Arco, *c.*1237-*c.*1309
|
Isabella d'Acquaviva, Countess of Celano, *c.*1262-?
|
Francesca di Celano, Countess of Anglone, 1310- *c.*1378
|
Jeanne Gorizia de Sabran, Countess of Nola, 1322-1379
|
Justine Sueva Orsini, Duchess of Andria, *c.*1365-*c.*1422
|
Margherita del Balzo, Countess of St Pol, 1394-1469
|
Jacquette de St Pol, Duchess of Bedford, Countess Rivers, *c.*1415-1472
|
Elizabeth Widville, Lady Grey

In her turn, Mary, Queen of France and Duchess of Suffolk subsequently transmitted the mtDNA which she had inherited via her daughter, Frances Brandon, to her all-female-line granddaughters, Lady Jane Grey and Lady Catherine Grey. Thus, in relation to the English throne, the mtDNA in question seem to have proved to be a rather ill-fated inheritance! Both Edward V and Jane Grey (the 'nine days' queen') only had very short and rather troubled 'reigns' as English monarchs. Both of them were proclaimed sovereigns of England. However, neither of them was ever crowned.

Mary herself had briefly been Queen of France, because she was married to the fifty-two-year-old King Louis XII. That was a political alliance, arranged by her brother, King Henry VIII. Following Louis' death, the young widowed queen had returned to England. There she contracted a second marriage – a love-match with Charles Brandon, Duke of Suffolk. Initially that infuriated her brother, Henry VIII. Eventually, however, he forgave the couple.

When Mary died she was interred with some splendour at Bury St Edmunds Abbey in Suffolk. And six years later, when the abbey was dissolved, Henry VIII had his sister's body rescued, and moved to the nearby church of St Mary, where it still lies.

The Queen (says Sir John Cullum's MS. account [*see below for details*]) died at the manor of Westhorpe, 25th June, 1553 [*sic*][4] and after being embalmed, lying in state, &c., was conducted to Bury with royal magnificence on the 21st of July following, and buried in the monastery there on the next day. (Sandford's *Geneal. Hist.*) Upon the dissolution of the monastery, but little more than six years' afterwards, her tomb was probably the only one that was saved from the destruction that involved the abbey and its noble church, with all its monuments, in one common ruin. This preservation was doubtless owing to the influence of her royal brother, and of her husband. It was a plain altar monument of stone, with the upper slab of Petworth marble, marked at each corner and at the centre with a small cross, which shows it was consecrated for an altar. It was removed to the north-east corner of the chancel of St. Mary's church, where it stood till September 6, 1784, as before mentioned. It was then taken down, and the coffin deposited in the same place, in a grave no deeper than was necessary for the slab to lie over it, level with the rest of the pavement.[5]

It had been in the early eighteenth century when the churchwardens of St Mary's church first had thoughts about moving Mary's standing tomb for a second time. That was because it was obstructing the north-east corner of the chancel. At that time, however, it was believed in Bury St Edmunds that the 'tomb' was not really Mary's burial site. It was thought to be merely a cenotaph. The general belief at that time was that Mary's body had actually been left lying in the abbey ruins and that only her empty monument had been moved to St Mary's church.

The altar tomb was first opened in 1731, when the churchwardens had a design to remove it, believing it to be only a cenotaph; but on the then discovery that it contained the coffin of the royal lady, they abandoned their intention. In 1758, the Rev. Dr. Symonds caused the tomb to be repaired at his own expence, and placed on its western face the inscribed marble tablet which is now let into the north wall of the chancel; but which, on the removal of the tomb in 1784, was placed in one of the panels of the tasteless woodwork which then existed at the back of the communion table.

The stone which surmounted the altar tomb, and had originally been an altar stone, as indicated by the five crosses yet remaining on it, still indicates the spot where the royal remains lie.[6]

In 1784, when the altar tomb was finally removed, and Mary's body was reburied in the ground beneath where it had stood, an account of the discovery was written by Sir John Cullum, Bt., who was present when the tomb superstructure was opened. His account reads as follows:

6th September, 1784. The Churchwardens of St. Mary's, at Bury St. Edmund's designing to remove the altar monument of the French Queen, which stood in the north-east corner of the chancel, and obstructed the approach to the rails of the communion table in that part, myself and a few more had notice of it.

The coffin rested on a plank within the tomb, not sunk into the ground; it was of lead, 6 feet 2 inches long, nearly of the shape of the body, with a coarse representation of the face, like the mummy coffins. Upon the breast, which had been smoothed and polished, was rudely scratched,
Mary Quene
1553 [*sic* – 1533][7]
of Ffraunc
Edmund H.

Upon opening the coffin, the corpse appeared of a deep chestnut colour: it had been embalmed, as Sandford says, but the whole was become extremely moist, perhaps from a small incision that had been made in the coffin about fifteen years before, which, though soldered up again, had doubtless admitted a fresh mass of air. What-ever gums and resins had been used, they had lost their tenacity. The swathings were of coarse linen, and, as well as their extreme tenderness would suffer me to handle a piece of them, seemed to be at least tenfold; they had given way about the stomach, by which it appeared that the inside of the body had been filled up with some calcareous substance, doubtless to absorb any moisture that might exude. The sockets of the eyes were also hued with the same substance, as was also probably the cranium, if the brains had been taken out; but this was not examined, as very little disturbance was given to the royal remains. The hair was perfectly sound, retaining the original strength, and adhering very closely to the skull. It was of considerable length, some perhaps near two feet long, and of a beauteous golden colour, as was that of her mother at the time of her marriage. (See Mr. Walpole's 'Anecdotes of Painting', vol. i. p. 51.) The teeth were all entire and even, both above and below.

Some parts of the envelopes [linen wrappings] had perforations in them of about the size of a small knitting needle; if these were made by insects (as they have the appearance) the eggs of these insects must have been deposited either before the original closing of the coffin, or at its opening about fifteen years ago, before mentioned. In either case, it is a curious instance how animal life can exist without the renovation of air.[8]

Samples of her hair were extracted before Mary's body was re-interred and the tomb closed. It is reported that a lock of Mary's hair was subsequently in the possession of the Duchess of Portland (sent to her by Sir John Cullum, together with the account quoted above). Other locks of her hair were held by Mr Pate, a Bury St Edmunds lawyer, and Revd George Ashby of Barrow. The lock of hair in the possession of Revd George Ashby passed subsequently to a Mr Deck. He presented it to Moyse's Hall Museum in Bury St Edmunds, where that specimen of Mary's hair can still be seen today (Acc. no. 1978.99; 1903 catalogue no. IV 688).

Other eighteenth-century accounts than Cullum's describe the hair found in the tomb as reddish rather than gold, and indeed the lock of hair now preserved at Moyse's Hall Museum, though possibly somewhat faded by exposure to the light, does appears to have a reddish tinge (see plate 22) – similar to what seems to have been the hair colour of Mary's maternal uncle King Edward V (see above, chapters 4 and 5). Henry VII's hair was very dark, but possibly Mary inherited her hair colour from her mother, Elizabeth of York.

I had long been aware that the locket containing a sample of Mary's hair was on display at Moyse's Hall Museum. So when I realised that Mary would have shared the mtDNA of her maternal uncles, the sons of Edward IV, that appeared to offer an intriguing possible way for me to reveal the mtDNA of the so-called 'princes in the Tower'. If the lock of Mary's hair could be extracted from its late eighteenth-century locket, then a few strands of it could be subjected to mtDNA analysis. It would then reveal the mtDNA of Mary, of her mother, Elizabeth of York, and of her uncles, Edward V and Richard of Shrewsbury.

In 2008 Moyse's Hall Museum kindly allowed the locket to be taken for a time to Colchester, where I was then working with the Museum Service on cataloguing their collection of medieval seals. There my friend Philip Wise, Collections and Curatorial Manager of Colchester and Ipswich Museum Service, then sought expert advice regarding possible ways of opening the locket for me, so that a few strands of hair could be carefully removed for scientific testing. Unfortunately, however, the locket proved to have been soldered shut in the eighteenth century. Thus it would have been impossible to open it without using heat. And of course, the risk was that heat might have damaged the contents.

Consequently the Moyse's Hall Museum locket was returned to Bury St Edmunds, and I was forced to do further research in an attempt to find some of the other locks of Mary's hair which had been extracted in 1784, as reported by Sir John Cullum. I discovered the following list of potential items, published in a mid-nineteenth-century account:

A locket containing a portion of hair which Mr. Hasted saw cut a few years since from the body of Thomas Beaufort, Duke of Exeter, who died in 1427, and was buried in the Abbatial Church of St. Edmund. The body was re-interred at the foot of the pillar in the grounds of J. Muskett, Esq.

A ring containing a portion of the hair of Mary Tudor, Queen of France, taken from her corpse when the leaden coffin in which it was interred in St. Mary's Church, Bury was opened. There can be no question as to the authenticity of this hair, it having been cut either by or in the presence of the Reader of the Parish, from whom Mr. Hasted inherited it.

Mr. S. Tymms observed that another lock of this hair, formerly in the possession of the Rev. George Ashby, of Barrow, was in the Bury and West Suffolk Museum, to which institution it had been presented by Mr. Deck; and several others were preserved in the town and neighbourhood. One lock, set in a plain gold locket, presented to Horace Walpole by Miss Fauquier, was sold, at the Strawberry Hill sale in 1842, to the Earl of Derby, for £2 12s 6d.

Another lock was presented to the Duchess Dowager of Portland, by the late Sir John Cullum, Bart., with an account, 'as meagre', he writes to her Grace, 'as the poor Queen's own skeleton,' of this royal lady, and 'the circumstances under which the coffin was opened'.

At the sale of the Duchess of Portland's effects, this lock of hair passed into the hands of the Duke of Chandos, under the circumstances related in the *following* letter of the agent employed by his Grace to purchase it : –

'Marqaret Street, May 8, 1786.
'*My* Lord Duke,
The ringlet of the French Queen's hair from which you are descended, the historical MS. account of her Majesty, and of the appearance of her body when the tomb was opened, together with Sir John Cullum's notes to the Duchess when he sent her the ringlet (which I required first of all to see, and to have with the lot), are now your Grace's own property in my possession and which I as firmly believe to have been cut from the head of the Queen as I believe my own existence. Upon my making that observation immediately after the lot was knocked down to me, a gentleman who sat next to me replied, 'Sir, that you may indeed, for I was with Sir John Cullum when he cut the hair off, as I did at the same time some for myself.' The gentleman's name was Orde, nephew to the Master in Chancery of that name, and lives near Bedford Row. Now, my Lord, for the purchase your Grace gave me leave to go as far as twenty pounds. At first, there was a smart bidding, but I pushed boldly with a determined face that I would have it, and which I got for £6 10s. If your Grace wishes to have them sent to Bath, I shall obey your commands, otherwise I shall keep the golden treasure at Castle Reynell, and venerate it with reverential regard each morning, till I deliver it into the hands of the 'pious Aeneas,' whose commands no one receives with more pleasure, whose health, with that of his Lavinia, none more fervently wishes, than,

'My Lord Duke,
'Your Grace's most obedient, and most humble seryant,
'RICHARD REYNELL'.

At the sale of the Duke of Buckingham's effects at Stowe, on September 13, 1848, this lock was sold for 7*l* 10*s* to Mr. Owen, of New Bond-street, London.

Of the colour of the hair there seems to have been a dispute. A MS. note of the Rev. George Ashby, of Barrow, in his copy of the 'Description of Bury', 1782, says 'Her hair, which was in quantity, was the *high red of a* lady living in Bury in 1789, who has often been asked to part with a lock to be passed off for the Queen's.

Miss Harmer, of Wattisfield, shewed me a lock, 'very clean and nice, a little curled, or in a ring [shape at the end]. It was certainly red and not auburn. Mr. Pate, attorney of Bury, assures me that he had some [which was cut off by Mr. Cooke, one of the then churchwardens] and that it was plainly of two colours, which he accounted for by the lower part lying immersed in pickle. He said one was of the colour of the lady's hair before mentioned'.[9]

It is intriguing – and rather worrying – to note that apparently not all the hair which was placed in lockets and other jewellery and reported to have belonged to Henry VIII's sister Mary really was hair from her dead body. However, hopefully the specific locks of hair mentioned in the mid-nineteenth-century report were believed to be authentic.

A ring containing a sample of Mary's hair appears to still exist. Of the other locks of Mary's hair mentioned in the report, the first which I sought to trace was the one which had originally been presented to the historian Horace Walpole and which had been sold, after Walpole's death, to the Earl of Derby, for £2 12*s* 6*d*. I then discovered that the present-day Rt Hon. the Earl of Derby still owns the locket which his ancestor had purchased from the estate of Horace Walpole. It is now kept at Knowsley Hall, near Liverpool. The inscription on the locket was obviously commissioned by Horace Walpole, and bears his initials, 'H. W.' (see plate 23).

With the kind help of the then Curator of Collections at Knowsley Hall, Emma McCarthy, and with the kind permission of her employer, the Earl of Derby, I was then able to travel up to Merseyside and, wearing a mask and surgical gloves, watch while Emma and her assistant (also wearing masks and gloves, and using tweezers) carefully extracted a few strands of hair from the locket, and sealed them in sterile containers which I had brought with me. Incidentally, this hair was also auburn (see plate 23) – similar to what seems to have been the hair colour of Mary's maternal uncle, Edward V. However the hair at Knowsley Hall is darker (probably less faded) than the lock of hair at Moyse's Hall Museum.

Initially I took the hair strands from Knowsley Hall home with me. I then set off on another journey in a different direction – to beautiful Leuven, in Belgium. At the university there I handed over one of my two sets of hair samples to Professor Jean-Jacques Cassiman, whose famous earlier work on the mtDNA of the prisoner child-king Louis XVII of France – which included mtDNA testing of hair samples of the boy's mother, Queen Marie-Antoinette – I was well aware of and greatly admired.

Unfortunately what emerged from Professor Cassiman's testing of the Knowsley Hall hair was the fact that the strands of Mary's hair had been contaminated as a result of their handling in the eighteenth century. Thus clear conclusions did not emerge in respect of their mtDNA. The report presented to me in 2009 by Professor Jean-Jacques Cassiman of the University of Leuven as a result of his analysis of the hair samples from the Knowsley Hall locket can be seen in full in appendix 4(a).

Subsequently, however, Glen Moran, who had been interested in my DNA work, also explored the possibility of tracing living all-female-line relations of Elizabeth Widville. He approached me and asked for my help in dealing with some fifteenth- and sixteenth-century Latin documents. Eventually, as a result, he found a living all-female line of descent from one of Elizabeth Widville's younger sisters. His findings were published in 2016 as follows:

> I started my own research into the mtDNA sequence of the 'princes in the Tower' in early 2016 and having failed to trace a line of descent from the sisters of Elizabeth Widville, I began to search for female-line relatives of her mother Jacquette of Luxembourg. Beyond the first few generations, information is not freely available

for the relatives of Jacquette (at least not in English). On closer inspection of the Widville family tree, it became clear that many of the Peerage collections that record the history of the noble families of England had made a significant mistake. Having identified the error in the historical records, a further female line was identified that opened up another possibility for the identification of an all-female line of descent and with it, the mtDNA sequence of the 'princes in the Tower'. After the discovery of this new all-female line, it was possible to identify a relative from whom mtDNA could be extracted and compared.[10]

This is an updated version of the key family tree discovered by Glen:

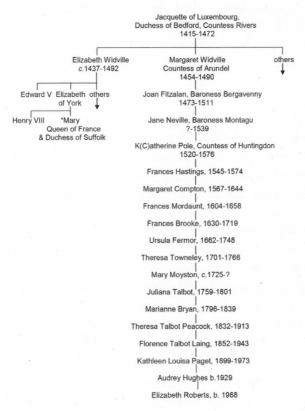

Jacquette of Luxembourg,
Duchess of Bedford, Countess Rivers
1415-1472

Elizabeth Widville
*c.*1437-1492

Margaret Widville
Countess of Arundel
1454-1490

others

Edward V   Elizabeth
of York   others

Joan Fitzalan, Baroness Bergavenny
1473-1511

Henry VIII   *Mary
Queen of France
& Duchess of Suffolk

Jane Neville, Baroness Montagu
?-1539

K(C)atherine Pole, Countess of Huntingdon
1520-1576

Frances Hastings, 1545-1574

Margaret Compton, 1567-1644

Frances Mordaunt, 1604-1658

Frances Brooke, 1630-1719

Ursula Fermor, 1662-1748

Theresa Towneley, 1701-1766

Mary Moyston, *c.*1725-?

Juliana Talbot, 1759-1801

Marianne Bryan, 1796-1839

Theresa Talbot Peacock, 1832-1913

Florence Talbot Laing, 1852-1943

Kathleen Louisa Paget, 1899-1973

Audrey Hughes b.1929

Elizabeth Roberts, b. 1968

* Source of the hair samples.

The line of descent from Margaret Widville, Countess of Arundel to Elizabeth Roberts.

Glen's newly discovered group of living all-female-line descendants of Margaret Widville, younger sister of Elizabeth, includes the opera singer Elizabeth Roberts, who gave me the following information about her immediate family.

> Kathleen Louise Paget married Jack Holt-Schooling and had one daughter, Jacqueline. Kathleen Holt-Schooling then married Allan Gibson Hughes (b1900) in 1928. They had two children, Audrey Rowena and Allan Berkeley Valentine Hughes. He was a solicitor in Shrewsbury and a registrar for county courts. He had been a captain in the King's Shropshire Light Infantry and served 1914-17, was injured at Paschendaele. Audrey was a commercial artist. She married Henry Edward 'Ted' Roberts in 1951. He was an advertising executive and then was ordained in 1956. They had five children: Jane, Simon, Kate, Peter and Elizabeth. A photo of all 7 of us is attached [plate 25].

Elizabeth Roberts had herself previously studied the history of the 'Wars of the Roses'. She told me that one of her mother's cousins had done some research years ago and had found some indication in respect of the family's ancestral connections with medieval English royalty, though 'we didn't realise it was such a direct connection.' Elizabeth then revealed that she was very interested in her maternal-line ancestry – the source of her mtDNA. In particular she was fascinated about the story of Jacquette of Luxembourg and her daughters having been water nymphs and witches! She also said, 'It's very interesting to see it in a different light now, to have more of a sense of the personal stories and of the political side-switching that was necessary for survival. I was very much aware that the Princes in the Tower story was unverified and potentially part of the anti-Yorkist propaganda by the Tudors but it's very difficult to work out what did happen, particularly since we don't have the voices of the women involved to give their side of events.'[11]

Once contact had been made with Elizabeth, she kindly provided samples for mtDNA testing to the University of Leuven, and she has now permitted this publication of the results. The full report from Professor Ronny Decorte can be seen in appendix 4(b). As for the relevant features of Elizabeth Roberts' mtDNA, they are reproduced in plate 27. Thus it is now clear that she belongs to a subgroup of the mtDNA haplogroup U, often known as 'Ursula' (see below).

In view of her female-line descent from a younger sister of Elizabeth Widville, it therefore appears to be the case that all of her ancestral female-line relatives, including Edward V; Richard of Shrewsbury, Duke of York; Elizabeth of York and all her sisters; Elizabeth of York's children, including King Henry VIII; and the female-line descendants of Elizabeth of York's daughters – including Lady Jane Grey, the 'nine days' queen', shared her mtDNA haplogroup, U5a2b.

In terms of their mtDNA it has been calculated that all modern humans are descended in an all-female line of descent from one common ancestress. That mother of all is known as 'Mitochondrial Eve', and it is estimated that she must have lived in Africa about 150,000 years ago. Of course, during her lifetime she would not have been the only living human female. Moreover, some of her contemporaries may also figure among our ancestresses in mixed (male/female) lines. However, subsequently a situation gradually arose, according to which 'Mitochondrial Eve' now happens to be the only one of her contemporaries to have living descendants in the *all-female* line. Indeed, she has been in that unique position for thousands of years.

Of course, the modern human population has a number of different lines of descent from 'Mitochondrial Eve', via various 'clan mothers'. Also, different 'clan mothers' predominate in the human ancestry in respect of the different continents. In Europe most of the 'native' population descends from 'Mitochondrial Eve' via one of seven 'clan mothers', who are thought to have lived at various different dates between 45,000 and 10,000 years ago. The seven clan mothers of Europe are referred to by letters, or by invented names, as follows:[12]

U ('Ursula') – ancestress of about 11% of the modern European population.

X ('Xenia') – ancestress of about 6% of the European population – mostly in central and eastern Europe.

H ('Helena') – ancestress of about 47% of the modern European population.

V ('Velda') – ancestress of about 5% of the modern European population – mainly in western Europe.

T ('Tara') – ancestress of about 9% of the modern European population – mostly along the Mediterranean coast or the western edge of the continent.

K ('Katrine') – ancestress of about 6% of the modern European population – mostly around the Mediterranean.

J ('Jasmine') – ancestress of about 17% of the modern European population.

In 2004, having discovered Joy Ibsen, all-female-line living descendant of Richard III's mother, I revealed her (and his) mtDNA haplgroup as J ('Jasmine'). That was not the most common group in Europe, and the mtDNA haplogroup later helped to identify the remains of Richard III when we (the Looking For Richard Project) found them in Leicester.

It now appears to have been revealed that, in terms of their mtDNA haplogroup, the children of Elizabeth Widville belonged to a slightly less common group than the children of Cecily Neville. The mtDNA haplogroup in question is the one which Elizabeth Roberts has now disclosed, namely U ('Ursula') – and specifically the subgroup U5a2b. However, initially there was a slight problem with this discovery, which was the same as a problem which occurred earlier on when I found Joy Ibsen.

As I made clear when reporting my earlier discovery of Joy Ibsen, she was initially the only living female-line descendant of Cecily Neville whom I had found. Thus, to confirm that Joy's mtDNA really was that of Cecily, ideally it was necessary to find another source to guarantee the evidence of her mtDNA haplogroup.[13] In 2007 I therefore reported that 'attempts are currently in progress to sequence mtDNA from a sample of Edward IV's hair, kindly supplied to the present writer by the Ashmolean Museum, Oxford.'[14]

Unfortunately, however, work on the Edward IV hair proved difficult. As we saw earlier in the case of the hair of Mary, Queen of France and Duchess of Suffolk, hair cut from dead bodies is frequently contaminated by the hands of those who carry out the cutting process. As a result the mtDNA of the hair sample becomes confused by the mtDNA of the hair cutter! Thus in Joy's case, the authenticity of her mtDNA could not be confirmed by the hair sample of Edward IV, because that hair was contaminated. In the end it was only absolutely confirmed when the

University of Leicester first traced another living female line of descent from Cecily Neville, and then found that the mtDNA of both the living descendants matched that of the bones of Richard III.

But although the 2009 results from two Knowsley Hall hair samples also proved those strands of hair to have been contaminated, in 2017 I received the newly revealed mtDNA result for Elizabeth Roberts. At that point some of the specific points revealed by the 2009 Knowsley Hall hair testing appeared to me to potentially correspond with those of the haplogroup which had just been revealed for Elizabeth.

INCOMPLETE SIGNS OF THE mtDNA OF MARY, QUEEN OF FRANCE AND DUCHESS OF SUFFOLK
Differences from the revised Cambridge Reference Sequence are shown highlighted in squares. This evidence was found in 2009 by testing contaminated hairs. Might Mary have belonged to the same mtDNA subgroup as Elizabeth Roberts (see plate 27)?

```
16021  CTGTTCTTTC  ATGGGGAAGC   AGATTTGGGT  ACCACCCAAG  TATTGACTCA  CCCATCAACA
16081  ACCGCTATGT  ATTTCGTACA   TTACTGCCAG  CCACCATGAA  TATTGTACGG  TACCATAAAT
16141  ACTTGACCAC  CTGTAGTACA   TAAAAACCCA  ATCCACATCA  AAACCCCCTC  C[T]CATGCTTA
16201  CAAGCAAGTA  CAGCAATCAA   CCCTCAACTA  TCACACATCA  ACTGCAACTC  CAAA[2]CACC
16261  CCTCACCCA[2] TAGGATACCA   ACAAACCTAC  CCACCCTTAA  CAGTACATAG  TACATAAAGC
16321  CATTTACCGT  ACATAGCACA   TTACAGTCAA  ATCCCTTCTC  GTCCCCATGG  ATGACCCCCC
```

A = ADENINE; C = CYTOSINE; G = GUANINE; T = THYMINE;
2 = two different results in one position – signs of contamination from handling of the hair.

Of course, I am not a scientific expert in this matter! However, I expected the hair from the Knowsley Hall locket to belong to the same subgroup of haplogroup U – even though confusion had been created by the contamination of the hair as a result of its handling in the eighteenth century. I therefore commissioned further testing by the University of Leuven, using my remaining hair samples from Knowsley Hall (plate 24). Professor Ronny Decorte told me that this time attempts would first be made to decontaminate the hair.

At present the work on the hair is still going on at the Centre of Human Genetics of the University of Leuven. I hope that in due course it will confirm that all the historical figures listed in the family tree on page 196 – including the so-called 'princes in the Tower' – belonged to the same mtDNA haplogroup as Elizabeth Roberts. In the future that scientific information could then be used to help to identify any of their remains. Of course, it would also be useful to trace other possible sources to confirm the mtDNA revealed by Elizabeth Roberts.

CONCLUSION

Hopefully it is now absolutely clear that there is no evidence that Edward V and Richard of Shrewsbury were ever called 'the princes in the Tower' during their own lifetimes. The evidence presented in chapter 2 showed that the appellation was only invented – and first applied to those two boys – late in the nineteenth century.

It should also now be clear that actually it is not at all a good term to apply to those two boys in respect of its historical accuracy. First, it suggests that because they were in the Tower of London, the two boys were prisoners. Also, because it applies to them the title 'princes', it implies that they were legitimate members of the royal family. But both of those points have now been shown to be contestable.

In respect of the notion that the two boys were confined in custody, it is of course true that the Tower of London – like other medieval castles – was sometimes used for the holding of prisoners. Primarily, however, the Tower was London's chief royal residence at that time. Indeed, it often housed members of the royal family, particularly new kings who were awaiting their coronations. Thus it was in preparation for the coronation of Edward V that he and his younger brother were installed there. And there is no clear contemporary evidence that either of the boys was ever imprisoned in the Tower.

In respect of the application of the title 'princes', Edward V and Richard of Shrewsbury definitely were the two sons of Edward IV who outlived their father. However, there are some important questions in respect of Edward IV. These include the precise date of his birth, the precise date of his death,[1] and the legality of his marriage to Elizabeth Widville.

It is universally acknowledged that Edward IV's marriage to Elizabeth Widville was carried out in secret. Subsequently, when their union was publicly announced, it is also clear that its validity was immediately questioned by some people. That problem is known to have seriously concerned Elizabeth Widville, both in respect of her own status, and in respect of the status of her royal children. It is also well known to have caused conflict within the royal family. Ultimately that conflict led to the execution of Edward IV's brother George, Duke of Clarence, and possibly also other deaths. The royal execution of the Duke of Clarence was clearly part of Elizabeth Widville's campaign to try to ensure that one of her sons by Edward IV would inherit the English crown in due course. Obviously she always feared that might not happen.

However, in 1483, after the death of Edward IV, a formal decision was reached by the three estates of the realm that the late king's legal wife had been Lady Eleanor Talbot (Lady Boteler), the beautiful daughter of the Earl of Shrewsbury. Although Eleanor was no longer living in 1483, she had still been alive when Edward IV had made his secret marriage with Elizabeth Widville. Therefore the decision arrived at by the three estates of the realm was that all the children of Edward IV and Elizabeth Widville – including the two boys – were bastards. In other words Edward V and Richard of Shrewsbury were not legal princes.

Consequently Edward V could not possibly be crowned as England's new king. It was therefore at that point that the crown was offered by the three estates to Edward IV's surviving younger brother, Richard, Duke of Gloucester (Richard III). Incidentally, there is not a shred of evidence indicating that Richard himself had ever conspired to acquire the crown, despite the existence of popular mythology in that respect. In fact it seems that several days were needed to persuade the Duke of Gloucester (as he then was) to accept the throne.

Curiously, however, many historians have alleged that, in the immediate aftermath of the death of Edward IV, Gloucester effectively staged a coup in order to make himself lord protector of the realm. Once again, not a single shred of evidence exists in that respect. Indeed, as the senior living prince of the blood royal, and in accordance with the precedents of the fourteenth and fifteenth centuries, the Duke of Gloucester would automatically have been the rightful person to act as lord protector during the minority of his nephew, Edward V. Precedent therefore *entitled* him to that position. However, actually he never appears to have used that title until he was formally appointed to the post by the royal council. And his appointment to the protectorship by the royal council only took place once he and his nephew, the young king, had arrived together in London.

Yet, strikingly, the real evidence in respect of the events of April 1483 makes it very clear that actually an attempt was then made to stage a coup, the purpose of which was to alter the identity of the individual who would exercise regency powers in England during the minority of Edward V. However, the coup in question was definitely not staged by the Duke of Gloucester. The actual attempted coup was organised by Elizabeth Widville. Nevertheless, she and her unpopular family then found themselves opposed once again – as they had been on previous occasions. As a result the attempted Widville coup failed.

Once the decision had been made that the legal consort of Edward IV had been Eleanor Talbot, and once Gloucester had been persuaded to become King Richard III, he was crowned at Westminster and then began a tour of parts of the kingdom. When he and his wife left the capital it appears that the two sons of Edward IV remained there, in residence at the palace of the Tower. One possible reason for leaving the two boys there at that stage might possibly have been the fact that the former Edward V was then suffering from ill health. Evidence exists in that respect in terms of the fact that the boy received regular visits from his doctor at about that time. Thus it is possible that he died of natural causes in the late summer or autumn of 1483. Significantly, no one ever subsequently claimed to be the living Edward V.

However, it is also clear that, in the summer of 1483, plots were made in some quarters to attempt to abduct the two sons of Edward IV from the Tower palace, presumably for political reasons. Some of those plots seem to have failed, but it is possible that one may have been successful, and that at least the younger son, Richard of Shrewsbury, may have been extracted from the Tower and taken elsewhere – possibly abroad. One pretender later claimed to be him, and was quite widely believed. Whether or not the young man in question really was Richard of Shrewsbury is not the most important point in the present context. Much more important is the fact that support for him clearly indicates that, in the 1490s, a number of Yorkists did believe that young Richard was still alive. In other words they did not then think that the two sons of Edward IV had been murdered.

Strangely enough, the only identifiable source during the reign of Richard III for a story that the two boys were *both* dead seems to have been supporters for the claim to the English throne of the 'Earl of Richmond' (later Henry VII). That claimant was then living in France, where the story of the boys' deaths was told to the French Estates General, and was also recorded in some French chronicles. However, no *detailed* account in respect of the boys' fate was then offered by Richmond's supporters. Also, of course, nothing was officially announced in England by Richard III, or by anyone else.

It is usually assumed that Richard III had been responsible for the death of the two boys. However there are three very important questions in that respect:

a) since it had been officially determined that the boys were bastards and had no legal claim to the throne, what reason would Richard have had to kill them?
b) If he had killed them for political reasons, surely the logical follow-up would have been to *announce* that they were dead – possibly by claiming that they had both died naturally. So why was no such claim ever made public by Richard III?
c) If Richard III had killed them, why did their mother subsequently continue to trust him in respect of her other children?

Later, when Richard III had himself been killed at the battle of Bosworth and the English throne had been usurped by Henry VII, initially the new monarch made no claim that the sons of Edward IV had been murdered. However, he did, very hastily, and very firmly, suppress the story of Edward IV's legal marriage to Eleanor Talbot. His motivation for that move comprised two points: first, to make Richard III appear to have been a usurper and second, to reinstate Elizabeth of York – his intended consort – as a legitimate princess. He then presented Elizabeth of York to the nation as the Yorkist heiress. His conduct in that respect could possibly be seen as implying that her two brothers were not around. However, no official announcement in that respect was made by Henry VII or his government at that point in time.

It was only nineteen years later – after Henry VII had been confronted by a young man who claimed to be the younger son of Edward IV, after he had been confronted by other Yorkist plots against him, and after he had found himself forced to struggle desperately to persuade the Spanish monarchs to complete a planned marriage of his own son and heir, Prince Arthur, with a Spanish infanta – that Henry's regime apparently began to spread a story on the diplomatic front which said that the recently executed Yorkist Sir James Tyrell had confessed to having murdered the sons of Edward IV on the orders of Richard III in 1483. However, not a single shred of real evidence exists in respect of that alleged confession. Moreover, it was never proclaimed, nor placed in the official indictment against Tyrell, nor in his attainder, as it should have been if the claim had been true.

Later Thomas More (who had significantly been educated by Cardinal John Morton) wrote a very full account of the story which had been put out diplomatically by Henry VII's regime in 1502. However, More wrote various versions. He also included elements of sarcastic humour in his accounts, he confused and conflated names and events, and he never published any of the accounts in his own lifetime, nor mentioned them in any of his many letters and communications.

Another significant point is the fact that it was according to More's account (as published after his own execution) that the story later spread which claimed that the bodies of the two boys had initially been interred in the Tower of London. However, More himself also reported clearly that the bodies had subsequently been moved elsewhere, and he stated firmly that their final resting place was unknown.

The first of those two points – the alleged burial at the Tower – has subsequently been taken very seriously. However, More's second point – that the bodies were not left lying in the Tower – has tended to be ignored. Thus when human and animal bones were discovered during building work, in 1674, lying deeply under a medieval staircase and ten feet down in the foundation level of the Tower, the human remains were identified as the sons of Edward IV, and were officially reburied under that identity in the Henry VII chapel at Westminster.

Those remains have only once been examined. And unfortunately the examination took place in the 1930s, when some elements of scientific methodology which are now available had not yet been discovered. At that time it was impossible to confirm that the remains were male. It was also impossible to assign them scientifically to a specific era, or to properly assess exactly how many sets of remains were included. More recent analysis of the examination report shows clearly that the remains found were not merely the bones of two human beings. Other remains were also present. Thus the fact that they were reportedly found buried so deeply under a medieval staircase strongly suggests that the remains could well be pre-medieval. Indeed at a similar level, more recent archaeological work in the Tower has uncovered human remains dating from earlier periods.

Nevertheless, the 1930s examination report assumed that the remains were those of two young males, of roughly the right ages for the two sons of Edward IV. Ironically, it also claimed that there was a possible bloodstain on one set of bones, which could prove that the owner of the bones in question had been suffocated. That particular claim seems very strange. After all, suffocation is not blood-shedding. In reality the stain might well have come from nails or peat, both of which were also found buried with the human remains. Moreover, suffocation would not produce such a mark on human *bones*. If any blood had been shed, at that point in time the bones would have been enclosed within the soft tissue. They would only have become exposed (as a result of the decomposition of soft tissue) at a time when there would no longer have been any blood present to stain them.

Both at the time of the examination, and later, it has also been claimed that the alleged two boys whose bones were examined had been relatives. One of the pieces of suggested evidence presented in that respect has been hypodontia. That was also found in the jaws of Anne Mowbray, second cousin once removed of Edward IV's two sons, and the child bride of Richard of Shrewsbury. However, a much closer relative of Edward IV's sons was Richard III, and his recently rediscovered body seems not to show signs of hypodontia. Moreover, there is evidence from Talbot sources which suggests that Anne Mowbray's congenital absence of certain teeth may have been inherited from an entirely different branch of her family – on her mother's side.

Thus there is, at present, no solid evidence to prove that the bones found at the Tower in 1674 belong to the sons of Edward IV, even though they lie buried at Westminster under those names. Only a re-examination of the bones in question will ever make it possible to clarify that issue. Moreover, a re-examination could now potentially be conducted very effectively, because this present study has revealed for the first time the mtDNA haplogroup to which the two sons of Edward IV and Elizabeth Widville would have belonged.

If a re-examination of the bones does now take place, the questions which need to be addressed are:

1. Can it be confirmed that the human bones belong to *two* young individuals?
2. Are the human bones male?
3. Do the human bones share mtDNA which matches that of Elizabeth Roberts?
4. At what ages did the individuals die?
5. At what period in history did they live and die?

If questions 1–3 were to receive affirmative answers, and if the answers to questions 4 and 5 were consistent with the ages, and the potential dates of death, of the sons of Edward IV, it would then be possible to advance a serious claim that the alleged identity of the remains had been proved. However, if even some of the answers varied, it could be argued that the alleged identity had been disproved.

Also, of course, even if the identity of the remains in the Westminster urn could be established, that would not resolve the issue of how the two sons of Edward IV came to die. In fact it would firmly prove that the account written by Thomas More cannot be trusted! After all, More stated that the remains of the sons of Edward IV were not left buried in the Tower of London. Yet that is the location in which the bones which now lie in the Westminster urn were discovered. And if Thomas More's account can be proved wrong in that respect, then why should it be believed in respect of any of its other points? In other words there is – and probably will always be – no solid evidence that the boys were murdered. There is also no evidence that Richard III ever harmed them.

Finally, as we have seen, there is no evidence that the boys were ever held as prisoners. However, there definitely is evidence – which was formally accepted by the three estates of the realm, and subsequently by parliament – that the two boys may never really have been true 'princes'.

Above left: 1. Real Evidence? Edward V as Prince of Wales, from a manuscript illumination commissioned by his maternal uncle, Anthony Widville, Earl Rivers. This shows the little boy with fairish ginger hair (much lighter in colour than that of his father, and his maternal uncle), but with dark eyes. (Courtesy Aibdescalzo, under Creative Commons)

Above right: 2. Real Evidence? Edward V depicted again with dark eyes, but this time with very fair hair. A posthumous fifteenth-century stained-glass window depiction at St Matthew's Church, Coldridge, Devon – a manor held by his half-brother Thomas Grey, Marquess of Dorset.

Right: 3. Real Evidence? The painted-screen posthumous image of Edward V, commissioned by Henry VII for St George's Chapel, Windsor. This shows young Edward with auburn hair, brown eyes and a long chin, similar to that of his father.

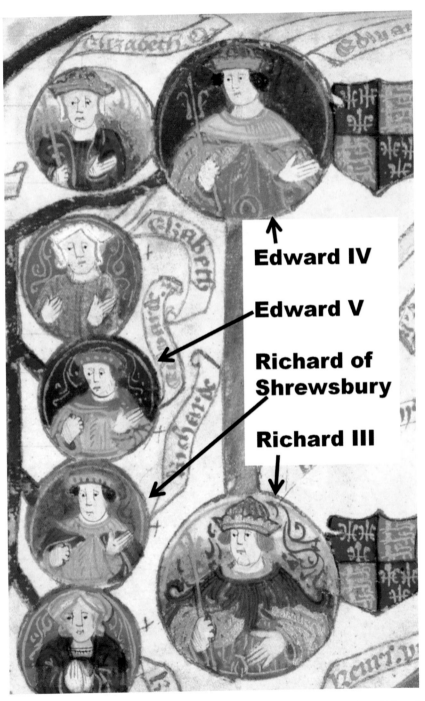

Edward IV

Edward V

Richard of Shrewsbury

Richard III

4. Real Evidence? Posthumous images of Edward IV, Richard III, Edward V and Richard of Shrewsbury from a family tree in a manuscript, commissioned in the reign of Henry VII. This shows Edward IV with dark hair, Richard III with fairish hair, Edward V with auburn hair, but his younger brother with very dark brown hair, similar to that of his father. (© The British Library, King MS 395, f. 33)

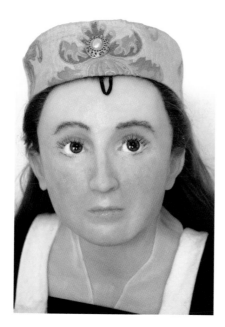

Above left: 5. Real Evidence: Anne Mowbray, Duchess of York and Norfolk, the niece of Eleanor Talbot, and the child-wife of Richard of Shrewsbury. She was also Richard's second cousin, and it has previously been alleged that she may have shared hypodontia with him and his elder brother. Facial reconstruction commissioned by the author from Amy Thornton, alumna of the Centre for Anatomy and Human Identification, University of Dundee. (© The King Richard III Visitor Centre Trust)

Above right: 6. Real Evidence: Eleanor Talbot, who was judged in 1483 to have been the legal wife of Edward IV – making the 'princes in the Tower' bastards. She was also the maternal aunt with whom Anne Mowbray may actually have shared her hypodontia. A modern painting commissioned by the author, based on the facial reconstruction of the CF2 skull at the Castle Museum in Norwich (which may be Eleanor's) and on portraits of Eleanor's closest relatives.

7. Real Evidence: Eleanor Talbot as a Carmelite tertiary, depicted in the Coventry Tapestry (*c.* 1500) with close relatives (her mother, her aunt and her sister). (Courtesy of St Mary's Guildhall and Coventry City Council)

8. Real Evidence: the royal arms of England as used by 'King Richard IV'. Reconstructed by the author based on the description of his seal.

9. Real Evidence: the heading for the year 1482–3 from the Colchester Oath Book. (Reproduced courtesy of Essex Record Office)

10. Real Evidence: magnified image of the erasure in the 1482–3 year heading of the Colchester Oath Book. In the lower version what appear to be surviving parts of erased letters have been tentatively reconstructed in red outline. And the missing letters have been inserted in pencil, to show that the word *Bastardi* would fit the space.

11. Real Evidence: the bones in the Clarence vault at Tewkesbury. They were generally thought to be remains of two individuals because two craniums are present. But when I had them re-examined in 2013 it was discovered that in reality parts of at least three individuals are present.

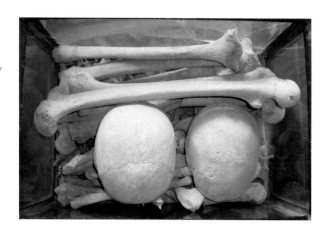

12. Real Evidence? A profile view of the more intact skull (TL1) found at the Tower of London in 1674. (© Dean and Chapter of Westminster)

13. Real Evidence? A rear view of the more intact skull (TL1) found at the Tower of London in 1674. (© Dean and Chapter of Westminster)

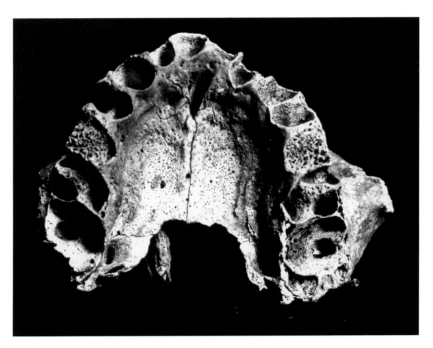

Above: 14. Real Evidence? The upper jaw of the more intact skull (TL1) found at the Tower of London in 1674. (© Dean and Chapter of Westminster)

Below: 15. Real Evidence? The lower jaw of the more intact skull (TL1) found at the Tower of London in 1674. (© Dean and Chapter of Westminster)

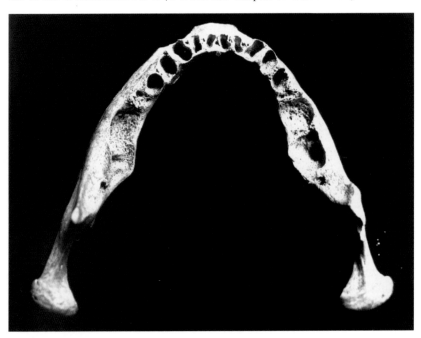

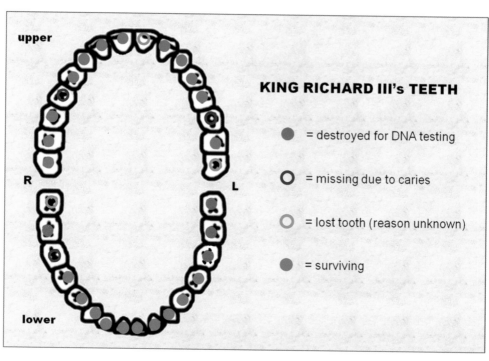

Above: 16. Real Evidence? The teeth of Richard III.

Below: 17. Real Evidence? X-Ray of the CF2 skull in Norwich (Eleanor Talbot?), showing her hypodontia.

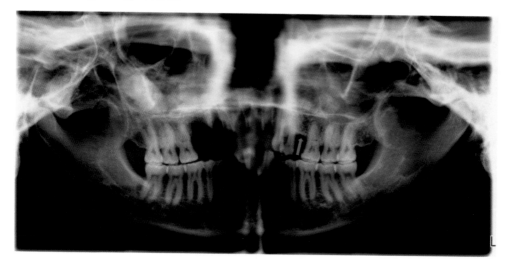

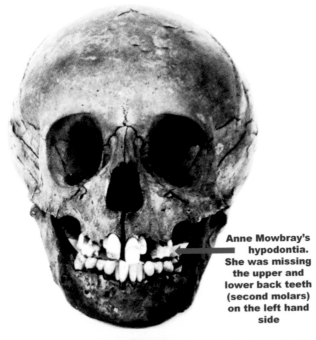

Anne Mowbray's hypodontia. She was missing the upper and lower back teeth (second molars) on the left hand side

18. Real Evidence? Anne Mowbray's hypodontia. (© Museum of London)

19. Real Evidence: Elizabeth Widville, the mother of the so-called 'princes in the Tower' and the source of their mtDNA. Her hair appears to be ginger or auburn – a colour which she seems to have passed on to her son Edward V, and to her granddaughter Mary, Queen of France and Duchess of Suffolk. Copy of a contemporary portrait, commissioned by the author and presented to Middleham.

20. Real Evidence: Mary, Queen of France and Duchess of Suffolk, who shared the mtDNA of her maternal uncles the 'princes in the Tower'. She also seems to have shared the ginger or auburn hair colour of her uncle Edward V, and her grandmother Elizabeth Widville. A copy of the portrait by Jean Perréal (commissioned by Louis XII of France as part of the preparations for their marriage), which is displayed beside Mary's tomb in Bury St Edmunds.

21. Real Evidence: the tomb at St Mary's Church, Bury St Edmunds, in which Mary, Queen of France and Duchess of Suffolk was reburied in 1784 – at which time some of her hair was taken.

22. Real Evidence: the locket at Bury St Edmunds which contains a lock of hair of Mary, Queen of France and Duchess of Suffolk (Moyse's Hall Museum, 1978.99; 1903). Though it has faded somewhat, the hair colour seems to have been ginger or auburn – similar to that of Mary's maternal uncle Edward V. (© Moyse's Hall Museum, St Edmundsbury Heritage Services)

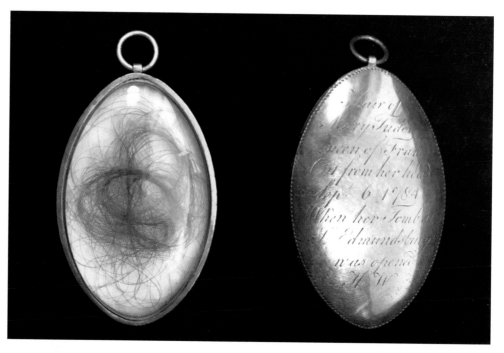

Above: 23. Real Evidence: the locket at Knowsley Hall which contains a lock of hair of Mary, Queen of France and Duchess of Suffolk. This hair has not faded, and is auburn – again, similar to that of Mary's maternal uncle Edward V. (Courtesy of the Rt Hon. the Earl of Derby, 2017)

Below: 24. Real Evidence: the hair from the Knowsley Hall locket which was retested in 2017.

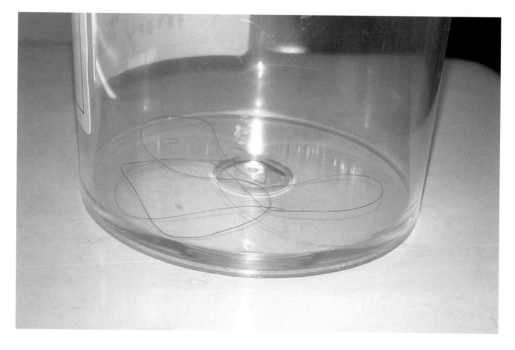

25. Real Evidence: Margaret Widville's all-female-line mtDNA descendant Audrey Hughes, together with her husband, Henry Edward 'Ted' Roberts, and their children Jane, Simon, Kate, Peter and Elizabeth. Elizabeth Roberts is the baby in the blanket.

26. Real Evidence: Elizabeth Roberts, singer, all-female-line descendant of Margaret Widville, Countess of Arundel, whose sample has revealed the mtDNA haplogroup of the 'princes in the Tower', together with her husband, Christopher Foster.

THE mtDNA REVEALED BY ELIZABETH ROBERTS' SAMPLES
This belongs to a subgroup of haplogroup U ('Ursula') - particularly U5a2b.
Differences from the revised Cambridge Reference Sequence are shown highlighted in red.

```
    1 GATCACAGGT  CTATCACCCT   ATTAACCACT  CACGGGAGCT  CTCCATGCAT  TTGGTATTTT
   61 CGTCTGGGGG  GTGTGCACGC   GATAGCATTG  CGAGACGCTG  GAGCCGGAGC  ACCCTATGTC
  121 GCAGTATCTG  TCTTTGATTC   CTGCCTCATC  CTATTATTTA  TCGCACCTAC  GTTCAATATT
  181 ACAGGCGAAC  ATACTTACTA   AAGTGTGTTA  ATTAATTAAT  GCTTGTAGGA  CATAATAATA
  241 ACAATTGAAT  GTCTGCACAG   CCGCTTTCCA  CACAGACATC  ATAACAAAAA  ATTTCCACCA
  301 AACCCCCCCT  CCCCCCGCTTC  TGGCCACAGC  ACTTAAACAC  ATCTCTGCCA  AACCCCAAAA
```

```
16021 CTGTTCTTTC  ATGGGGAAGC   AGATTTGGGT  ACCACCCAAG  TATTGACTCA  CCCATCAACA
16081 ACCGCTATGT  ATTTCGTACA   TTACTGCCAG  CCACCATGAA  TATTGTACGG  TACCATAAAT
16141 ACTTGACCAC  CTGTAGTACA   TAAAAACTCA  ATCCACATCA  AAACCCCCTC  CTCATGCTTA
16201 CAAGCAAGTA  CAGCAATCAA   CCCTCAACTA  TCACACATCA  ACTGCAACTC  CAAAGTCACC
16261 CCTCACCCAT  TAGGATACCA   ACAAACCTAC  CCACCCTTAA  CAGTACATAG  TACATAAAGC
16321 CATTTACCGT  ACATAGCACA   TTACAGTCAA  ATCCCTTCTC  GTCCCCATGG  ATGACCCCCC
```

A = ADENINE; C = CYTOSINE; G = GUANINE; T = THYMINE

Above: 27. Real Evidence: the mtDNA revealed by Elizabeth Roberts' samples.

Below: 28. Part of the mythology: Paul Delaroche's 1831 painting of *Les Enfants d'Edouard* ('Edward's Children'). (Courtesy Scailyna, under Creative Commons)

Left: 29. Part of the mythology: Sir John Everett Millais' 1878 depiction of Edward and Richard, showing them both with the wrong hair colour and hairstyle.

Below: 30. Part of the mythology: the mid-nineteenth-century brass plaque, wrongly positioned in the White Tower.

THE TRADITION of the TOWER has ALWAYS POINTED out THIS, as the STAIR UNDER WHICH the BONES of EDWARD the 5th and his BROTHER WERE FOUND in CHARLES the 2nds TIME, and from WHENCE THEY WERE REMOVED to WESTMINSTER ABBEY.

31. Part of the mythology: the alleged 'Richard IV silver groat' of 1494. (© Fitzwilliam Museum, Cambridge)

32. Part of the mythology: a drawing of the alleged *Vive Perkin* Tournai jetton of *c.* 1497–98, as published in 1860 by Longpérier. But a jetton bearing this inscription seems never really to have existed.

33. For example, here is a genuine Tournai jetton of the same period, and of the same basic design. But it does not bear the alleged *Vive Perkin* inscription. (Author's collection)

Left: 34. Part of the mythology: the ruins of St Mary's Church at Eastwell in Kent, home to the alleged tomb of 'Rychard Platagenet'. (Courtesy of Barry Marsh)

Below: 35. Part of the mythology: the alleged tomb itself.

APPENDIX 1

THE REIGN OF EDWARD V

a) Dates and sources for the reign of Edward V and for subsequent references to him

1483
MARCH

Sun 30   Edward IV ill.[1]
Mon 31

APRIL

Tues 1   Edward IV died? (If York requiem held on day 7).[2]
Wed 2
Thurs 3   Edward IV died?[3]
Fri 4   Edward IV died?[4]
Sat 5   Edward IV died? (If York requiem held on day 3).[5]
Sun 6   News reached the mayor of York that Edward IV had died.[6]
Mon 7   Edward IV died?[7]
Tues 8   Edward IV died?[8]
        Requiem mass for Edward IV in York.[9] (3rd or 7th day after death?)[10]
        The Duke of Gloucester had oaths of loyalty taken to Edward V?[11]
        Lord Howard reached London.[12]
Wed 9   Edward IV died?[13] Official announcement of death given out.
        Lord Howard visiting the Palace of Westminster?[14]

Thurs 10	Privy Council met in London?[15]
	Lord Howard visiting the Palace of Westminster?[16]
Sun 13	Lord Hastings was in conflict with the Widvilles.
	He sent information to Gloucester.
Mon 14	News of his father's death reached Edward V at Ludlow.[17]
Tues 15	
Wed 16	Edward V wrote from Ludlow to the mayor of Lynn about his plans for his coronation.[18] About this date Buckingham contacted Gloucester.[19]
Thurs 17	
Fri 18	Edward IV buried at Windsor.
Mon 21	Gloucester said to be 'protector' – but no evidence has been found.[20]
	Government appointments made in London (under Elizabeth Widville).
Tues 22	Rotherham still Chancellor.[21]
Wed 23	About this date Gloucester arranged to meet Edward V on his way to London.[22]
Thur 24	Edward V and Lord Rivers left Ludlow for London.
	Gloucester left York for London.
Fri 25	
Sat 26	Gloucester expected in Nottingham.[23]
Sun 27	Royal commissions in London (Elizabeth Widville).
Mon 28	
Tues 29	Gloucester met Buckingham and Rivers at Northampton.
Wed 30	Rivers and Sir Richard Grey arrested.[24]
	Edward V met Gloucester and Buckingham at Stony Stratford.[25]
	Edward Widville made off with the fleet and treasure.[26]

MAY

Thurs 1	Elizabeth Widville went into sanctuary at Westminster.[27]
	Edward V and Gloucester spent the night in Northampton.
Fri 2	Gloucester said to be 'protector' – but no evidence has been found.[28]
	Edward V wrote asking Cardinal Bourchier to take care of the Great Seal.[29]
Sat 3	Edward V and Gloucester at St Albans Abbey.

Sun 4   The first planned coronation date for Edward V.[30]

        Edward V received in London (at the Bishop's palace).[31]

Mon 5   Edward V at the Bishop's palace.

Tues 6   Edward V at the Bishop's palace.

Wed 7   Edward V at the Bishop's palace.

        Meeting of Edward IV's executors (and others) at Baynard's Castle.

        Cardinal Bourchier took custody of the Great Seal.[32]

Thurs 8   Edward V at the Bishop's palace.

Fri 9   Edward V at the Bishop's palace.

Sat 10   Russell appointed Chancellor.[33]

        Edward V moved to the King's Lodgings at the Tower of London.

        Pursuit of Edward Widville.[34]

Tues 13   Parliament summoned for 25 June (following the new planned date for the coronation).[35]

Wed 14   Commission to pursue Edward Widville.[36]

        Gloucester was definitely protector by this date.[37]

Thurs 15   Gloucester made grants to Buckingham.

Fri 16   Gloucester made more grants to Buckingham.

Tues 20   Those eligible for knighthood at Edward V's coronation invited to London by 18 June.

Wed 21   Gloucester made more grants to Buckingham

Thurs 22

Fri 23   Attempt to persuade Elizabeth Widville out of sanctuary.[38]

JUNE

Thurs 5   Anne Neville, Duchess of Gloucester, arrived in London.[39]

        Edward V wrote letters inviting prospective knights to his coronation.

        Lord Howard liaised with his co-Mowbray heir, Lord Berkley.

Mon 9   Coronation problem at Council meeting (Stillington?)[40]

        Elizabeth Widville still in sanctuary at Westminster.[41]

        Edward V at the Tower of London.[42]

Tues 10   Gloucester sent a request for military help to York.[43]

Wed 11   Gloucester asked for help against a Widville plot.[44]

        Hastings changed sides.[45]

Thurs 12

Fri 13   Hastings attempted a coup at the Tower council meeting and was killed by guards.[46]

Rotherham and Morton arrested.

Sat 14

Sun 15   Gloucester's request for military help received by the mayor of York.[47]

Mon 16   Elizabeth Widville handed over Richard, Duke of York.[48]

Tues 17   Final document in the *CPR* naming Edward V as king.[49]

Fri 20   Last London documents in *CCR* naming Edward V as king.[50]

Edward V was apparently officially removed from the throne.[51]

Sat 21   Further pursuit of Edward Widville.[52]

Archbishop Rotherham and Bishop Morton both prisoners in the Tower.[53]

Elizabeth Shore (*née* Lambert), mistress of Hastings & Dorset, was in prison.[54]

Sun 22   St Paul's sermon preached by Dr Shaa.

Mon 23

Tues 24   [Second planned coronation date for Edward V.[55]]

Wed 25   [planned date for state opening of Edward V's first parliament.[56]]

Execution of Rivers and Grey.[57]

Buckingham and others presented a petition to Gloucester at Baynard's Castle asking him to accept the crown.

Thurs 26   Gloucester became King Richard III.[58]

First Richard III document in CPR.[59]

Fri 27   Last document in *CCR* naming Edward V as king – but it was issued in Cambridge.[60]

Sat 28

JULY

Sat 5   Official reference to the reign of Edward V (in the reign of Richard III).[61]

Sun 6   Richard III's coronation.

c. Th. 10   Official reference to 'Edward Bastard late called king Edward the Vth'.[62]

Tues 15   Buckingham created Lord High Constable of England.

Mon 21   Richard III and party left Windsor Castle for Reading.
Tues 22   Richard III sent the Duke of Norfolk back to London for
          some reason.
Sat 26   Norfolk was at Crosby's Place, Bishopsgate.
Tues 29   Letter from Richard III to the Lord Chancellor (re. trial at
          Bishopsgate?)

About this stage Buckingham left for home.

AUGUST
Fri 1   Norfolk at Crosby's Place, Bishopsgate.
Tues 5   Norfolk at Crosby's Place, Bishopsgate.
Sun 10   Payment by Norfolk for the 'sege' at Crosby's Place.
Mon 11   Norfolk left London for Suffolk.
Wed 27   Richard III made grants to Buckingham.

SEPTEMBER
Tues 23   Papal Requiem Mass for King Edward at the Sistine
          Chapel.
Mon 29   Official reference to *Regis Edwardi Bastardi quinti nuper
          filii domini Edwardi quarti* ('the Bastard King Edward V,
          late son of the lord Edward IV').[63]

DECEMBER
Tues 16   Official reference to *Edwardi Bastardi nuper Regis
          Anglie quinti* ('Edward V, the Bastard, late King of
          England').[64]

b) Evidence for the final dates of the reign of Edward V
Calendar of Patent Rolls, 1476–1485
The latest document listed under EDWARD V (p. 352) is dated 17
June 1483

   The earliest documents listed under RICHARD III (p. 360) are
dated 26 June 1483.

Calendar of Close Rolls, 1476–1485
The latest document listed under EDWARD V (no. 1028, p. 304) is
dated 27 June 1483. However, it does not specifically mention the

name or regnal year of the king. The document in question was issued in the name of a Cambridge resident.

The latest documents which actually *mention* Edward V are 1036, 1037 and 1038 (p. 306), all of which are dated '20 June, 1 Edward V'. 1038 also has a memorandum of acknowledgement which is apparently dated 21 June, 1 Edward V. 1036 and 1038 were clearly issued in London.

The earliest document listed under RICHARD III (no. 1049) appears to be dated 26 June, but it does not appear to specifically mention the king's name anywhere.

It therefore seems that in London Edward V was still acknowledged as king on 20 June 1483, and possibly also on 21 June 1483.

It also seems that in Cambridge he was still acknowledged as king on 27 June 1483.

APPENDIX 2

TANNER

The original footnotes, which were included in the article by Tanner, have the letter 'T' added before their number, as reproduced here, to distinguish them from the new (end) notes which the present writer has added, and they are reproduced (as in Tanner's original publication) at the end of each page within his text.

Also, in the original publication, on his pages numbered 8 and 13, Tanner's notes were long, so the final sentences of his notes on those pages were published at the foot of the following pages. Here the final part of those notes have been moved to the foot of the page to which they refer. However, their page numbers in respect of the original publication have been noted.

Recent Investigations regarding the fate of the Princes in the Tower.
By Lawrence E. Tanner, Esq., M.V.O., M.A., F.S.A,
and Professor William Wright, F.R.C.S., F.S.A.

Read 30ᵗʰ November 1933

p. 1

I

HISTORICAL

'EDWARD Vth ended his reign on the 25th [of June 1483], and with his brother, Richard, then disappears from authentic history. How long the boys lived in captivity and how they died is a matter on which legend and conjecture have been rife with no approach to certainty. Most men believed, and still believe, that they died a violent death by their Uncle's order.' In these words Bishop Stubbs[T1] summed up a mystery which has never failed to fascinate those who have attempted to probe it.

The only two certain facts are, first, that from the day when Richard, duke of York, joined his brother in the Tower of London neither of the brothers was ever seen again outside its walls,[1] and, secondly, that in 1674 some bones were found by chance under a staircase in the White Tower at the Tower of London which were assumed to be those of the young princes and were buried as such by Charles II's order in Henry VII's chapel, Westminster Abbey.

The questions arise, therefore, what relationship, if any, is there between these two facts? Were the bones which were found in 1674 animal bones, as has been more than once hinted by reputable historians, or were they human bones? If they were human bones, were they the bones of two boys of about the reputed age of the two princes, and were the 'most certain indications' (to quote the epitaph on the monument in the abbey) which convinced Charles II that they were indeed the bones of the princes, likely to be such as would commend themselves to modern medical science? And, lastly, if the bones were scientifically examined to-day could anything be deduced from them which might throw light on the mystery surrounding the fate of the princes in the Tower?

Strong representations of the importance of the questions under review having been made by responsible persons to our Fellow the dean of West-

T1 *Constitutional Hist. of England*, iii, 231.

p. 2

minster, he determined in July 1933 (though not without hesitation) to open the urn, in which the bones were alleged to have been deposited, in order that the matter might be fully investigated. It is the result of that investigation which Professor Wright and myself have the honour of laying before the Society.

Professor Wright's paper describes in detail what was actually found, but here it may be said at once that the bones which filled the urn were unquestionably those of two children of approximately the ages of the princes.[2] Such being the case, it seemed desirable to re-investigate such aspects of the story as might either throw light on, or receive corroboration from, what was found.[T1]

The outstanding question, of course, is the responsibility for the murder[3] or, to put it in a more popular way, the guilt or innocence of King Richard III. It cannot be denied that there is a considerable body of evidence to show that suspicion rested upon him from the earliest times,[T2] and it is certainly most remarkable that so responsible a person as the Chancellor of France should have mentioned the murder as a fact in addressing the Estates General which met at Tours in the January following the presumed date of the murder.[T3]

But none the less there have been many both before and since who have shared the 'Historic Doubts' of Horace Walpole, and our late Fellow Sir Clements Markham endeavoured to fasten the guilt for the murder on Henry VII.[T4] It is, I think, generally held by responsible historians that Dr. Gairdner, who remains the chief modern authority on the reign, successfully disposed of these doubts and theories. [T5] Nevertheless a book has been recently published, which asserts with considerable vigour that Henry VII was responsible, and gives a circumstantial and picturesque account of the murder, which the author definitely states took place in June or July 1486.[T6]

T1 It may be noted that Professor Wright and myself worked independently and did not compare our results until we had arrived at our conclusions.

T2 The evidence may be conveniently found in Ramsay, Lancaster and York, ii, 510 and notes; Kingsford, English Historical Literature in the Fifteenth Century, pp. 101, 183 fl., 184 n.; Calendar of State Papers – Milanese i, 299; The Great Chronicle of London ('But afftyr Estyrn [1484] much whysperyng was among the people yt the kyng hadd put the childyr of King Edward to deth'), f. ccix b. By the kindness of the authorities of the Guildhall Library I have been allowed to examine and quote from the manuscript of the Great Chronicle which is now being transcribed for publication.

T3 'Aspicite, quaeso, quidnam post mortem regis Eduardi in ea terra contigerit; ejus sciiicetjarn adultos et egregios liberos impune trucidari et regni diadema in horum extinctorem, populis faventibus, delatum.' Journal des Etats-Généraux de France, tenus à Tours, 1483-4, by Jehan Musselin (Documents Inédits), p. 39.

T4 *Eng. Hist. Review*, vi, 250 et seq.

T5 *Ibid.*, vi, 444 et seq., and Richard III (1898), pp. 119—28.

T6 Philip Lindsay, *King Richard III. A Chronicle* (1933), p. 325. It is fair to say that the author frankly admits that his book 'is not written for students of history but for the public' (p. 43). Mr. Lindsay has since published a pamphlet entitled On Some Bones in Westminster Abbey, giving his views on the subject of this paper.

p. 3

It is unnecessary for us to reopen this controversy except as a pure matter of dates. For if it can be shown from historical sources that the ages of the princes at the generally presumed date of the murder, August 1483, correspond almost exactly with the ages of the two children whose bones rest in Westminster Abbey, and if, further, it can be shown that there is a reasonable probability that those bones are in fact the bones of the princes, then it is obvious that the murder must have taken place before the close of the reign of Richard III (August 1485).[4]

On October 1st, 1470, after the flight of her husband Edward IV, the queen, Elizabeth Woodville, together with her three daughters, fled from the Tower at the approach of Warwick the King-Maker, and took sanctuary at Westminster. According to Westminster tradition she was lodged in the Abbot's House, and there, on November 2nd she gave birth to a son, the future Edward V. It is unfortunate that no reference to these events appears among the Abbey muniments,[T1] but though the Chronicles disagree as to the exact day of the birth, Miss Scofield has pointed out an entry in the Patent Roll for 1472 whereby a grant of the issues of the Duchy of Cornwall is made to the young prince from Michaelmas 10 Edward IV, to the 2nd of November following, 'on which day he was born'.[T2] He was probably baptized privately – for the sacrist makes no entry of it on his Account Roll for that year – but we know that the abbot, Thomas Millyng, and the prior, John Estney, were godfathers, and Lady Scrope was the godmother. The next year Edward IV returned in triumph. In gratitude for the hospitality extended to her at Westminster, the queen founded the chantry and chapel of St. Erasmus which was attached to the old Lady Chapel; the king promised a donation of l. 100 per annum towards the rebuilding of the nave, while a promise was made on the young prince's behalf that as soon as he was four years of age he would contribute an annual donation for the same purpose. Unfortunately the king's promise was kept but fitfully and, more often than not, the keeper of the New Work had to add to his Account Roll the entry: 'De dono domini Regis centum librarum – nihil hoc anno'. An annual and judicious 'regard' to the prince's treasurer, however, ensured the fulfilment of the prince's promise until 1481 – 2.[T3]

T1 But the sacrist, treasurer and infirmarer paid small sums towards guarding the church and sanctuary *'tempore advent'* Kanciencium (W. A. M. 19717, 23085, and 19452).
T2 Scofield, Edward IV, i, 546 n., quoting Cal. Pat. Rolls, 1467-77, p. 365.
T3 Rackham, Nave of Westminster, p. 33. The Queen while she was in Sanctuary made a donation of 60s. 'pro diversis lesionibus in voltis ecclesie' (W. A. M. 19717).

p. 4

The date of the birth of the younger prince, Richard, is more difficult to determine. There is no doubt that he was born at Shrewsbury, but the exact year has given rise to considerable controversy. The commonly accepted date, 17th August 1472, based upon the supposed authority of a contemporary manuscript list of Edward IV's children which seems to have belonged to Sir William Dethick, Garter, and is now among the Add. MSS.[T1] at the British Museum, is impossible, for the Princess Margaret was quite certainly born on 10th April of that year.[T2] There exists, however, a chronicle at Shrewsbury, which, although it was written in the sixteenth century, appears to be based on local traditions, and contains entries of notable events in the history of the town. These entries are given under the names of the bailiffs of the town who were elected annually in September. Under the year September 1472 to September 1473 there is the following entry: 'This yeare the ducke of yorcke was borne in the blacke frears wthin the towne of Shrewsbery the wche frears standethe under Sainct Marys churche in the sayde towne estwards'.[T3]

This entry, coupled with the fact that the queen was certainly at Shrewsbury in August 1473, and that Edward IV joined her there for some weeks, suggests that the prince was born in August of that year, and that the king went to Shrewsbury in order to be present at the birth.[T4] On the other hand Perkin Warbeck in the document which he signed on 24th January in which he made over his rights to the crown of England, in case of his death, to Maximilian, king of the Romans, describes himself as 'under age' at that date, i.e. that he believed himself to have been born not earlier than 1474.[T5] The unlikelihood that in so important a document he would have made a mistake in the right age of the prince whom he was impersonating – a mistake which would have exposed him at once as an impostor – has led to the suggestion[T6] that the prince's birth really took place between January 1474 and

T1 Adds MSS. 6i 13. See also *Gent. Mag.*, 1831, i, 24; *Notes and Queries*, 8th series, ix, i; and 7th series, vi, 386; G.E.C. Complete Peerage.

T2 Scofield, *Edward IV* ii, 60 n. Ramsay, *Lancaster and York*, ii, 469 and, note. The princess was buried in Westminster Abbey on Dec. ii, 1472. For inscription formerly on her tomb see Dart, *Westminster Abbey*, i, 29.

T3 I am indebted to Mr. J. B. Oldham, librarian of Shrewsbury School, for kindly copying for me this entry from the Taylor MS. in that library. In a subsequent letter to *The Times* dated December 12, 1933: he pointed out that the Taylor MS. is obviously 'based in its earlier portion upon Holinshed, and that Holinshed makes no mention of the birth of Prince Richard. This goes far to prove that in this particular case of putting the birth between September 1472 and September '473, the local Chronicler was following local tradition. Unfortunately there is nothing in the Shrewsbury Borough records to throw any light on the question.'

T4 Scofield, ii, 60 and note.

T5 Gairdner, *Richard III*, pp. 290, 291.

T6 Mr. Gilbert West in *Notes and Queries*, cliii, 381.

p. 5

28th May 1474, on which date the prince was created duke of York. Dr. Gairdner, however, thinks that Warbeck made the mistake in ignorance.[T1]

The question of the month and the year seems to be settled, however, by a document (pl. i, fig. I) in the possession of Mr. W. Westley Manning, in which Chester Herald, Thomas Utine (Whiting), acknowledges the gift of a sum of money from the duke of Burgundy, 'que mon dit seigneur ma de sa grace donnee pour une foiz quant en ce present mois de septembre je suis venu pardevers lui en sa ville darlon [Luxembourg] et lui apporte lettres du dit Roy d'Angleterre par lesquelles il signiffie a icellui seigneur de ses nouvelles et mesmement la nativite de son second filz.'

The document is dated 'le troisme jour du dit mois de septembre lan mil quatre cent soixante treize'.[T2] The birth of the prince, therefore, almost certainly took place in August 1473 and probably on the 17th of that month.[T3]

We may now pass on to the crucial year 1483. On 1st May of that year the queen, Elizabeth Woodville, on hearing that the duke of Gloucester had seized his nephew the young king, 'in gret fright and heuines, bewailing her childes ruin, her frendes mischance, and her own infortune, damning the time that euer shee diswaded the gatheryng of power aboute the kinge, gate herselfe in all the haste possible with her yonger sonne and her doughters oute of the Palyce of Westminster in whiche shee then laye, into the Sainctuarye, lodginge her selfe and her coumpanye there in the Abbottes place'.[T4]

There shortly before dawn she was visited by the archbishop of York, Chancellor of England, who delivered to her the Great Seal. More states that the archbishop found the queen surrounded by' muche heauinesse, rumble, haste and businesse, carriage and conueyaunce of her stuffe into Sainctuary, chestes, coffers, packes, fardelles, trusses, all on mennes backes, no manne vnoccupyed, somme lading, somme goying, somme descharging, somme cornmynge for more, some breakinge downe the walles to bring in the nexte waye ... The Quene her self satte alone alowe on the rishes all desolate and dismayde, whome the Archebishoppe coumforted in the best manner hee coulde, shewinge her that hee trusted the matter was nothynge soe sore as shee tooke it for'.[T5]

On 4th May Gloucester and the young king reached London, and on the

T1 Gairdner, p. 290 fl.
T2 Mr. Manning sent a copy of this document to *The Times* (December 12, 1933). He has kindly allowed me to examine the original, which is unquestionably genuine, and to have it photographed.
T3 With regard to the actual day, it is worth noting that on 17th August, 1480, the duke of York received from the king 'as a gift' a purple velvet gown and the Garter, while the king, the prince of

Wales, the marquess of Dorset and Earl Rivers (the queen's brother) all had new robes. It suggests a birthday celebration. N. H. Nicolas, *Wardrobe Accounts of Edward IV,* pp. 160, 161.
T4 Sir Thomas More, *Workes,* 1557, p. 42.
T5 *Ibid.*, p. 43

p. 6

19th the king was lodged in the Tower, ostensibly to be in readiness for his coronation.[5] On 16th June the queen was induced to surrender the little duke of York, perhaps, as More suggests, because it was told her that 'the king lacketh a playfelowye' and needed 'disporte and recreacion'. Thereupon he was taken first to his uncle, Gloucester, who received him at the door of the Star Chamber with 'many lovynge wordys', and thence 'through the citie honourably into the Tower.' where he joined the king, and from which neither of them ever emerged alive.[T1 6] We have one pathetic glimpse of the princes after the gates of the Tower closed upon them.[7] In the Great Chronicle of London it is noted that 'duryng this mayris yere the childyr of Kyng Edward were seen shotyng and playyng in the Gardyn of the Towyr by sundry tymys'.[T2 8]

No one knows, no one ever will know exactly, what happened subsequently. Our only apparent authority is that remarkable work, Sir Thomas More's *Historie of Kyng Rycharde the Thirde,* and the historical value of the circumstantial account of the murder which he gives has been much disputed. More himself was only a boy in 1483, but he was brought up in the household of Cardinal Morton, who was in a position to know the facts,[9] and it is supposed that More derived his information in part from the cardinal. In the definitive edition of the *English Works of Sir Thomas More,* now in course of publication, Dr. R. W. Chambers and Mr. W. A. G. Doyle-Davidson discuss the literary value of the *History* and the textual problems involved, and they have little difficulty in showing that both the English and Latin versions were, in fact; written by More probably from information derived from Morton, and almost certainly in 1513. But they do not discuss the historical value of the *History.*[T3] Dr. Gairdner believed that the account 'must bear some resemblance to the truth. It is mainly founded upon the confession of two of the murderers, and is given by the writer as the most trustworthy report he had met with'.[T4] Sir James Ramsay called it an 'uncritical narrative' but 'believed it to rest on substantial fact'.[T5 10]

If, then, we may follow More's account[T6] very briefly, he tells us that Sir James Tyrell was sent by Richard III with a letter to the Constable of the Tower, Sir Robert Brackenbury,[T7] directing him to deliver up the keys to the

T1 Ramsay, 11, 486.

T2 f.ccix b.' Sir Edmund Shaa, Mayor 1482–3

T3 *The English Works of Sir Thomas More* (Eyre and Spottiswood, i3I), ed. W. E. Campbell, pp. 26, 34, 42. See also A. F. Pollard in *History*, xvii, 317.

T4. *Richard III*, p. 119.

T5. *Lancaster and York*, ii, 512,. 514. Cf. C. L. Kingsford, *English Historical Literature of Fifteenth Century*, pp. 185–90; Oman, *Political History of England* iv, 481 and note.

T6 *Workes*, 1557, pp. 67 *et seq.*

T7 In *The Times* of December 7, 1933, Mr. K. F. Brackenbury drew attention to the remarkable (and perhaps significant) series of rewards given to Sir Robert Brackenbury in 1484.

p. 7

bearer for one night. Thereupon Tyrell took possession and directed Miles Forrest, Forrest, one of the princes' attendants, 'a felowe fleshed in murther before time', and John Dighton, 'a big brode square strong knaue', to smother them in their sleep. They 'about midnight' (the sely children lying in their beddes) came into the chamber, and sodainly lapped them vp among the clothes, so bewrapped them and entangled them, keping down by force the fetherbed and pillowes hard vnto their mouthes, that within a while smored and stifled, theyr breath failing, thei gaue vp to God their innocent soules...'. The murderers then called in Tyrell, who 'vpon the sight of them, caused those murtherers to burye them at the stayre foote, metely depe in' the grounde vnder a great heape of stones'. Tyrell then rode off to King Richard, who gaue hym gret thanks', but 'allowed not, as I haue heard, the burying in so vile a corner, saying he woulde haue them buried in a better place, because thei wer a kinges sonnes, ...whereupon thei say that a prieste of syr Robert Brackenbury toke vp the bodyes again, and secretely entered them in such place, as by the occasion of his deathe, whiche onely knew it, could neuer synce come to light. Very trouthe is it and well knowen, that at such time as syr James Tirell was in the Tower, for Treason committed agaynste the moste famous prince" king Henry the seuenth [i.e. in 1502], bothe Dighton and he were examined, and confessed the murther in maner aboue writen, but whither the bodies were remoued thei could nothing tel.' More adds that he had learned all this 'of them that much knew and little cause had to lye'.[T1]

Before we pass to the finding of the bones there is one point of interest to be noted. If More's account of the murder can be trusted,[11] when did it take place? The question is fully discussed by Sir James Ramsay in an Appendix to his *Lancaster and York*.[T2] It will be sufficient to say that from four practically contemporary sources he was led to place the murder between the end of July and the end of September 1483 – the 'most probable dates being between 7th August and 15th August when Richard III was at Warwick, from which place More states that Tyrell was despatched to the Tower.

If this is so Edward V was twelve years and nine months old and Richard,

T1 The Great Chronicle of London has the following entry, which to some extent supports More's account and is interesting as giving the rumours of the time : 'Concideryng the deth of Kyng Edwardys chyldyr Of whom as than men Ferid not opynly to saye that they were Rydd owth of this world. But of theyr dethis maner was many opynyons For some said they were murderid atwene ii Fethyr beddis, some said they were drownyd in malvesy and some said that they were stykkid wyth a venymous pocion, But how soo evyr they were put to deth Certayn it was that before that daye they were departid From this world. Of which cruell dede Sr Jamys Tyrell was Reportid to be the doer, but other putt that wygth upon an old servaunt of kyng Rychardes nãmyd [blank]...' (f.ccxii.b and ccxiii).[12]

T2 ii, 510 *et seq*. The authorities were Sir T. More; the Croyland writer; John Ross; and Jean Molinet.

p. 8
duke of York (if we take 1473 as the date of his birth) was within a few days of his tenth birthday at the time of their murder.

Our chief authority for the discovery in 1674 of the bones now in Westminster Abbey is Sandford,[T1] who, writing in 1677, gives the following account:

'Upon Friday the [17th] day of July. An. 1674 (take this Relation from a gentleman, an eyewitness, and principally concerned in the whole scrutiny) in the margin is printed John Knight Esq., Principal Chirurgeon to His Majesty King Charles II [T2] in order to the rebuilding of the several Offices in the Tower, and to clear the white Tower from all contiguous Buildings, digging down the Stairs (which led from the King's Lodgings, to the Chappel in the said Tower, about ten foot in the ground, were found the Bones of two striplings in (as it seemed) a wooden Chest, which upon the survey were found proportionable to the ages of those two Brothers viz about thirteen and eleven years. The Skul of the one bein entire, the other broken,[T3] as were indeed many of the other Bones, as also the Chest, by the violence of the Labourers, who not being sensible of what they had in hand, cast the rubbish and them away together, wherefore they were caused to sift the rubbish, and by that means preserved all the Bones. The Circumstances from the Story being considered, and the same often discoursed with the Right Honourable Sir Thomas Chichley Kt., Master of the Ordnance, by whose industry the new Buildings were then in carrying on, and by whom this matter was reported to the King: upon the presumptions that these were the Bones of the said Princes, His Majesty King Charles II, was graciously pleased to command that the said Bones should be put into a Marble Urn, and deposited among the Reliques of the Royal Family in the Chapel of King Henry the Seventh, in Westminster Abbey.'[T4]

T1 Sandford, *Genealogical History of the Kings of England* (1677), p. 402.

T2 In a copy of Yorke's *The Union of Honour* (1640) in the possession of Mr. Leslie W. Wegg there is the following manuscript note (p. 42 beneath the account of Edward V) in Knight's handwriting and signed by him: 'A° 1674. In digging down a pair of stone staires leading from the Kings Lodgings to the chappel in the white tower ther were found the bones of two striplings in (as it seemed) a wooden chest w upon the presumptions that they were the bones of this king and his brother Rich: D. of York, were by the command of K. Charles the 2d put into a marble Vrn and deposited amongst the R: Family in H: 7th Chappel in Westminster at my importunity. Jo. Knight.'

T3 In a copy of 'a Catalogue and succession of the Kings ... of England' which belonged to John Gibbon, Bluemantle, and is now at the College of Arms, is the following autograph note: 'Die Veneris July 17 Anno 1674 in digging some foundaċons in ye Tower, were discoverd ye bodies of Edw 5 and his Brother murdred 1483. I my selfe handled ye Bones Especially ye Kings Skull, ye other wch. was lesser was Broken in ye digging. Johan Gybbon, Blewmantle.'

T4 Wren in the *Parentalia* gives a similar account. He states that the bones were found 'about 10 feet deep in the ground ... as the workmen were taking away the stairs, which led from the [*Original published at the bottom of p. 9*] royal Lodgings into the Chapel of the Whitetower', p. 333. Kennett *(History of England*, 1719), i, 551 n., describing the finding of the bones, writes that 'when ... great heaps of records of bills and answers lying in the Six Clarkes office were removed thence to be reposited in the white Tower and a new pair of stairs were making into the Chappel there, for the easier conveyance of them thither, the labourers in digging at the foot of the old stairs came to the bones of consumed Corps, cover'd with an heap of stones'.

p. 9

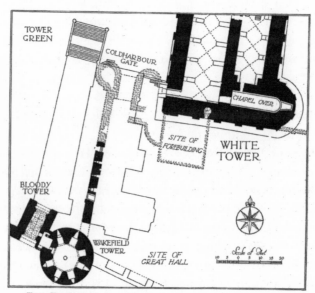

Fig. 1. Plan of part of the Tower of London, showing site of demolished forebuilding, etc.

Tanner's plan of the Tower (p. 9).

With this we may compare another contemporary account quoted by Mr. Richard Davey in his *Tower of London*.[T1] He writes: 'on the margin of one of the pages of a curious MS. on Heraldry inherited by the writer from his Grandfather,[T2] the following note in an ancient handwriting appears: "This day I, standing by the opening, saw working men dig out of a stairway in the White Tower, the bones of those two Princes who were foully murdered by

T1 pp. 22–3.
T2 I have been unable to trace the present location of this manuscript.

p.10
Richard III ... they were small bones, of lads in their teens and there were pieces of rag and velvet about them ... Being fully recognised to be the bones of those two Princes, they were carefully put aside in a stone coffin or coffer".'

John Knight, principal surgeon to Charles II, from whom Sandford derived his account, was a well-known man whose career can easily be traced, and at his death he left a remarkable collection of Heraldic manuscripts in some sixty volumes to Caius College, Cambridge.[T1] I have searched these without finding any references to the princes, but it is not improbable that the unknown writer of the note on the margin of the Heraldic manuscript quoted by Mr. Davey was Knight himself. At any rate if any formal written report on the discovery was made to Charles II it does not appear to be in existence.

It is not clear whether the bones were found in a hole in the staircase actually within the White Tower or somewhere beneath the stairs just outside the actual building.[13] Lord De Ros (who became Lieutenant-Governor of the Tower in 1852) writing in 1866 states: 'it was by Charles II's orders, as tradition went, that Sir Thomas Chicheley, his Master General of the Ordnance, planted a mulberry tree on the spot where the Princes bodies were found; but with a vandalism to which the Tower has been too often subjected, a staircase was built up in 1674 against the wall, which caused the rapid decay of the mulberry tree. There was, however, in 1853 an old Warder who well recollected to have seen the stump still embedded in the landing of the stairs.' [T2]

About 14 ft. up the face of the south wall of the White Tower there is to-day a door[T3] which opens on a small landing of a now blocked spiral staircase. This staircase gave access from the forebuilding of the keep to the chapel of St. John, and was originally the private way from the King's Lodgings. A tablet (dating probably from Lord De Ros's tenure of office) is fixed on the wall of the staircase and has the following inscription: 'the tradition of the Tower has always pointed out this as the Stair under which the bones of Edward the Vth and his brother were found in Charles the 2nd's time and from whence they were removed to Westminster Abbey'.

The tradition is not entirely satisfactory for the staircase at this point is cut out of a solid eleventh-century wall, and it could hardly have provided an adequate place for burial. If we take all the contemporary accounts together

T1 Venn, *Alumni Cantabrigiensis*. Cf. 'Medical Court Roll' by S. D. Clippingdaie, M.D. (manu. script in the Royal College of Surgeons Library), etc.

T2 De Ros, *Tower of London*, p. 45.

T3 The stairs which led to it were removed some years ago and it can now only be reached by a ladder. I am much indebted to Lt.-Col. W. F. O. Faviell, D.S.O., the Major and Resident Governor of the Tower, who kindly gave every facility to Professor Wright and myself to examine the actual place. See fig. 1, and illustration on p. 46 of De Ros, which shows the door and old stairway.

p. 11

it is perhaps more reasonable to suppose that the bones were actually buried at the foot of the steps which then led up to the present door. It would appear that in 1674 the old stairs were done away with, and that the White Tower was cleared of 'all contiguous buildings'. The place of burial would thereby become open ground. 'In digging down' these foundations the children's bones might well have been found, as Sandford says, 'about ten feet in the ground', and might be said to be 'alte defossa in ruderibus scalarum' (as is stated in the inscription on the monument in the abbey), and they would have been found sufficiently near to the stair in the south wall to be said to have been buried beneath it, and to enable a mulberry tree to have been planted to mark the spot.

However that may be; it would appear that the bones remained for a few months in the custody Of Sir Thomas Chicheley.[T1] On '8th

February, 1675, the following warrant[T2] was issued to Sir Christopher Wren, as Surveyor General:

A Marble Coffin for two princes
These are to signifie his Maiesties pleasure that you provide a white Marble Coffin for the supposed bodyes of ye two Princes lately found in ye Tower of London and that you cause the same to be intered in Henry ye 7th Chappell in such convenient place as the Deane of Westminster shall appoynt. And this shalbe yor warrant.
Given under my hand this 18th day of February 1674/5

To Sir Christopher Wren   ARLINGTON
Surveyor General of His Majesties Workes

At the same time a further warrant was issued to the dean of Westminster[T3] informing him that Sir Christopher Wren had been desired 'to attend yor Lordshipp for yor Order and direction for a convenient place for ye Interment'. Sir Christopher Wren thereupon designed the existing monument (pl. 1, fig. 3), which was actually carried out by Joshua Marshall, the King's Master Mason.[T4] It was erected in 1678, and in the meanwhile the bones seem to have been

T1 Sir Winston Churchill in *Divi Britannici* (1675) writes 'within these very few weeks when some occasionally digging in the Tower ... found the coffin, and in it the bones of both the Princes ... which (I take it) are yet to be seen, or were very lately, in the custody of Sir Thomas Chicheley, the Master of the Ordnance'.
T2 P.R.O., Lord Chamberlain's Warrants, 1674–76, L.C. 5. 141. Cf. Wren's *Parentalia*, p. 333.
T3 John Dolben, dean of Westminster and bishop of Rochester.
T4 Cf. *Parentalia,* p. 333 P.R.O., Audit Accounts 2439/103-5.

p. 12
temporarily interred in General Monck's vault nearby.[T1] The inscription is as follows:

H.S S
Reliquae

EDWARDI Vti REGIS ANGLIAE ET RICHARDI DVCIS
EBORACENSIS
HOS, FRATRES GERMANOS, TVRRE LONDIN[si] CONCLVSOS
INIECTISQ CVLCITRIS SVFFOCATOS
ABDITE ET INHONESTE TVMVLARI IVSSIT
PATRVVS RICHARDVS PERFIDVSREGNI PRAEDO
OSSA DESIDERATORVM, DIV ET MVLTVM QVAESITA
POST ANNOS CXC &I
SCALARVM IN RVDERIBVS (SCALAE ISTAE AD SACELLVM
TVRRIS ALBAE NVPER DVCEBANT)
ALTE DEFOSSA, INDICIIS CERTISSIMIS sunt REPERTA
XVII DIE IVLII A°. D[ni] MDCLXXIIII
CAROLVS II REX CLEMENTISSIMVS, ACERBAM SORTEM
MISERATVS
INTER AVITA MONVMENA[T2] PRINCIPIBVS INFELICISSIMIS
IVSTA PERSOLVIT
ANNO DOM[I] 1678 REGNI SVI 30.[T3]

We may now consider where the murder took place. A tradition at the Tower of London associates it with a room in the Bloody Tower. [T4] This tower was then known as the Garden Tower, and at that time had no particularly dismal associations. Indeed, with its outlook to the river and to the lieutenant's garden, it was no unlikely place for the princes to have been lodged. There is a further tradition that after the murder they were buried first under or near the Bloody Tower, in a place which is still pointed out, and that they were then removed by a priest and buried under the staircase in the White Tower beneath the place now marked by the tablet we have already mentioned. The supposition is that this was the nearest spot to consecrated ground which the priest could find where he could bury them secretly.[14]

It may have been so; but it is important to bear in mind that the identification of the Bloody Tower as the scene of the murder rests only on a late tradition. The first reference to it appears to be in 1604, when, in an address of welcome to King James I, the chaplain of the tower, William Hubbocke, described it as the tower which 'our elders tearmed the Bloody Tower for the

T1 Dart, *Westminster Abbey*, i, 167.[15]
T2 *sic.* The punctuation throughout is as it is on the Monument.

T3 As designed by Wren the urn was surmounted by two palm leaves and a crown. The marks for these still remain.
T4 De Ros, *Tower of London,* p. 44.[16]

p. 13

bloodshed, as they say, of those infant princes of Edward IV'.[T1] We may, perhaps, remark that between 1483 and 1604 there were all too good reasons, apart from the princes, for changing the name of the Garden Tower and for associating it with deeds of blood.

More makes no attempt to identify the scene of the murder – he merely calls it a 'chamber', and he was evidently doubtful about the story of the priest, for he guards himself by adding 'as I haue heard' and 'thei say'.[T2] On the other hand he states definitely, and apparently quoting from the murderers' confessions, that they were ordered 'to burye them at the stayre foote, metely depe in the grounde under a great heap of stones', and the important fact seems to be that it was in a situation exactly corresponding to this that the bones now in Westminster Abbey were found in the White Tower in 1674.

It is not easy to see how, if the princes were buried first at the foot of the Bloody Tower, they would have been found in 1674 at the foot of the White Tower in a position so closely corresponding to More's account of the first interment. Possibly the murder took place in the Bloody Tower and the bodies were then carried across to the foot of the White Tower for burial.

There is, however, a sentence in the very important contemporary manuscript 'De Occupatione regni Anglie per Riccardum tercium', written by Dominic Mancini and recently discovered in the Lille Municipal 'Library by Mr. C. A. J Armstrong, Fellow of Hertford College, Oxford which offers a more reasonable solution of the problem. Mancini obviously writes with authority on the events he records. He relates that at first the young king was treated with every mark of respect, but that after the execution of Hastings (13th June, 1483) his attendants were forbidden to see him, and he and his brother were moved to 'the more central and less accessible parts of the tower'. Each day they were seen less and less often behind the bars and windows, until at last they ceased to appear.[T3] Mancini himself had no doubt that they were murdered, although he was never able to obtain definite proof.[17] But he states

T1 Nichols, *Progresses of King James I*, i, 326*.[18]

T2 Hardyng has another story in his Chronicle: 'The very trueth could never yet be very wel and perfectly knowen, for some say that Kyng Richard caused the priest to take them up and close them in lead, and to put them in a coffyne full of holes hoked at the endes, with ij hokes of yron, and so to castthem into a place called the Blacke depes at the Thames mouth so that they should never rise up nor be sene agayne.' It shows at least the uncertainty and that several stories were current.[19]

T3 Mr. Armstrong, who is editing Mancini's Manuscript (the existence of which he made public in an article in *The Times* of May 26, 1934), has very kindly allowed me not only to see his transcript but to quote the relevant sentences which are as follows: – 'Sed postquam Astinco amotus est; omnes familiares qui regulo inservierant ab eius accessu prohibiti sunt; Ipse cum fratre in penitiores ipsius turns edes reducti, rarius per cancellas et fenestras in dies conspici ceperunt; usque adoe ut penitus desierint apparere.' The Great Chronicle of London also states that 'afftyr this [the execution of Hastings] were the prince and the duke of York holdyn more streygth (f. ccvii). [*Original published at the bottom of p. 14*] There is apparently a slight confusion in dates. Hastings was executed on June 13, 1483, and it was not until June 16 that the duke of York joined his brother in the Tower. More, however, infers that the younger prince was already in the Tower at the time of Hastings' execution.

p. 14
that he had discussed the matter with several people who could not restrain their tears when speaking of the mystery of their disappearance.

We may perhaps conjecture that the young king was lodged at first in the Garden or 'Bloody' Tower. There on 16th June he was probably joined by the duke of York, and for the first week or two they were seen 'shooting and playing' in the garden—it will be remembered that one of the reasons which induced the queen to part with the duke of York was said to have been that his brother wanted a playfellow and needed 'desporte and recreacion'.[T1] But on 26th June (after Dr. Shaw on 22nd June had openly preached at St. Paul's on the illegitimacy of the princes in the presence of Richard) Richard formally assumed the crown and Edward V's short reign came to an end. It would surely not be unnatural that the princes should have been then 'holden more streygth' and should have been removed to the 'more central and less accessible parts of the Tower (in penitiores ipsius turris edes, i.e. the White Tower), where they were gradually less and less seen,[T2] and where finally perhaps the murder actually took place. If this was really so, and if they were buried 'at the stayre foot 'of the White Tower, where in fact the bones of two children of approximately the ages of the princes were found in 1674 – one of whom, as Professor Wright suggests, had almost certainly (from the stain on the jaw) met with a violent end – then the story does appear to become a coherent whole.[20]

On Thursday, 6th July, 1933, the urn in Henry VII's chapel was opened in the presence of the dean of Westminster (Dr. W. Foxley Norris), the Lord Moynihan, Sir Edward Knapp-Fisher (Chapter clerk), myself, Professor W. Wright, Mr. Aymer Vallance, F.S.A., the clerk of the works (Mr. W. Bishop), the dean's verger (Mr. G. C. Drake), and four of the Abbey staff. It was found that the bones filled an oblong cavity within the urn. It was at once apparent that they belonged to two human beings, for a fairly complete skull and a portion of another lay upon the top.[21] Many bones were found to be missing, but this is accounted for by the fact, as stated in Sandford, that the bones at first were thrown away by the workmen and had subsequently to be recovered.

T1 If, as the Great Chronicle says, they were thus seen playing during the mayoralty of Sir Edmund Shaa (1482–3), the only possible dates are between June 16 and October 28, when his year of office came to an end. It may be remarked, too, that it would obviously be to Richard's advantage to allow them to be seen playing together and thus allay suspicion of his designs on the crown as long as he could.[22]

T2 It is most remarkable that on June 28 John, Lord Howard was actually created duke of York [sic – Norfolk] by Richard.

p. 15

from a heap of rubbish.[T1] Among the dust at the bottom of the urn we found three much rusted nails, which may possibly have belonged to the original chest in which the bones were buried, No portion of rag, velvet or any other material was found. The bones were carefully lifted out and placed upon a table nearby. The chapel was closed to the public, and every facility was provided to enable Professor Wright to make a detailed examination.

On 11th July, the examination having been concluded and photographs having been taken, the bones of the two children were placed separately on the table and were wrapped in the finest lawn. The dean himself replaced the bones within the urn, together with a statement written on parchment recording what had been done.

The dean then read part of the Burial Service, and the urn was finally re-sealed in our presence.

L.E.T.

II
ANATOMICAL

It will be evident from Mr. Tanner's historical statement that the reason for opening the urn was to see if it contained bones which, on anatomical examination, would confirm the very definite statement in the epitaph – ossa...indiciis certissimis sunt reperta – that they were those of the princes. Were such confirmation forthcoming, a further question would present itself – could the ages of the princes at the time of their death be determined; were they, in short, alive or dead at the time of the battle of Bosworth?

An examination of the contents of the urn proved beyond all doubt that there were only two human beings represented: that the bones were those of children differing some two or three years in age as judged by the length of their bones, and that the elder child was still in the puberty period, since the elements forming the sockets of the shoulder and hip joints showed no signs of union.

An attempt to fix the age of the elder child more precisely was rewarded

T1 Others were probably given away by Sir Thomas Chicheley, for
  Hearne *(Collections, X, 86, Oxford Hist. Soc.)* has the following

note under Jan. 10, 1728/9: 'Td enquire of Mr. Whiteside about some of the bones of Ed. V and of his brother Richard Duke of York, found in the Tower of London, temp. Car. II, part whereof were sent (as Dr. Plot in his MSS. memoirs says) by Mr. Ashmole to his Museum at Oxford'. The next day Hearne called at the Ashmolean 'on purpose to see the bones of Edw. V and his brother Richard D. of York. Mr. Whiteside told me they had somewhere or other such bones very small, particularly the finger bones, and that Sandford had mentioned them as being there in his *Gen. History,* but Mr. Whiteside did not produce them.' The present Keeper of the Ashmolean, Mr. E. T. Leeds, F.S.A., kindly made every effort to trace them for me, but like his predecessor, Mr. Whiteside, was unable to produce them when I called on purpose to see them! [23]

p. 16

by the discovery of two bones which furnished the necessary evidence – an axis or second cervical vertebra and a first sacral vertebra.

The axis was without the apical part of its odontoid process, a state which makes it possible to say with every confidence that it belonged to a child who had not yet attained the age of thirteen. The bone undoubtedly belonged to the elder child: this conclusion was based on the following observations – there were two atlases or first cervical vertebrae found in the urn, one in an almost perfect state of preservation, the other in fragments; when corresponding parts of the two atlases were measured it was found that the more complete one was the larger, and belonged therefore to the elder child. It seemed in consequence reasonable to infer that the well-preserved second cervical vertebra belonged to the same skeleton as the well-preserved first cervical vertebra. Any doubt on the matter which there may have been was removed when it was found not only that the two bones – the complete atlas and axis – fitted perfectly together, but that in addition there was a dark brown stain which was common to both bones, and continuous from one to the other.

Corroborative evidence of some value as to the correctness of the estimate of the age of the elder child was obtained from the first sacral vertebra which almost certainly belonged to his skeleton, since his two ilia – bones with which the sacrurn articulates – were present, whereas only a portion of one ilium of the younger child's skeleton was found. The laminae of this vertebra were still half an inch or so apart, indicating a probable age of less than thirteen.

Of all methods of determining the age of children none is more helpful and reliable than the examination of the teeth. So impressed was I by the importance of the method that I at once sought the assistance of one of the leading authorities on the dentition of children, Dr. George Northcroft, an ex-President of the British Society of Orthodontics and the immediate ex-President of the British Dental Association. Dr. Northcroft with characteristic generosity placed his time and knowledge, based on a long and wide experience, freely at my service, and it is largely, I might almost say entirely, due to his invaluable help that I am able to write on this matter with great confidence.

To present the dental evidence as clearly as possible I give it in a tabulated form, prefacing my remarks with the statement that only the right half of the lower jaw of the younger child, whom I shall now presume to call Richard, was present, and that although both jaws of the elder child, Edward, were present in their entirety, they contained no teeth.[24] Fortunately the empty sockets of the teeth in all cases were in good condition, so, that it was not difficult to determine the state of development of the missing teeth.

p. 17
The teeth of Richard, duke of York:

Incisors. Completely formed.
Canine. Unerupted, pulp cavity open, root about two-thirds formed.
First prernolar. Unerupted, pulp cavity open, root about half formed.
Second premolar. Unerupted, only its crown formed, and only discovered by radiography: it lay in its bony crypt under bone of considerable thickness and density.
First molar. Erupted, completely formed, as shown by the sockets for its, roots.
Second molar. Found loose in the urn, crown only formed, no sign of any root formation.

The canine and first premolar teeth could be seen in their crypts behind the crown of the unerupted canine tooth the socket of the anterior root of the first deciduous molar could be seen, proving that this tooth had either been in part present at the time of death, or had only recently been lost,

These data taken separately and together, after making all due allowance for deviation from the normal, permit of the determination of Richards age as being about mid-way between nine and eleven.

The teeth of Edward V as judged by the state of their sockets:

Incisors. Completely formed.
Canines. Upper or maxillary not completely formed.
Lower or mandibular completely formed.
First premolars. Upper or maxillary – not completely formed.
Lower or mandibular completely formed.
Second premolars. Upper or maxillary both teeth entirely absent.
Lower or mandibular not completely formed.
First molars. Completely formed.
Second molars. Not completely formed.
Third molars. The crown of the upper or maxillary tooth of the left
    side about one-third formed: it was found loose in the urn. No
    trace of the tooth of the right side.
Lower – no trace of this on either side as proved by radiography.

The second upper or maxillary deciduous molars had either been in part present at the time of death, or had only recently been lost, seeing that the sockets of their palatine roots were still clearly discernible. The sockets of the posterior roots of the corresponding lower molars were also apparent.

These data, taken separately and together, permit of Edward's age being determined as somewhere between the ages of twelve and thirteen.

In seeking to identify the remains, evidence of consanguinity obviously has considerable weight. Such evidence, drawn as it must be solely from the examination of the bones, is naturally difficult to obtain. I would refer, how-

p. 18

ever, to two features of no small significance—the presence of Wormian bones of unusual size and of almost identical shape in the lambdoid sutures of both Edward's and Richard's crania, and the absence of the upper second premolars in Edward and of the lower second deciduous molar in Richard. Although the absence of the last-named tooth is excessively rare,[T1] and although absence would be expected to be associated with a forward movement of the first permanent molar, a movement of which there is no indication, both Dr. Northcroft and I are of opinion, after most careful examination, that Richard had never had a deciduous second molar; there was no trace of any socket, while the alveolar margin instead of being flattened, as would be expected if any tooth had been present, was rounded and somewhat compressed. If the tooth had been present it must, in view of the appearance of the alveolar margin, have been lost at an early age. The retention of certain roots of Edward's second upper and lower milk molars, and of Richard's first milk molar, do not suggest any tendency in either child to early loss of their milk dentition. If we assume that the second deciduous molar was absent in Richard we would have an instance, not only of tooth-suppression in both children, but of tooth-suppression occurring in the same regional plane.

There is undoubted evidence of Edward having suffered from extensive disease affecting almost equally both sides of the lower jaw, originating in or around the molar teeth, from the sockets of which the inter-radicular septa had been entirely absorbed. On the left side the disease had spread to such an extent that it had destroyed the inter-dental septum between the first and second molar teeth. The disease was of a chronic nature and could not fail to have affected his general health. It may well have accounted, in part at least, for the depression from which he is said to have suffered, for the relief of which his mother is said to have agreed to part with her younger son.

A remarkable feature of Edward's facial skeleton was an extensive stain reaching from just below the orbits to the angles of the lower jaw. The stain was of a distinctly blood-red colour above, of a dirty brown colour below, and was obviously, as shown by the gradual fading away of its margins; of fluid origin. I have no doubt it was a blood stain.[T2] Its presence, together with the complete separation of the facial skeleton, lends support to the traditional account of the manner of the brothers' death – suffocated 'under feather bed and pillows, kept down by force hard unto their mouths'.[25]

T1 Cases of absence of deciduous molars are recorded in Colyer and Sprawson's *Dental Surgery and Pathology.*

T2 I endeavoured to obtain corroborative evidence of its nature by scraping the parts but failed to obtain more than a little powdered bone which subjected to spectroscopic examination, gave no results.

p. 19

Suffocation by such means is well known to be associated with intense congestion of the face, When Humphrey, duke of Gloucester, met his death in this way at Bury St. Edmunds, and his body was brought into the presence of Henry VI, Shakespeare puts into the mouth of Warwick the following lines: 'See how the blood is settled in his fade', and a little later, 'But see his face is black and full of blood'.[26]

The evidence that the bones in the urn are those of the princes is in my judgement as conclusive as could be desired, and definitely more conclusive than could, considering everything, have reasonably been expected. Further, their ages were such that I can say with complete confidence that their death occurred during the reign of their usurping uncle, Richard III.[27]

As to the appearance of the princes they were in height probably 4 ft 10 in. and 4 ft. 6½ in, From the size of such bones as the collar bones, shoulder blades, and hip bones, we may conclude that they were of slender form. An examination of their mouths would show Edward to have all his teeth in position except his second maxillary pre-molars, their places possibly being taken by the partially absorbed second deciduous molars; Richard to have a distinct gap between his right lower lateral incisor and his first molar, with possibly the partially absorbed canine and first deciduous molar occupying the interval. The gums of Edward in the lower molar region would be inflamed, swollen, and septic, and be no doubt associated with discomfort and irritability.

As to what happened after their death no one now can say, but I imagine that when placed in the elm chest in which they were found,[28] Edward lay at the bottom on his back with possibly a slight tilt his left, that Richard lay above him face to face, and that when the chest was discovered in the seventeenth century the workmen broke into it from above and near its middle. I am led to these conclusions from the fact that much more of Edward's skeleton is present than of Richard's, since presumably lying deeper it was less disturbed, and from the fact that the extreme upper and lower portions (viz, the head and feet) of Edward's skeleton are so well preserved. The singular fact that of the atypical ribs no less than six should have been found, and that of these six, three were of the left side and belonged to Edward's skeleton, three of the right side and belonged to Richard's, and that similarly only the left clavicle of Edward and the right clavicle of Richard were present, strongly suggests that the left shoulder of Edward must have been in close contact with the right shoulder of Richard, as would have been the case had they lain face to face.[29]

The chest containing the bodies was, so I believe, buried in a hole which, with the accumulation of surface soil which naturally occurs during the

p. 20

centuries, would gradually have become deeper and deeper, particularly as there is reason to think that the surface received a considerable amount of kitchen refuse.[30] It is difficult otherwise to explain why, when the chest was found, it was said to have been taken from a deep hole, 'alte defossa', and why the urn should have contained, in addition to the human bones, a large variety of other bones such as those of fish, duck, chicken, rabbit, sheep, pig, and ox.[TI] These animal bones were presumably picked up with the scattered human bones in the seventeenth century and taken to the abbey.[31]

The bones in the urn were arranged in no particular order, but on the whole the human cranial bones were uppermost. With the bones were a few rusted iron nails, two small pieces of sandstone, a peat-stained piece of wood, a few flakes of marble from the marble of the urn, and a number of irregularly shaped pieces of lead evidently from the sealing of the urn.

After the examination of the contents of the urn had been completed and the interior of the urn cleaned, the human bones wrapped in white lawn were replaced—first the bones of Richard, then the limb and body bones of Edward, and finally the bones of his skull. The cover of the urn was then replaced and the urn was again sealed.[32]

Many years ago a Latin poet, meditating on the strange and varied fortunes of the dead, reflected that while 'Licinus a freedman sleeps

248

in a marble tomb, Cato had a small one, Pompey none'. Where, he asks, are the gods? To which in Delphic fashion may we not reply that while the bones of Richard III have long since disappeared, trampled into common clay, those of the princes freed from all undignified associations rest secure, in the company of those of their mighty ancestors, at the very heart of the national shrine?[33]

T1 I am indebted to Dr. Hopwood of the Natural History Museum for their identification.

p. 21

RELIQUIAE

'EDWARD V'	'RICHARD DUKE OF YORK'
Skull	
The cranial vault complete from the supraorbital region to the posterior margin of the foramen magnum (opisthion) and from the middle line to the parieto-squamous suture.	The cranial vault incomplete and in fragments, the largest parts being the frontal bone in two pieces, and the parietal bone of the right side. A trace of the metopic suture still apparent at its lower end.
The cranial base complete except in the ethmoidal region but its various parts – sphenoidal, temporal and occipital – separate.	The cranial base only represented by the temporal bone of the right side and fragments of other bones.
The upper facial skeleton complete except for the nasal bones and for the bones forming the adjoining regions of the orbits: the bones still articulated with each other but separate from the remainder of the skull.	
The lower jaw in two pieces.	Part of the right half of the lower jaw.

Vertebral Column.	
The first cervical vertebra or atlas.	The first cervical vertebra or atlas in fragments.
The second cervical vertebra or axis.	
The first sacral vertebra.	

Thoracic Skeleton.	
The first rib of the left side.	The first rib of the right side.
The second rib of the left side-incomplete.	The second rib of the right side—incomplete.
The eleventh rib of the left side.	The eleventh rib of the right side.

Bones of the Upper Limb.	
The clavicle of the left side.	The clavicle of the right side.
The scapulae of both sides.	The glenoid part of the left scapula.
The humeri of both sides.	The humeri of both sides.
The radius of the right side—upper part.	The radius of the right side–upper part.
The radius of the left side—lower part	The radius of the left side.
The ulna of the right side	The ulna of the right side in fragments.
The ulna of the left side.	The ulna of the left side.

Bones of the Lower Limb.	
The ilia of both sides.	Part of one ilium.
The ischium of the right side.	
The femora of both sides.	The femora of both sides
The tibiae of both sides.	The tibiae of both sides.
The fibulae of both sides.	The fibulae of both sides.
The tarsus of both sides.	Part of the tarsi–the larger bones.
The metatarsus of both sides.	Part of the metatarsi.

The epiphyses of the long bones of the limbs were well represented but in no case had fusion with the diaphyses occurred.

p. 22

BONES OF WHICH THE EXACT IDENTIFICATION
IS UNCERTAIN[34]

Vertebral Column.

Fragments of various vertebrae including two lower cervical, two mid-thoracic, the last thoracic, and three lumbar of which one was the fifth: the lines of union of the three primary parts of the vertebrae still apparent: probably most, if not all of them, formed part of the skeleton of the king seeing that his skeleton and particularly certain identifiable parts of his vertebral column, viz, the atlas, axis, and first sacral vertebra are so much better preserved than the corresponding parts of Richard's skeleton.

Thoracic Skeleton.

Fragments of a number of ribs: two long ribs, almost complete, had a chordal measurement across their arches of 193 mm. and 179 mm. respectively: they were both of the left side: probably they were the seventh and eighth ribs and formed with the mid-thoracic vertebrae already mentioned part of the skeleton of the king.

Bones of the Upper and Lower Limbs.

Of the twenty bones constituting the metacarpi only one—a third—could be definitely identified. A number of fragmentary phalanges mainly those of the toes, but including two of the fingers.

ADDITIONAL OBSERVATIONS

Skull.

The small wings of the sphenoid of Edward's skull were united in the middle line forming a *jugum sphenoidale* which was incompletely fused with the underlying portion of the body of the sphenoid (presphenoid). The spheno-turbinate bones were fused with the sphenoid, and the sphenoidal sinuses were well developed.

Owing to the detachment of the upper facial skeleton it was possible to obtain a good view of the maxillary antra, the left being considerably larger than the right. The right inferior turbinate bone was in an almost perfect state of preservation and was still firmly articulated with the corresponding maxilla.

The squamo-zygomatic portion of the glenoid cavity of the temporal bones was unusually deep, particularly on the right side – a condition which may possibly be attributed to the dental disease from which he suffered, disease which must, I imagine, have entailed irregular movement at the temporo-mandibular joints.

The left half of the interior of Edward's cranium was stained a dirty brown colour suggesting that in the chest in which he was originally placed he lay with an inclination to the left – a theory which receives some confirmation from the fact that somewhat more of the left side of his skeleton than of his right is preserved.

It will be noticed that Edward's skeleton is much better preserved than Richard's: this statement applies particularly to the skull, the vertebral column, and the bones of the feet. In the case of Richard the right parts of the skull and trunk are better preserved than the left. The absence, from both skeletons of the sterna, patellae, and scaphoid bones of the tarsus is probably attributable to their cancellous structure and in the case of the last two to their relatively small size. The general absence of carpi and metacarpi may be in part at any rate similarly explained.

CONDITION OF THE BONES

While as a general rule the bones were dry and of a light brown colour, being obviously largely if not entirely destitute of organic matter, the single metacarpal bone and to a less degree the two phalanges of the fingers were exceptional in being of an ivory-white colour suggesting that a certain

p. 23

amount of organic matter was still present. Such a difference may be attributable to the three bones in question having been in some way protected from the more complete desiccation which the other bones had undergone. If, as I conjecture, the two bodies lay face to face with the hands folded between them the conditions necessary for the more perfect preservation of the three bones may have been present.

MEASUREMENTS

	'EDWARD V'.	'RICHARD DUKE OF YORK'
Cranium.		
Ophryo-inial length	173 mm	
Biparietal width	27 mm	
Wormian bone at bregma	27 x 20 mm	
	Wormian bones symmetrical in shape, size, and position in lamb doid sutures, maximum diameter 34 mm	Wormian bone broken, but fitting into lambdoid suture on the right side; approximately of the same shape and size as those in Edward's cranium.
Atlas.[T1]		
Width of vertebrarterial groove	9 mm	7 mm
Transverse diameter of inferior facet	16 mm	13 mm
Antero-posterior diameter of inferior facet	20 mm	18 mm
First Rib.		
Chordal length across arch	58 mm	55 mm
Eleventh Rib.		
Chordal length across arch	153 mm	146 mm
Clavicle.		
Length without epiphysis	113 mm	96 mm
Humerus.		
Length without epiphyses	242 mm	222 mm
Ulna.		
Length without epiphyses	195mm	182 mm

	Femur.	
Length from great trochanter to articular surface of lower epiphysis	383 mm	345 mm
	Tibia.	
Length including epiphyses	306 mm	274 mm
	Astragalus and Caicaneuni.	
Vertical height with the two bones in their normal positions	66 mm	60 mm

T1 Owing to fragmentation of Richard's atlas, only certain parts were available for comparison.

p. 24

Particular importance attaches to the measurements of the bones of the lower limb since they afford valuable evidence as to stature. If to the above measurements we make an allowance for Edward of 14 mm. and for Richard of 12 mm. in respect of cartilages and of soft parts at the heel, we arrive at an estimate for the length of Edward's leg measured from the top Of the great trochanter to the sole of the foot of 769 mm. and of Richard's of 691 mm. According to figures based. on many measurements, given in Rudolph Martin's *Lehrbuck der Anthropologie,* the proportion which the length of the lower limb as measured bears to stature is at the age of 13, 52 per cent., at the age of 10, 50 per cent. Using these figures I estimate Edward's stature to have been approximately 4 ft. 10 in. and Richard's 4 ft 6 in. Aware of the possibility of individual and racial variation, I still think it probable that the margin of error is extremely small.

The skiagrams (pl. vi) were taken for me by Dr. George Northcroft, to whom I am greatly indebted.

I am also indebted to Mr. Henry George, a member of the staff of the Royal College of Surgeons, for the other photographs (pls. ii—v); these were taken under great difficulties since it was not possible to remove the bones from the chapel.

W.W.

III
SUMMARY

We are now in a position to sum up very briefly the results of this investigation:

(1) On the historical side there is at least a reasonable probability that the traditional story of the murder, as told by More, is in its main outlines true.[35] It has further been, shown that the bones were in fact found in a position at the Tower which approximates to the place where the princes were supposed to have been buried.[36]

(2) The bones which were found in the Tower in 1674, and now rest in the urn in Westminster Abbey, have been definitely proved to be those of two children.[37]

(3) Professor Wright, as a result of his anatomical examination, has been able to trace evidence of consanguinity with, features 'of no small significance' in the bones and jaws of these two children.[T1]

(4) Professor Wright has drawn attention to a red stain across the facial bones of the elder child which, he had no doubt, was a blood stain, and was probably caused by suffocation.[T2] One of these children, therefore, probably died a violent death.[T3] The princes were traditionally said to have been smothered with a feather bed and pillows.[T4] [38]

(5) Professor Wright has been able to show that the age of the elder child was 'somewhere between the ages of twelve and thirteen'.[T5]

T1 pp. 17–18.

T2 p. 18.

T3 There was nothing to suggest how the younger child met his death.

T4 p. 7.

T5 pp. 15, 17.

p. 25

There is no doubt that the age of King Edward V, at the presumed date of the murder, was twelve years and nine months old.[T1]

(6) Professor Wright has been able to show that the age of the younger child was 'about mid-way between nine and eleven'.[T2]

Working independently on the historical evidence, I came to the conclusion that the hitherto disputed age of Richard, duke of York, at the presumed date of the murder, was 'within a few days of his tenth birthday'.[T3]

It follows from the above that if these bones are really those of the princes, and Professor Wright concludes that not only is there nothing from a scientific point of view against it, but that the evidence is 'definitely more conclusive than could, considering everything, have reasonably been expected',[T4] then we can say with confidence that by no possibility could either, or both, have been still alive on the 22nd August 1485, the date of Henry VII's accession.

L.E.T.

T1 p. 7.
T2 p. 17.
T3 p. 8.
T4 p. 19.

p. 26

We may note two occasions prior to 1674 when bones were found in the Tower and were thought to be those of either one or both of the princes.

Sir George Buck (d. 1623), in his *History of the Life and Reign of Richard III*, first issued in 1646, mentions 'certaine bones like to the bones of a Child being found lately in a high desolate 'Turret [in the Tower of London], supposed to be the bones of one of these Princes.; others are of opinion it was the carcasse of an Ape kept in the Tower'. He adds that the turret was 'a vast and damned place for the hight, and hard accesse, no body in many yeares looking into it'.

The other occasion was far more interesting and curious. The only record of it appears to be a MS. note on the flyleaf of a copy of *The*

Historie of the Pitiful Life … of Edward V by Sir Thomas More published in 1641.[T1] It is as follows:

'August ye 17th 1647. Mr Johnson a Counsellor sonne of Sr Robert Johnson affirmed to mee and others when in Company that when ye Lo. Grey of Wilton and Sr Walter Raleigh were prisoners in ye Tower, the wall of ye passage to ye Kings Lodgings there sounding hollow was taken downe and at ye place marked A was found a little roome about 7 or 8 fo. square, wherein there stood a Table and uppon it ye bones of two Children supposed of 6 or 8 yeeres of Age which by ye aforesayd noble and all present were credibly beeleeved to bee ye Carcasses of Edward ye 5th and his brother the: then Duke of Yorke. This gent was also an eyewitnesse at ye opening of it, with Mr Palmer and Mr Henry Cogan, officers of ye minte and others with whom having since discoursed hereof they affirmed ye same and yt they saw the Skeletons. Jo. Webb.'

On the opposite page of the book is a neat little plan of the King's Lodgings:

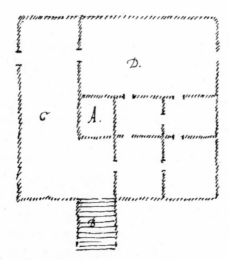

A. The ' little roome '.
B. The Stayres leading out of Cole Harbour to ye Kings Lodgings.
C. Passage to ye Kings Lodgings.
D. Ye Guard Chamber.

John Webb's plan showing room 'A' where bones were found at the Tower *c.*1610.

T1 In the possession of Miss Gwladys E. Daniel, who has kindly allowed me to examine it and have the entry photographed (pl. 1, fig. 2).

APPENDIX 3

THE MEANING OF THE LATIN WORD *NUPER*

In chapter 17 the Colchester Oath Book was quoted as applying the Latin word *nuper* to Edward V at the end of September 1483. The question was then raised as to whether the use of that word meant that the elder of the two sons of Edward IV was then known (or believed) to be dead. In addition to the evidence presented in chapter 17, the following evidence helps to clarify how the word nuper was used in England in the fifteenth, sixteenth and early seventeenth centuries.

In the original Latin text of his *Historia Regni Henrici Septimi Regis Angliae* (*History of the Reign of Henry the Seventh, King of England*), dedicated to Charles I (born 1600, king 1625–49) as Prince of Wales, Francis Bacon (1561–1626) included numerous uses of the Latin word *nuper* with the clear meaning 'late/deceased'. Examples of that use of *nuper* by Bacon include:

filius et haeres Georgii nuper Clarentiae ducis
'the son and heir of the late George, Duke of Clarence'

parlamento condemnati sunt nuper dux Glocestriae Richardum Tertium se appellans
'the parliament attainted the late Duke of Gloucester calling himself Richard the Third'
nuper regis Henrici
'the late King Henry [VI]'

Edwardus Quartus, nuper Angliae rex
'Edward the Fourth, late King of England'

It is therefore obvious that by the first quarter of the seventeenth century 'late/deceased' was one standard use for the word *nuper*.

Bacon had used Polydore Vergil as one of his sources, and Vergil also occasionally used *nuper* to mean 'late/deceased':

Gulielmi archiepiscopi Eboracensis nuper demortui
'William archebisshop of York, lately deade'[1]

However, Vergil's uses of the word *nuper* to mean 'late/deceased' are much less frequent than those of Bacon.

That could be taken to mean that earlier, when Vergil was writing, 'late/deceased' was not the usual meaning for *nuper*, at least in contexts where the writer was not a native speaker of English (Vergil was Italian). However, the slightly earlier English records of the first parliament of King Henry VII contain the following uses of *nuper*.[2]

Henricum Clyfford, filium seniorem Johannis nuper domini Clyfford
'Henry Clyfford, eldest son to John late Lord Clyfford'

Edwardo filio et herede Henrici nuper ducis Buk'.
'Edward Stafford knyght, son and heir of blode of Henry late duke of Bukyngham'

Though a third use of *nuper* as used in the parliamentary records of 1485 has a different meaning:

Elizabethe regine nuper uxoris regis Edwardi .iiij.[ti].
'[Queen] Elizabeth late wif of Edward the .iiij.[th]'

In the first two of these *nuper* clearly means 'late/deceased'. However, the third example does not mean that Elizabeth Widville was dead in 1485, but simply that she had *formerly* been the wife of Edward IV.

About two years earlier (in January 1483/4) the parliament of Richard III had also employed the word *nuper* to mean 'late/deceased':[3]

Henricus nuper dux Exon
'Herry late duc of Excestr'

Pro executore Johannis Don, nuper de London mercer.
[*For the executor of*] 'John Don, late of London, mercer'.

Earlier still, the parliaments of Edward IV had also used the word *nuper* to mean 'late/deceased' in the context of kingly status, for example:[4]

Henricus quintus, nuper de facto et non de jure rex Anglie defunctus
'Henry V, late in fact, but not in law, king of England, deceased'

In standard classical Latin–English dictionaries the adverb *nuper* is translated as meaning 'newly', 'lately', 'recently', and 'not long ago'.[5] However, Henry V had died fifty years earlier, in 1422. Thus in 1472 his passing was by no means recent, and none of the four standard classical Latin translations could logically be employed in respect of the above quotation relating to him. Moreover Henry IV, who died in 1413, was also described by the parliament of 1472 using the same words as those applied to his son. It therefore seems that by the 1460s and 1470s the classical Latin word *nuper*, as employed by English writers, had definitely changed to some extent and acquired a new meaning.

Edward IV's parliament also employed the word *nuper* regarding inheritance issues in respect of:

Henrico Percy milite, primogenito Henrici Percy nuper comitis Northumbr
'Henry Percy knyght, first begoten son of Henry Percy late erle of Northumberlond'

Everardi Dygby, nuper de Stokdrye in comitatu Rotel armigeri
'Everard Dygby late of Stokdrye in the shire of Rutland squier'

and

Johannis Nevyll militis, nuper domini Nevyll
'John Nevyll knyght, late Lord Nevyll'

Also on 18 August 1471, a few months after the death of King Henry VI (who died on an unconfirmed date in about May 1471), he was described by Edward IV as 'late king'.[6]

It therefore seems clear that, when applied to a human being, the word *nuper* usually did mean 'late' in the sense of 'deceased' by the last quarter of the fifteenth century.

APPENDIX 4

LEUVEN REPORTS

a) Professor Cassiman's 2009 Report on the First Hair Testing
UZ LEUVEN
FORENSICHE GENEESKUNDE

REPORT G5546 -1

Prof. dr. med. Jean-Jacques Cassiman, consulent Activiteitencentrum Forensische Genetica en Moleculaire Archeologie, Forensische Geneeskunde, UZ St Fafaël
has been requested by Dr. L.J.F. Ashdown-Hill, 8 Thurlston Close, Colchester Co4 3HF, UK, to perform a mitochondrial DNA analysis on the "Mary Tudor hairs"

Two strands of hair (Mary Tudor, Queen of France) enclosed in a sealed envelope have been delivered on January 30, 2009. The samples have been given the internal code G5546-1. The two hairs (G5546-1.1 and -1.2) have been used at different time points for DNA isolation according to ISO17025 accredited protocols (procedure ISO9):

- G5546-1.1 brown hair with a length of 5 cm; completely used for DNA isolation
- G5546-1.2 brown hair with a length of 4 cm; completely used for DNA isolation

The two different DNA extracts have been analysed by two different lab technicians:

- DNA amplification of one hypervariable region (HV1 between positions 16008 and 16366) of the mtDNA in 5 overlapping DNA fragments
- Sequence analysis of both strands (forward and reverse strand) of the amplified DNA fragments (procedure MT SEQ1)
- Separation of the sequencing fragments on an ABI PRISM 3130xl Genetic Analyser (procedure MT ABI2)
- Interpretation of the results and comparison with the Cambridge reference sequence of human mitochondrial DNA (procedure MT ANA2 and INTERPRETATIE2)

This procedure has been performed twice for each of the DNA extracts (PCR1 and PCR2).

Discussion:

For two hairs (G5546-1.1 and -1.2) a mitochondrial sequence has been determined. A consensus sequence was obtained for each analysis (PCR 1 and PCR 2) which was based on the analysis of 5 overlapping DNA fragments and forward and reverse sequencing of the two strands. In one analysis (G5546-1.1 – PCR 1), it was not possible to determine the complete sequence between the positions 16008 and 16366 of the mitochondrial DNA, indicating that the amount of mitochondrial DNA was low in this DNA extract.

A comparison between the consensus sequences obtained reveals several differences:

- Several positions show 2 nucleotides (N) indicating the presence of mitochondrial DNA from two different persons. One of these persons has probably contaminated the hairs and this contamination was not removed by the procedures employed in the laboratory to 'clean' the hair shaft from contaminating cellular material.
- Only one mutation (C16192T) was confirmed in a second analysis of the same DNA extract, but this position was not confirmed

by the analysis of the second hair sample (G5546-1.2). Other mutations in the first analysis of DNA extract G5546- 1.1 were not observed in the other analysis performed on the same DNA extract and on the second DNA extract (G5546-1.2).

These results indicate that the quality of the hairs (including the mitochondrial DNA present in these hairs) were insufficient for obtaining a reproducible mitochondrial DNA sequence. The presence of contaminating cellular material on the hair shaft complicates the interpretation of the results and also does not allow us to determine the exact composition of the mutations for the donor of the hair. There is also no evidence to conclude that the two hairs belong to the same person.

Conclusion:

It was not possible to determine a reproducible mitochondrial DNA sequence for the two hairs of "Mary Tudor". The results obtained cannot be used for a comparison to other mitochondrial DNA sequences in order to establish any maternal relationship.

Leuven 8/10/2009
em. Prof. dr. med. Jean-Jacques Cassiman

mtDNA – HV1 (16008-16366)

Sample	Position 1	Position 2	Position 3	Position 4	Position 5	Position 6	Position 7	Position 8	Position 9	Position 10	Postion 11
5546-1.1 – PCR 1	C16111T	C16192T	C16223T	16229		16285	C16290N	C16294N	*	*	*
5546-1.1 – PCR 2	*	C16192T	*	C16256N	C16266N	C16270N	*	*	*	*	A16316N
5546-1.2 – PCR 1	*	*	*	*	*	*	*	C16294N	C16296N	T16304N	*
5546-1.2 – PCR 2	*	*	*	*	*	*	*	C16294N	C16296N	T16304N	*

* = position identical to the Cambridge reference sequence of mtDNA
■ = sequence could not be determined

Leuven University's 2009 test results for the hair from Knowsley Hall.

b)
UZ LEUVEN
FORENSICHE GENEESKUNDE

REPORT G-9433 1 FG 010520 DP 1

The undersigned, Prof. dr. Ronny Decorte, labohoofd Activiteitencentrum Forensische Genetica en Moleculaire Archeologie, Forensische Geneeskunde, has been requested on 20/02/2017 by

Dr. L.J.F. Ashdown-Hill to establish a mitochondrial DNA profile for Elizabeth Roberts and to compare this profile with the results obtained for two strands of the "Mary Tudor hairs" (report G5546-1 of Prof. Jean-Jacques Casiman).

Opdrachtgever: Dr. L.J.F. Ashdown-Hill
[address]

The following sample has been received on 30/03/2017 together with a signed consent for the DNA analysis:
G9433-l Elizabeth Roberts [address] UK
Two buccal swabs

The two buccal swabs have been used for DNA extraction and analysis of two segments of the mitochondrial DNA genome according to the following procedures: *AC LFOR-MT079- PR, AC LFOR-MT038-PR, AC LFOR-MT045-PR, AC LFOR-MT047-PR and AC LFOR-MT049-PR* (annex 1):

Results:
HV1 (16024-16390)

Sample number	Name	Position 1	Position 2	Position 3	Position 4
9433-1	Elizabeth Roberts	16168T	16192T	16256T	16270T

HV1 (61-367)

Sample number	Name	Position 1	Position 2	Position 3
9433-1	Elizabeth Roberts	73G	263G	315.1C

Remark: The positions in the table are those positions in the mitochondrial DNA sequence where a difference is seen with the internationally used "Anderson reference sequence".

Discussion:
A mitochondrial DNA profile was established for Elizabeth Roberts. This sequence is a typical West-Eurasian type and has a frequency of

0,013% in the West-Eurasian population (Database EMPOP Release 11; 15,271 unrelated individuals).

In report G5546-1 of Prof. Jean-Jacques Cassiman, the results were reported of the mitochondrial DNA analysis of two strands of "Mary Tudor hairs". These results are however not reproducible for the same hairs and between the hairs. This indicates that the DNA of these hairs are not suitable for establishing a reliable mitochondrial DNA profile (authentic for the hairs) and that probably the hairs are contaminated by cellular material of unknown human origin. Therefore, any comparison of these results with mitochondrial DNA sequences of known individuals should be done with care.

Three positions for HV1 in the mitochondrial DNA profile of Elisabeth Roberts are also present in one of the two hairs analyzed previously. The fourth position is not present in this hair and therefore may exclude any maternal relationship between Elizabeth Roberts and the donor of these hairs.

Conclusions:

A mitochondrial DNA profile was established for Elizabeth Roberts.

The mitochondrial DNA results obtained previously for the two strands of "Mary Tudor hairs" do not allow us to conclude that they belong to the same maternal lineage as Elizabeth Roberts. In case of improvement of the methodology for analyzing these hairs in the future, it is recommended to analyze additional hairs which might give a reproducible sequence that can be used in a comparative analysis with different maternal lineages.

ABBREVIATIONS

Armstrong/Mancini – C. A. J. Armstrong, ed., D. Mancini, *The Usurpation* [*sic*] *of Richard III*

CCR – Calendar of Close Rolls

CPR – Calendar of Patent Rolls

Crowland Chronicle Continuations – Pronay & Cox, eds, *The Crowland Chronicle Continuations*

Davies, *York Records* – R. Davies, *Extracts from the Municipal Records of the City of York during the Reigns of Edward IV, Edward V and Richard III*

Ellis/Vergil – H. Ellis, ed., *Three Books of Polydore Vergil's English History*

Gairdner, *Richard III* – J. Gairdner, *History of the Life and Reign of Richard the Third*

Harleian MS 433 – R. Horrox & P. W. Hammond, eds., *British Library Harleian Manuscript 433* (4 volumes)

HHB – A. Crawford, ed., *The Household Books of John Howard, Duke of Norfolk, 1462–71, 1481–83*

PROME – C. Given-Watson, ed., *The Parliament Rolls of Medieval England*

R3MK – A. Carson, *Richard III The Maligned King*

Soc. Ant. – Society of Antiquaries

Stonor Letters – C. L. Kingsford, ed., *The Stonor Letters and Papers*

NOTES

Introduction

1. R. Horrox & P. W. Hammond, eds., *British Library Harleian Manuscript 433* (hereinafter *Harleian MS 433*), vol. 3, London/Gloucester 1982, p. 190 (f. 308v).

2. D. M. Kleyn, *Richard of England*, Oxford 1990, p. 43.

3. J. Ashdown-Hill, 'The Full Itinerary of Edward IV', https://www.amberley-books.com/community-john-ashdown-hill

4. *remanserunt duo praedicti Regis Edwardi filii sub certa deputata custodia infra Turrim Londoniarum.* N. Pronay & J. Cox, eds, *The Crowland Chronicle Continuations 1459-1486*, London 1986, p. 162 – my translation.

5. *Ipse cum fratre in penitiores ipsius turris edes reducti, rarius per cancellos et fenestras in dies conspici ceperunt; usque adeo ut penitus desierint apparere.* C. A. J. Armstrong, ed., D. Mancini, *The Usurpation [sic] of Richard III*, Gloucester 1989 (hereinafter Armstrong/Mancini), p. 92 – my translation.

6. For the evidence in that respect see J. Ashdown-Hill, *The Dublin King*, Stroud 2015.

7. For the full evidence in respect of 'Plantagenet', see J. Ashdown-Hill, *The Private Life of Edward IV*, Stroud 2016, pp. 3–6.

8. Correctly highlighted by Ian Mortimer, *The Fears of Henry IV*, London 2007, plate 7.

1. Who were the so-called 'Princes in the Tower'?

1. Her maiden surname is often given as 'Woodville'. However there is very little fifteenth-century evidence for *wood* as the sound of the first syllable of that name. Most contemporary spellings employed 'i' or 'y' in the first syllable, suggesting that the normal sound was *wid*.

2. Ashdown-Hill, *The Private Life of Edward IV*, chapter 3; J. Ashdown-Hill, *Cecily Neville Mother of Richard III*, Barnsley/Havertown PA 2018, pp. 38–49, 51, 136–8.

3. For Eleanor's story and the date evidence in respect of the royal marriage see Ashdown-Hill, *The Private Life of Edward IV*, chapter 7.

4. J. Gairdner, ed., *The Historical Collections of a Citizen of London in the Fifteenth Century* [Gregory's Chronicle], London 1876, pp. 219–22.

5. This quote comes from *La Regina d'ingliterra* ('The Queen of England'), part of a poem which was written between 1466 and 1468 by Antonio Cornazzano. C. Fahy, 'The marriage of Edward IV and Elizabeth Woodville: a new Italian source', *English Historical Review*, vol. 76 (1960), p. 672, lines 214–18, accessed courtesy of JSTOR.

6. C. L. Kingsford, *Chronicles of London*, Oxford 1905, p. 183.

2. Who invented the term 'Princes in the Tower', and when?

1. S. Bentley, ed., *Excerpta Historica*, London 1831, pp. 366–79, citing Rymer, BL, Add. MS 4615 (part of his miscellaneous collections for the *Foedera*).

2. Bentley, ed., *Excerpta Historica*, pp. 366–79, citing Rymer, BL, Add. MS 4615 (part of his miscellaneous collections for the *Foedera*).

3. https://fr.wikipedia.org/wiki/Angelo_Catho_de_Supino (consulted August 2017); M. Jones, ed., Philippe de Commynes, *Memoirs*, Harmondsworth 1972, pp. 26; 383.

4. Armstrong/Mancini, pp. 58–61.

5. Armstrong/Mancini, pp. 88–9.

6. Pronay & Cox, eds, *The Crowland Chronicle Continuations*, London 1986 (hereinafter *Crowland Chronicle Continuations*), pp. 156–5.

7. *Crowland Chronicle Continuations*, pp. 158–9.

8. *Crowland Chronicle Continuations*, pp. 162–3.

9. H. Ellis, ed., *Three Books of Polydore Vergil's English History* (hereinafter Ellis/Vergil), London 1844, p. 188.

10. R. S. Sylvester, ed., St Thomas More, *The History of King Richard III*, New Haven & London 1976, pp. 87–8.

11. A. R. Myers, ed., G. Buck, *The History of the Life and Reigne of Richard the Third*, London 1973, pp. 83–4.

12. This book was published in London in 1707.

13. See below, Appendix 2.

3. What does the term 'Princes in the Tower' imply?

1. W. Fleetwood (alleged ed.), *Les Reports des Cases en les ans des Roys Edward v. Richard iij. Henrie vij & Henrie viij.*, London 1679, p. 24 (Henry VII, Year 1, p. 5 – Hilary Term, plea 1).

2. M. Jones, ed., P. de Commynes, *Memoirs*, Harmondsworth 1972, pp. 353–4; *Crowland Chronicle Continuations*, pp. 160–1.

3. J. Ashdown-Hill, 'The Inquisition *Post Mortem* of Eleanor Talbot, Lady Butler, 1468 (PRO C 140/29/39)', *The Ricardian*, vol. 12, No. 159, December 2002, pp. 563–73.

4. H. Ellis, ed., R. Fabyan, *The New Chronicles of England and France*, London 1811 (text of Fabyan's 1516 edition), p. 654.

5. *Crowland Chronicle Continuations*, pp. 160–1.
6. PROME, Edward IV, April 1463, October 1472.
7. J. Gairdner, ed., *Letters and Papers, Foreign and Domestic: Henry VIII*, vol. 6, London 1882, p. 618.

4. *What was young Edward really like?*
1. Ashdown-Hill, *The Private Life of Edward IV*, p. 173.
2. Ashdown-Hill, *The Private Life of Edward IV*, pp. 181–2.
3. Ashdown-Hill, *The Private Life of Edward IV*, p. 182.
4. C. L. Scofield, *The Life and Reign of Edward the Fourth*, 2 vols., London 1923; 1967, vol. 2, p. 55.
5. A. Cheetham, *The Life and Times of Richard III*, London 1972, p. 78.

5. *What was young Richard really like?*
1. Ashdown-Hill, *The Private Life of Edward IV*, p. 176.
2. Ashdown-Hill, *The Private Life of Edward IV*, p. 177.
3. York City Archives, 1487 (York House Book 6, f. 97r); Ashdown-Hill, *The Dublin King*, pp. 42–3.
4. The Latin inscription of the seal was '*SECRETVM SIGILLVM RICARDI QVARTI REGIS ANGLIE ET FRANCIE ET DOMINI HIBERNIE*'. Gudenus, *Codex Diplomaticus*, vol. 4, Frankfurt & Leipzig 1758, p. 505. Gudenus also records the seal description.

6. *How was young Edward brought up?*
1. Thomas Vaughan had been the boy's chamberlain since before 6 August 1471 – CCR 1468–1476, p. 196, no. 722; p. 227, no. 849.
2. A Suffolk lawyer in the service of Sir John Howard (later Duke of Norfolk) and of Richard, Duke of Gloucester: J. Ashdown-Hill, *Richard III's 'Beloved Cousyn': John Howard and the House of York*, Stroud 2009, pp. 28–9 (2015 edition, p. 37), and *Cecily Neville*, p. 145, 146, 149–51.
3. CPR 1467–1477, p. 366.
4. https://en.wikipedia.org/wiki/John_Talbot,_3rd_Earl_of_Shrewsbury (consulted October 2017).
5. Ashdown-Hill, *Cecily Neville*, pp. 8, 9, 12, 231.
6. 3 July 1471, and 24 February 1474/5, CCR 1468–1476, p. 229, no. 858, p. 381, no. 1380.
7. https://en.wikipedia.org/wiki/Walter_Devereux,_7th_Baron_Ferrers_of_Chartley (consulted September 2017).
8. CCR 1468–1476, p. 44, no. 172.
9. *Harleian MS 433*, vol. 2, London/Gloucester 1980, p. 48.
10. *Harleian MS 433*, vol. 1, London/Gloucester 1979, p. 267.

11. https://en.wikipedia.org/wiki/John_Fogge (consulted September 2017).

12. https://en.wikipedia.org/wiki/John_Scott_(died_1485) (consulted September 2017).

13. *Harleian MS 433*, vol. 1, p. 123.

14. *CCR 1468–1476*, p. 196, no. 722; p. 227, no. 849.

15. *Harleian MS 433*, vol. 1, p. 42.

16. *CCR 1468–1476*, p. 159, no. 602; p. 250, no. 923.

17. *CCR 1468–1476*, p. 12, no. 37; p. 219, no. 812; p. 323, no. 1178.

18. *Harleian MS 433*, vol. 1, p. 110.

19. *CCR 1468–1476*, p. 264, no. 972.

20. *CCR 1468–1476*, p. 412, no. 1474.

21. *CPR 1476–1485*, p. 345.

22. *CCR 1468–1476*, pp. 380–1, nos 1379–81.

23. *Harleian MS 433*, vol. 4, London/Gloucester 1983, p. 94.

24. *CPR 1476–1485*, p. 543.

25. See above, chapter 6, note 2.

26. Scofield, *Edward IV*, vol. 2, p. 54.

27. *CPR 1467–1477*, p. 401.

28. *CPR 1467–1477*, p. 417.

29. Ashdown-Hill, *'Beloved Cousyn'*, 2009 edition, pp. 28–9; 2015 edition, p. 37.

30. Scofield, *Edward IV*, vol. 2, pp. 55–6, citing Signed Bills, file 1506, no. 4578.

31. 12 November 1472, *CPR 1467–1477*, p. 358; 26 October 1473, *CCR 1468–1476*, p. 289, no. 1057 and 17 April 1481, *CPR 1476–1485*, p. 259. Avice is named as 'nurse' of Edward (not his *former* nurse) on each of those occasions.

7. *What provisions were made for young Richard?*

1. N. Davis, ed., *Paston Letters and Papers of the Fifteenth Century*, 2 vols., Oxford 1971 and 1976, volume 1, p. 489.

2. Davis, *Paston Letters*, volume 1, p. 492.

3. The date of the birth of Richard of Shrewsbury, Duke of York has been given as 17 August 1472, but this cannot be accurate, and 17 August 1473 is probably the correct date. See C. Scofield, *The Life and Reign of Edward IV*, 2 vols., London 1923, vol. 2, p. 60. Also G. Smith, 'Lambert Simnel and the King from Dublin', *Ricardian* vol. 10, no. 135, December 1996, p. 500 and n. 12.

4. *Calendar of Papal Registers, vol. 13, part 1, Papal Letters 1471–1484*, London 1955, p. 236.

5. *CPR 1476–85*, p. 75.

6. F. Sandford, *Genealogical History of England*, London 1707, p. 416.

7. J. Ashdown-Hill, *The Third Plantagenet, George, Duke of Clarence, Brother of Richard III*, Stroud 2014, p. 133.

8. Ashdown-Hill, *'Beloved Cousyn'*, pp. 101–2.

8. When did King Edward IV die?

1. *Crowland Chronicle Continuations*, p. 151 (written 1486); Great Chronicle of London (as cited – but not *quoted* in respect of the *date* – in K. Dockray, *Edward IV, a source book*, Stroud 1999, p. 146); H. Ellis, ed., R. Fabyan, *The New Chronicles of England and France*, London 1811, p. 667 (Fabyan died *c.* 1512, however, his Chronicle, as published concludes with the year 1540 – so it appears not to be contemporary.); C. L. Kingsford, ed., *Chronicles of London*, Oxford 1905, pp. 189, 278 (Vitellius A XVI – not contemporary – the Chronicle continues to the end of the reign of Henry VII); E. Hall, *Chronicle*, London 1809, p. 341 (published 1548; 1550 – so not contemporary).

2. L. Lyell & F. D.Watney, eds, *Acts of Court of the Mercers' Company 1453–1527*, Cambridge 1936, p. 146.

3. E. Carusi, ed., Jacopo Gherardi da Volterra, *Il Diario Romano dal 7 Settembre 1479 al 12 Agosto 1484*, Castello 1904, p. 116.

4. R. Davies, *Extracts from the Municipal Records of the City of York during the Reigns of Edward IV, Edward V and Richard III* (hereinafter Davies, *York Records*), London 1843, pp 142, 143, and footnote.

5. '*il termina le quatrième jour après Pasques*'. J-A. Buchon, ed., *Chroniques de Jean Molinet*, vol. 2, Paris 1828, p. 376.

6. '*infra dies octo ... vita finivit*'. J. Quicherat, ed., T. Basin, *Histoire des règnes de Charles VII et de Louis XI*, vol. 3, Paris 1857, p. 134.

7. Armstrong/Mancini, p. 59.

8. Hence its assertion that the reign of his son, Edward V, lasted two months and eight days: *Obitus Edwardi V^{ti} xxij° mens [sic for mensis] Junij regnavit ij menses et viij° dies set non coronatus fuit occisus et nemo s[c]it ubi sepultus.* [The death of Edward V: 22 of the month of June, he reigned two months and eight days but was not crowned, he was killed, and no one knows where he was buried.] However, that (and other claims of the Anlaby Cartulary in respect of dates) is very dubious. Fitzwilliam Museum, Cambridge, Ms. 329, f. 7r.

9. Armstrong/Mancini, pp. 62–3.

10. *Crowland Chronicle Continuations*, pp. 154–5.

11. Armstrong/Mancini, p. 106, note 2.

12. P.M. Kendall, *Richard the Third*, London 1955; 1976, p. 173.

13. CPR *1476–1485*, pp. 350–1.

14. CPR *1476–1485*, p. 354.

15. *Crowland Chronicle Continuations*, pp. 154–5.; Ellis/Vergil, p. 175.

16. Kendall, *Richard the Third*, p. 178.

17. The French threat would certainly account for Edward Widville's sailing. The fact that he took with him a significant part of the contents of the royal treasury is perhaps less easily explained.

18. Armstrong/Mancini, p. 81.

19. Armstrong/Mancini, pp. 119–20, note 59.

9. *Were the two boys captured in April 1483?*

1. Ellis/Vergil, p. 175.

2. *Crowland Chronicle Continuations*, pp. 154–5.

3. Armstrong/Mancini, pp. 70–1; *Crowland Chronicle Continuations*, pp. 154–5.

4. Kendall, *Richard the Third*, p. 164.

5. *Crowland Chronicle Continuations*, pp. 154–5.

6. R. Edwards, *The Itinerary of King Richard III 1483–1485*, London 1983, p. 1.

7. Kendall, *Richard the Third*, pp. 164, 173; Edwards, *The Itinerary of King Richard III*, p. 1.

8. *Crowland Chronicle Continuations*, pp. 154–5.

9. *Crowland Chronicle Continuations*, pp. 154–5.

10. Kendall, *Richard the Third*, p. 176; Edwards, *The Itinerary of King Richard III*, p. 2.

11. Armstrong/Mancini, pp. 76–9.

12. *Crowland Chronicle Continuations*, pp. 154–5.

13. Armstrong/Mancini, pp. 78–9.

14. Armstrong/Mancini, pp. 78–9.

15. 'comitem de Ripariis et Richardum, nepotem suum fratem regis ... arestantes', *Crowland Chronicle Continuations*, pp. 156–7.

16. TNA, SC 1/45/236.

10. *What did their mother do?*

1. Armstrong/Mancini, p. 114, note 42, citing *CPR 1467–77*, pp. 534–5; Rymer, *Foedera*, xii, 13, & Cotton MS Vespasian C. xiv, f. 272v.

2. Armstong translated the phrase ... *ab eorum manu in libertatem* ... as '... set free ... from the clutches ...'. But the present writer prefers to use 'release ... from the hands'.

3. Armstrong/Mancini, pp. 78–9, with the present writer's correction to the English translation as noted above.

4. *Crowland Chronicle Continuations*, pp. 156–7.

5. *Crowland Chronicle Continuations*, pp. 156–7.

6. Edwards, *The Itinerary of King Richard III*, p. 2.

7. Kendall, *Richard the Third*, p. 182.

8. Edwards, *The Itinerary of King Richard III*, p. 2.

9. P. W. Hammond, & A. F. Sutton, *Richard III: The Road to Bosworth*, London 1985, p. 99; *Crowland Chronicle Continuations*, pp. 156–7. The palace was destroyed during the seventeenth-century Civil War.

10. Soc. Ant., MS 77, f. 57r; A. Crawford, ed., *The Household Books of John Howard, Duke of Norfolk, 1462–71, 1481–83*, Stroud 1992, part 2, p. 390.

11. *Crowland Chronicle Continuations*, pp. 156–7.

12. Armstrong/Mancini, p. 120, note 63.

13. *Crowland Chronicle Continuations*, pp. 156–7.

14. *Isto die lectum fuit iuramentum Richardi ducis Gloucestriae protectoris Anglie, Thomae archiepiscopi Cantuariensis, Thomae archiepiscopi Eboracensis, Henrici ducis Buckinghamiae et dominorum nuper factum domino nostro Regi. Item iuramentum quod dicti domini facere voluissent domine Elizabethae regine Anglie modo existenti in sanctuario Sancti Petri Westminster, si eadem domina privilegium eiusdem loci reliquere voluerit.* Armstrong/Mancini, pp. 124–5, n. 74, citing minutes of the City Council of London (London Guildhall, MS., Journal 9, f. 23v).

15. Mancini, pp. 88–9.

16. *Crowland Chronicle Continuations*, pp. 158–9.

17. Mancini, pp. 62–3.

18. The first evidence in respect of that name dates from 1544.

19. Harl. 433, f. 308v; *Harleian Manuscript 433*, vol. 3, p. 190.

20. *Harleian Manuscript 433*, vol. 3, p. 190 (f. 308v).

21. Kendall, *Richard the Third*, p. 287; Ellis/Vergil, p. 210.

22. For references to Cecily's Scrope marriage see: Ellis/Vergil, p. 215, P. Sheppard Routh '"Lady Scroop Daughter of K. Edward": an Enquiry', *The Ricardian* vol. 9, no. 121, June 1993, pp. 410–16 (pp. 412, 416, n. 12) and J. L. Laynesmith, *The Last Medieval Queens*, Oxford 2004, p. 199.

23. '*casamento da filha delRej Duarte de Inglaterra ... com o duque de Beja Dom Manuel ... o qual casamento antes fora a elRej apontado por Duarte Brandão sendo uindo por embaixador delRej Richarte jrmão do ditto Rej Duarte a jurar as ligas e commeter casamento com a Iffante Dona Joana*'. A. Mestrinho Salgado and Salgado, Álvaro Lopes de Chaves, *Livro de Apontamentos (1438-1489)*, as cited in A.S. Marques, 'Álvaro Lopes de Cheves [*sic*]: A Portuguese Source', *Ricardian Bulletin*, Autumn 2008, pp. 25–7.

24. Ellis/Vergil, p. 210.

25. J. Ashdown-Hill, *The Mythology of Richard III*, Stroud 2015, p. 50.

11. Why were the 'princes' declared bastards?

1. *Crowland Chronicle Continuations*, pp. 158–59; Armstrong/Mancini, p. 123, n. 72.

2. Armstrong/Mancini, p. 129, note 94.

3. Armstrong/Mancini, p. 123, note 72.

4. C. A. Halsted, *Richard III as Duke of Gloucester and King of England*, 2 vols., London 1844, vol. 2, p. 515, citing Harl. Ms. 433, p. 227.

5. Ashdown-Hill, *The Private Life of Edward IV*, chapter 7.

6. J. Ashdown-Hill, *The Secret Queen*, Stroud 2016, pp. 147–8.

7. *CCR 1468–1476*, p. 264, no. 972.

8. *CPR 1476–85*, p. 102.

9. *CPR 1476–85*, p. 241.

10. For details of the council meeting, see Ashdown-Hill, *Richard III's 'Beloved Cousyn'*, p. 93.

11. Ashdown-Hill, *Cecily Neville*, chapter 9, citing Sylvester, ed., St Thomas More, *The History of King Richard III and Selections from the English and Latin Poems*, London 1976, p. 65.

12. Armstrong/Mancini, pp. 62–3.

13. Armstrong/Mancini, pp. 62–3.

14. C. L. Kingsford, ed., *The Stonor Letters and Papers*, vol. 2, Camden third series, XXX, London 1919, p. 160.

15. Ashdown-Hill, *The Secret Queen*, pp. 148–9, citing N. Adams and C. Donahue, eds., *Select Cases from the Ecclesiastical Courts of the Province of Canterbury, c. 1200–1301*, London 1981.

16. Hammond & Sutton, *The Road to Bosworth*, p. 103.

17. *Crowland Chronicle Continuations*, pp. 158–9.

18. Shakespeare, *The Tragedy of King Richard III*, act III, scene VII.

19. J. Ashdown-Hill, 'Norfolk Requiem: the Passing of the House of Mowbray', *The Ricardian*, 12 (March 2001), pp. 198–217 (p. 208).

12. *What did Lord Hastings do?*

1. See R. Horrox, *ODNB*, 'Shore (*née* Lambert), Elizabeth', and Ashdown-Hill, *The Private Life of Edward IV*, chapter 22.

2. Armstrong/Mancini, pp. 90–1.

3. Kendall, *Richard the Third*, p. 207. Kendall dates these meetings to Thursday 12 June.

4. Hammond & Sutton, *The Road to Bosworth*, p. 105, citing R. Firth Green, 'Historical Notes of a London Citizen 1483–8', *English Historical Review*, vol. 96 (1981), p. 588. The extant copy of this account probably dates from the early sixteenth century, but is believed to reproduce earlier material: *R3MK*, p. 289.

5. *Crowland Chronicle Continuations*, pp. 158–9.

6. *Acclamat protector insidias sibi instructas esse, eosque cum armis latentibus nenisse ut primi vim facere inciperent. Tunc milites, qui per dominum dispositi erant, et duc Buckingamie accurentes, sub falso proditionis nomine Astinconem gladio obtruncant. Certos detinent, quibus religionis et sacerdotii reverentiam vite causam fuisse arbitrantur.* Armstrong/Mancini, p. 90, my translation.

7. Hammond & Sutton, *The Road to Bosworth*, p. 113.

8. Edwards, *The Itinerary of King Richard III*, p. 3.

9. *CPR 1476–1485*, p. 360.

10. J. Kirby, ed., *The Plumpton Letters and Papers*, Cambridge 1996, pp. 59–60.

13. What does the Cely Note mean?

1. TNA SC1/53/19A

2. Armstrong/Mancini, p. 128, n. 91; A. Hanham, ed., *The Cely Letters 1472–1488*, London 1975, pp. 184–5; pp. 285–6. Also A. Hanham, *The Celys and their World*, Cambridge 1985, p. 287.

14. Would Richard III have had the boys killed?

1. Hammond & Sutton, *The Road to Bosworth*, p. 99; *Crowland Chronicle Continuations*, pp. 156–7.

2. Armstrong/Mancini, p. 121, citing *Registrum Thome Bourgchier*, pp. 52–3.

3. R. Edwards, *The Itinerary of King Richard III 1483–1485*, London 1983, pp. 2 & 3.

4. The Book of Wisdom has always formed part of the Bible as defined by the Catholic and Orthodox churches, though it was removed from the Protestant Bible in the sixteenth century, at the Reformation.

5. Ellis/Vergil, p. 183. For the evidence which shows that the story which alleged that Edward IV was illegitimate was merely a myth, see Ashdown-Hill, *The Private Life of Edward IV*, pp. 19–21, and Ashdown-Hill, *Cecily Neville*, chapter 11.

6. *Harleian Manuscript 433*, vol. 2, p. 2.

7. For example, CCR *1476–1485*, p. 309, no. 1049; p. 312, no. 1052; p. 313, no. 1057; p. 315, no. 1064; p. 316, no. 1068; p. 320, no. 1081; p. 321, nos. 1082-1086; p. 322, nos 1087 & 1089; p. 323, no. 1090; p. 324, nos 1093 & 1094; p. 325, no. 1098; p. 326, nos. 1103 & 1104; p. 328, no. 1106; p. 332, no. 1125; p. 343, no. 1156; p. 353, no. 1191; p. 355, no. 1201; p. 357, no. 1208; p. 371, nos. 1266, 1267, 1268; p. 375, no. 1282; p. 376, no. 1284; p. 377, no. 1288; p. 379, no. 1293; p. 380, no. 1299; p. 381, no. 1301; p. 392, no. 1329; p. 403, no. 1368 – all of which refer to actions taken in the reign of Edward IV without questioning in any way his status as a legal King of England.

8. *Nullum superesse e regio genere preter Ricardum ducem Closestrie, qui per leges mereatur, et per virtutem posit corone onera sustinere. Anteactam eius vitam moresque integros certissimum esse pignus rei bene administrande: eum vero, etsi huiusmodi onus recuset, posse tamen animum flectere, si a principibus rogetur. His auditis, princeps, exemplo Astinconis admoniti, et videntes duos duces convenire, quorum viribus propter militum multitudinem resistere difficile et periculosum esset,se vero quasi circumventos eorum minibus teneri, proprie saluti consuluerunt; et Ricardum regem declarandum rogandumque ut onus suscipiat, censuerunt. Postridio in domum matris ad quam consulto se contulerat Ricardus, ne in turri ubi regulus detinebatur ea fierent, omnes principles convenerunt, ubi omnia tranacta sunt; iuramenta enim fidelitas prestita et cetera, que exiguntur, ordine perfecta;* Armstrong/Mancini, p. 96 – my translation.

9. Ashdown-Hill, *'Beloved Cousyn'*, pp. 47, 113.

10. J. Gairdner, ed., *The Paston Letters*, Gloucester 1983, vol. 6, p. 85.

11. Armstrong/Mancini, p. 131, note 100.

12. CCR *1476–1485*, no. 1170.

13. Edwards, *The Itinerary of King Richard III*, p. 4 is of that opinion. Annette Carson assumes that Richard resided at his rented London accommodation, Crosby's Place, while using his mother's home as his headquarters (A. Carson, *Richard III the Maligned King*, Stroud 2008, p. 99; 2013 edition, p. 116). Actually, however, there is no solid evidence to *prove* where he resided from late May until early July 1483.

14. Ellis/Vergil, pp. 188–9.

15. Did 'Edward V' attend Richard III's coronation?

1. P. W. Hammond, ed., H. Walpole, *Historic Doubts on the Life and Reign of King Richard the Third*, Gloucester 1987 (originally published 1768), p. 66.

2. A. F. Sutton & P. W. Hammond, *The Coronation of Richard III: the Extant Documents*, London 1984, p. 171.

3. Sutton & Hammond, *The Coronation of Richard III*, p. 80.

4. Halsted, *Richard III as Duke of Gloucester and King of England*, vol. 2, p. 516.

5. Revd Dr Milles, 'Observations on the Wardrobe Account', *Archaeologia*, vol. i (1770), pp. 364–79 (p. 361).

16. What was the Duke of Buckingham up to?

1. *Rex fecit Henricum, ducem Bukes, maritare sororem reginae Elizabethae.* William Worcester, *Annales*, published in J. Stevenson, ed., *Letters and Papers Illustrative of the Wars of the English in France during the Reign of Henry the Sixth, vol, 2, part 2*, London 1864, p. 785.

2. C. Rawcliffe, *The Staffords, Earls of Stafford and Dukes of Buckingham 1394–1521*, Cambridge 1978, p. 28.

3. Rawcliffe, *The Staffords*, p. 28.

4. H. Ellis, ed., *The Chronicle of John Hardyng, together with the Continuation of Richard Grafton*, London 1812, p. 475.

5. Rawcliffe, *The Staffords*, p. 29.

6. Kendall, *Richard III*, p. 191, citing CPR; Nichols, *Grants &c ... Edward V*, pp. 5–11.

7. CPR *1476–1485*, pp. 349, 356.

8. Nichols, *Grants &c ... Edward V*, pp. 31–7.

9. Nichols, *Grants &c ... Edward V*, pp. 49–50.

10. Rawcliffe, *The Staffords*, pp. 31–2, citing J. G. Nichols, *Grants from the Crown during the Reign of Edward V*, London 1854.

11. Edwards, *The Itinerary of King Richard III*, pp. 4–5.

12. Edwards, *The Itinerary of King Richard III*, p. 6.

13. CPR *1476–85*, pp. 465–6.

14. Carson, *Maligned King*, chapter 11, n. 2, citing Harley 433, vol. 1, pp. 3–4.

15. Edwards, *The Itinerary of King Richard III*, p. 7. Hammond & Sutton, *The Road to Bosworth*, pp. 140–1.

16. Edwards, *The Itinerary of King Richard III*, pp. 7–8.

17. Carson, *Maligned King*, 2008 ed., p. 212 (2013 ed., p. 246).

18. Hammond & Sutton, *The Road to Bosworth*, p. 14 – but no contemporary source is cited.

19. https://en.wikipedia.org/wiki/Buckingham%27s_rebellion (consulted August 2017).

20. *Crowland Chronicle Continuations*, pp. 162–3.

21. *CPR 1476–85*, p. 361.

22. P. W. Hammond, 'Richard III: Dutch Sources', *The Ricardian*, vol. 3, no. 46, September 1974, pp. 12–13.

17. Did young Edward die in 1483?

1. A. R. Myers, ed., G. Buck, *The History of the Life and Reigne of Richard the Third* (text first published London 1646), Wakefield 1973, p. 85.

2. One twentieth-century writer wondered whether the first Yorkist pretender of 1486–87 might have claimed to be Edward V, but his royal appellation was actually 'Edward VI', and it is clear that he claimed to be Clarence's son, Edward, Earl of Warwick. See Ashdown-Hill, *The Dublin King*, pp. 42–3.

3. W. G. Benham, ed., *The Oath Book, or Red Parchment Book of Colchester*, Colchester 1907, p. 134.

4. J. Ashdown-Hill, 'The Death of Edward V – new evidence from Colchester', *Essex Archaeology & History* 35 2004, pp. 226–30.

5. Hervy had previously served both John Howard (Duke of Norfolk), and the family of Howard's cousin by marriage, John de Vere, 12th Earl of Oxford. J. Ashdown-Hill, 'The client network, connections and patronage of Sir John Howard (Lord Howard, first Duke of Norfolk) in north-east Essex and south Suffolk', PhD thesis, University of Essex 2008, p. 226, section 4.15.4.

6. See above, chapter 8.

7. 'the viij th day of Aprile the king Edward the iiij th dyed at Westminster', L. Toulmin Smith, ed., R. Ricart, *The Maire of Bristowe is Kalendar*, London 1872, p. 46.

8. *CCR 1476–1485*, p. 306, nos. 1036, 1037 and 1038.

9. R. H. Britnell, 'The Oath Book of Colchester and the Borough Constitution, 1372-1404', *EAH*, 14, 1982, pp. 94–101 (p. 96).

10. Colchester Oath Book f.107r (modern foliation).

11. John Bisshop and Thomas Cristemesse were prominent Colcestrians of the time. John Bisshop had served as bailiff on several previous occasions. Thomas Cristemesse had not held this office before, but he was to hold it again later, and interestingly he was also subsequently elected to represent Colchester in the first parliament of Henry VII.

12. Ashdown-Hill, 'The Death of Edward V'.

13. *CCR 1476–1485*, p. 328, no. 1108.

14. *Harleian Manuscript 433*, vol. 2, p. 2.

15. G. McKelvie, 'The Bastardy of Edward V in 1484: New Evidence of its Reception in the Inquisitions Post Mortem of William, Lord Hastings', p. 74 – http://www.rsj.winchester.ac.uk/index.php/rsj/article/view/75 (consulted August 2017) – citing *CPR 1476–1485*, p. 375. I am grateful to Philippa Langley for bringing this point to my attention.

16. TNA, C 66/553. I am grateful to The National Archives for helping me check this original document.

17. *CPR 1466–1476*, p. 279.

18. I am very grateful to the Essex Record Office for all the help I was given in this respect.

19. *CCR 1476–1485*, p. 396, no. 1346.

20. 'Edward bastard late called kyng of Englond the v^the' is the formula of the original text (TNA, C 54/337).

21. *CCR 1476–1485*, p. 328, no. 1108.

22. *Harleian Manuscript 433*, vol. 2, p. 2.

23. Oath Book f.107r (modern foliation).

24. TNA, C 66/553.

25. TNA, C 54/337.

26. Mancini's report was published by Armstrong in 1969, but his English translation contains some inaccuracies – including his wording of the title! C. A. J. Armstrong, ed., D. Mancini, *The Usurpation [sic] of Richard III*, Oxford 1969, reprinted Gloucester 1989.

27. This is my translation of Mancini's original text: *Non paucos homines in lacrymas et fletus prorupisse vidi, cum eius memoria fieret postquam a conspectibus hominum est amotus, et iam suspitio foret esse sublatum. An autem sublatus sit, et quo genere mortis nihil adhuc compertum habeo.* The Latin text is published in Armstrong/Mancini, p. 92, but I do not agree with Armstrong's English translation.

28. ... *quod mortem sibi instare putaret.* Armstrong/Mancini, p. 92 – my translation.

29. *Obitus Edwardi V^ti xxij° mens [sic for mensis] Junij regnavit ij menses et viij° dies set non coronatus fuit occisus et nemo s[c]it ubi sepultus.* [The death of Edward V: 22 of the month of June, he reigned two months and eight days but was not crowned, he was killed, and no one knows where he was buried.] Fitzwilliam Museum, Cambridge, Ms. 329, f. 8r.

30. Ashdown-Hill, *The Private Life of Edward IV*, p. 210. I am grateful to the Fitzwilliam Museum for allowing me to inspect the Anlaby Cartulary.

31. *Eduardo Anglie regi parentatum hodie septembris XXIII in maiori sacrario, pontifice et patribus presentibus, rem divinam egit Christophorus episcopus Modrusiensis. Sed novissima persolvit pontifex, vaparato thure et aqua sancta*

inspersa, non pluviali sed purpurea cappa circumdatus. C. S. L. Davies, 'A Requiem for King Edward', *Ricardian*, vol. 9, no. 114, September 1991, pp 102–05 (p. 102).

32. Ashdown-Hill, *Eleanor*, pp. 207 & 241.

33. Saturday 3 May 1483. Ashdown-Hill, '*Beloved Cousyn*', p. 85, citing Crawford, *Howard Household Books*, part 2, p. 389.

34. Davies, 'A Requiem for King Edward', p. 103.

18. Did young Richard survive beyond 1483?

1. *Crowland Chronicle Continuations*, p. 162 – my translation.

2. Toulmin Smith, ed., Ricart, *The Maire of Bristowe is Kalendar*, p. 46.

3. M. Hicks, *Richard III*, Stroud, 2000, p. 242.

4. Soc. Ant., MS 77, f. 62v ; *HHB*, part 2, p. 399.

5. A. Crawford, 'The Mowbray Inheritance', *The Ricardian*, vol. 5, no. 73 (June 1981), pp. 334–40 (p. 338).

6. Kendall, *Richard the Third*, p. 227; *CPR 1476–1485*, p. 358; *Calendar of Charter Rolls*, vol. 6, 1427–1516, p. 258.

7. Ashdown-Hill, 'Norfolk Requiem'.

8. Buchon, ed., *Chroniques de Jean Molinet*, vol. 2, p. 402. Molinet thought the elder son was called Peter and the younger, George.

9. Kingsford, ed., *The Stonor Letters and Papers*, vol. 2, p. 161.

10. *Crowland Chronicle Continuations*, pp. 158–9.

11. *HHB*, part 2, p. 348.

19. What did the Duke of Norfolk do in late July/August 1483?

1. *duo praedicti Regis Edwardi filii sub certa deputata custodia infra Turrim Londoniarum pro quorum ab huiusmodi captivitate liberation coeperunt populi Australes et Occidentales regni plurima submurmurare inire coetus et conventicula multa secreto aliqua que palam innotuerant in hunc finem tractare maxime hi qui per franchesias et sanctuaria propter metum dispersi sunt.* Crowland Chronicle Continuations, p. 162 – my translation.

2. M. Hicks, 'Unweaving the Web: The Plot of July 1483 against Richard III and its Wider Significance', *The Ricardian*, vol 9, no. 114 (September 1991) pp. 106–09 (p. 107).

3. J. Stow, *Annales, or a General Chronicle of England*, London 1631, p. 459.

4. Hicks, 'Unweaving the Web', p. 107, citing Stow, *Annales*, p. 459.

5. Edwards, *Itinerary R3*, p. 5.

6. Edwards, *Itinerary R3*, p. 5.

7. Edwards, *Itinerary R3*, p. 5.

8. Soc. Ant., MS 77, f. 71v ; *HHB*, part 2, p. 416.

9. This building survives, in part, though it was moved to Chelsea in 1908–10. Incidentally the house is variously known in modern texts as 'Crosby Place' and 'Crosby Hall', but the fifteenth-century Howard accounts invariably refer to it as 'Crosby's Place'.

10. Edwards, *Itinerary R3*, p. 5.

11. Edwards, *Itinerary R3*, p. 5.

12. TNA, C81/1392 No. 1; P. Tudor-Craig, *Richard III* (catalogue for the National Portrait Gallery exhibition June–October 1973), p. 98 (punctuation modernised); see also A. J. Pollard, *Richard III and the Princes in the Tower*, Stroud, 1991, p. 109. Kendall, not Herbert, was Richard III's usual secretary. I am grateful to Annette Carson for drawing my attention to this letter.

13. Tudor-Craig, *Richard III*, pp. 54–5 and appendix 4.

14. See above, note 12.

15. Hanham, *Richard III and his Early Historians 1483–1535*, p. 49.

16. J. J. Smith, *Essentials of Early English*, Oxford 1999, 2005, p. 115.

17. Personal communication from Marie Barnfield.

18. See, for example, the use of the word 'hadde' in the heralds' account of the 1476 Garter ceremonies at Windsor: '… Entred into the Chapter-house with the Soveraign and Knyghts of the Order; And thro the Chapter-house into the quier to evensonge, which donne they rode uppe to the Castle againe in their habitts according to the Statutes, and there hadde voyde of Espices &c'. I am grateful to Marie Barnfield for drawing my attention to this.

19. http://www.oed.com/view/Entry/67478?rskey=AV1wfu&result=1#eid (consulted September 2014).

20. Tudor-Craig, *Richard III*, p. 55.

21. *Crowland Chronicle Continuations*, pp. 162–3.

22. *Harleian Manuscript 433*, vol. 1, Gloucester/London 1979, pp. 87, 121, 143, 209; vol. 4 Gloucester 1983, p. 141.

23. *Harleian Manuscript 433*, vol. 2, p. 190.

24. Soc. Ant., MS 77, f. 73r; *HHB*, part 2, p. 419.

25. Soc. Ant., MS 77, f. 73v; *HHB*, part 2, p. 420.

26. Soc. Ant., MS 77, f. 75v; *HHB*, part 2, p. 423.

27. Soc. Ant., MS 77, f. 76r; *HHB*, part 2, p. 424.

20. Would Henry VII have had the boys killed?

1. Maxwell-Lyte, ed., *The Registers of Robert Stillington, Bishop of Bath and Wells 1466–1491 and Richard Fox, Bishop of Bath and Wells 1492–1494*, p. xiii.

2. J. Strachey, ed., *Rotuli Parliamentorum; ut et Petitiones, et Placita in Parliamento*, vol. 6, London 1777, p. 289.

3. 'The real reason for describing Eleanor's family connections in such detail seems rather to relate to a world in which Lady Eleanor's name had been brought briefly

into the limelight and had then been deliberately obscured and even confused with the name of Elizabeth Lucy'. J. Ashdown-Hill, 'The Endowments of Lady Eleanor Talbot and of Elizabeth Talbot, Duchess of Norfolk, at Corpus Christi College Cambridge', *The Ricardian*, vol. 14, 2004, pp. 82–94 (p. 90).

4. G. Smith, 'Lambert Simnel and the King from Dublin', *Ricardian* 10 (December 1996), pp. 498–536, p. 499.

5. Kleyn, *Richard of England*, p. 64.

6. In France he had claimed that he was 'the son of the late King Henry [VI] of England'. J. Ashdown-Hill, *The Wars of the Roses*, Stroud 2015, p. 190; M. Jones, *Bosworth 1485: Psychology of a Battle*, Stroud 2002, pp. 124–5.

21. *What myths are told about 'Richard of England'?*

1. A. Wroe, *Perkin – a story of deception*, London 2003, p. 183 – present writer's emphasis of the place name. Kleyn, *Richard of England*, chapter 12, and I. Arthurson, *The Perkin Warbeck Conspiracy 1491–1499*, Stroud 1994; 1997, p. 79, offer slightly more accurate accounts of the claimant's movements in 1495.

2. Officially in 1495 the Easter octave (= *eight* days after Easter) ended on Monday 27 April, so that year the Monday *after* the octave would probably have been 4 May.

3. The Haarlem Commandery of the Knights Hospitaller was one of the ten houses of St John under the authority of the Utrecht priory of that Order. https://en.wikipedia.org/wiki/Commanderies_of_the_Order_of_Saint_John and https://en.wikipedia.org/wiki/Order_of_Saint_John_(Bailiwick_of_Brandenburg) (both consulted October 2017).

4. *In den jare M IIII C ende XCV, des maendages na der octaven van Paesschen, des avonts laet, is binnen der stede van Haerlem gecomen Ritzaert, des conincs Eduwaerts soen van Engelant, die men gemeenlic noemt die Witte Roese; daer hij een wijl tijts lach logeert totten heren van Sint Jans oerde, om te verwachten sijn volc ende ander gereetscap ten oerloge dienende, daer hi mede over in Engelant reysen woude om sijn vaderlike erve ende crone te conquesteren, die hem van rechtsweghen toebehoerde.* Cornelius Aurelius, *Divisiekroniek*, f. 416r, http://resources.huygens.knaw.nl/retroboeken/divisiekroniek/#page=842&accessor=thumbnails&source=1&view=imagePane (consulted October 2017). I am very grateful to my cousin, Jacqueline Enkelaar, for checking my translation.

5. Dutch National Archives, *Grafelijkheidsrekenkamer Rekeningen » Inventaris nr. 191, Accounts of Thomas Beukelaar, Steward-General, 1495*. The relevant paragraph contains the date 18 April, but that has been crossed out. I am grateful to the members of the Dutch team (W.H. Wiss, N.G.M. Nijman-Biekendaal, J. Roefstra and A.J. de Rooij) of Philippa Langley's 'Missing Princes Project' for sending me this unpublished information from their on-going archival research in the Low Countries. This original research is investigating the journey made by Richard of England through Zeeland and Holland in 1495.

6. They suggested that he was a baby smuggled into the royal bed of the queen, his mother, in a warming pan.

7. Soc. Ant. MSS 116. The text is published in H. Symonds, 'The Irish Silver Coinage of Edward IV', *Numismatic Chronicle*, series 5, no. 1 (1921), pp. 108–25 (pp. 122–3), though M. Dolley, '*Tre Kronor Trí Choróin*, a note on the date of the "three crown" coinage of Ireland', *Numismatiska Meddelanden*, vol. 30 (1965), pp. 103–12 (pp. 109–10) offers some corrections and demonstrates that the marginal drawings of a penny and half groat of the 'three crowns' issue which now accompanies the manuscript text of the indenture is a nineteenth-century interpolation.

8. 'As a final act Edward IV attempted another revision of the Irish coinage before his death in 1483. But this new coinage did not emerge until after his death. Richard III did implement his brother Edward IV's new coinage (see next section) but the earliest coins in his name are of the last type of Edward (with Richard's name often stamped over Edward's on the die)'. http://www.irishcoinage.com/HAMMERED. HTM (consulted August 2017).

9. For a more detailed account in respect of the coinage of 'Edward VI', see Ashdown-Hill, *The Dublin King*, pp 136–41.

10. Wroe, *Perkin a story of deception*, between pp. 182–3.

11. Spink, auction sale report, 31 March 2004: http://www.coinarchives.com/w/lotviewer.php?LotID=148309&AucID=121&Lot=86 (consulted October 2008). In 1464 Edward IV had reduced the weight of the English groat from 60 grains to 48 grains. The Irish groat had fluctuated somewhat in weight, but John Tiptoft (as lieutenant of Ireland) stabilised it at 45 grains from about 1468. An undated *gros* of Charles the Bold issued between 1467 and 1477 and currently in the author's collection weighs 3.3g (or approximately 51 grains).

12. http://www.medievalcoinage.com/earlydated/ (consulted September 2017).

13. See, for example, C. E. Blunt, 'The medallic jetton of Perkin Warbeck', *British Numismatic Journal*, 26 (1949–51), pp. 215–16 (p. 215).

14. D. M. Metcalf, *Sylloge of Coins of the British Isles 23. Ashmolean Museum, Oxford. Part III. Coins of Henry VII*, London, 1976, xxiii–xxiv, xxix, xxxvii.

15. The nearest approach to such iconography on Yorkist coins is the reverse of the Yorkist gold ryal (or rose noble). Following a tradition dating from the reign of Edward III this displayed leopards in the angles of a cross fleury, thus hinting at the juxtaposition of leopard and fleur-de-lis.

16. Although Edward IV owned bed covers (*tapettes*) in the Yorkist livery colours, adorned with roses and crowns, the two symbols seem to have figured on the fabric separately, and not in the form of crowned roses: N. H. Nicolas, ed., *Privy Purse Expenses of Elizabeth of York: Wardrobe Accounts of Edward the Fourth*, London 1830, p. 144.

17. Personal communication from Marion Archibald (to whom my thanks are due for kind permission to cite her then unpublished research). She also found that the

punches used for the 1494 pieces showed no connections with those used to create dies for the Burgundian coinage.

18. A. de Longpérier, 'Perkin Werbecque', *Revue Numismatique* (1860), pp. 384–95, plate xvii, no. 2.

19. M. Mitchiner, *Jetons, Medalets and Tokens*, vol. 1, *The Medieval Period and Nuremberg*, London 1988, pp. 242–5.

20. See, for instance, the gradual degradation of the inscriptions on 'ship'-type jettons, where the obverse inscription began as *Vive le bon roi de France*, but later deteriorated to *Vive le bon foi de banc*, *Vive le cou ugone de nance* and other such drivel. Mitchiner, *op. cit.*, pp. 365–6.

21. Mitchiner lists no examples of jettons bearing the spelling IETOIS. On the other hand the spellings GETTOIS, GETTORS, GECTOIRS, IECTOIRS, IETTORS, IETTON and IETTONS are all attested, as are inscriptions beginning JE SUI[S] ... : Mitchiner, *op. cit.*, pp. 687–8.

22. W. H. D. Longstaffe 'Misplaced Coins – Richard IV's Groat', *Numismatic Chronicle*, 3rd series, vol. 9 (1889), pp. 363–4. Longstaffe himself expressed doubts as to the authenticity of this piece.

22. *What myths are told about 'Richard of Eastwell'?*

1. D. Baldwin, *The Lost Prince – the survival of Richard of York*, Stroud 2007, p. 29.

2. Baldwin, *The Lost Prince*, p. 26, citing F. Peck, *Desiderata Curiosa*, vol. 2 (1779), pp. 249–51.

3. Baldwin, *The Lost Prince*, p. 36 et seq.

4. Baldwin, *The Lost Prince*, p. 36, citing C. Igglesden, *A Saunter through Kent with Pen and Pencil*, vol. 3, Ashford 1901, p. 16.

5. See *R3MK*, pp. 262, 264.

6. Lyell & Watney, eds, *Acts of Court of the Mercers' Company 1453-1527*, pp. 173-4.

7. *Crowland Chronicle Continuations*, pp. 176-77.

8. Hammond & Sutton, *The Road to Bosworth*, pp. 205-6.

9. Baldwin, *The Lost Prince*, p. 90.

10. Ashdown-Hill, *'Beloved Cousyn'*, p. 42.

11. 'There were two types of sanctuary in medieval England.' Any church could offer some degree of protection, but 'some abbeys and minsters had special rites of sanctuary ... anyone who took refuge in such a sanctuary could remain there with impunity for life'. R. F. Hunnisett, *The Medieval Coroner* (Cambridge: CUP, 1961, reprinted Florida 1986), p. 37. Colchester Abbey had been granted such extraordinary rights of sanctuary in 1109 [J. C. Cox, *The Sanctuaries and Sanctuary Seekers of Mediaeval England* (London: Allen, 1911), p. 197] but these rights seem to have been contested. Abbot Ardeley appealed to Henry VI for the abbey's rights of sanctuary to be confirmed, on the grounds that during the king's incapacity,

the community at St John's had expended much time and effort in praying for his recovery, and on 13 May 1453 the king obliged: *CPR 1452–1461*, p. 80.

12. BL, Add. MS 46349, f. 25v; *HHB*, part 1, p. 186.

13. The surname Stansted is otherwise unrecorded in Colchester at this period, implying that the new abbot was born elsewhere, and indeed, Stansted, like Ardeley, could be a toponym, related to either Stanstead Mountfichet in Essex, or Stansted in Suffolk. Of the two the latter seems the more likely point of origin for the new abbot. It is known that Sir John Howard had some connection with the manor of Stansted.

14. Howard himself, however, was summoned to this parliament: Crawford, 'Howard, John' (*ODNB*). Abbot Stansted did sit in subsequent, Yorkist parliaments. It is a fact that some religious houses were partisan. Clare Priory, in Suffolk, for example, clearly favoured the house of York, and deployed the not inconsiderable writing talents of Friar Osbern Bokenham OSA in support of this cause.

15. 'Lovell our dog' of the famous 'Cat and Rat' rhyme.

16. The duchess (possibly for political reasons) did not mention St John's Abbey in her own will. However, her executor, the dean of her Chapel, Richard Lessy, evidently acting upon her instructions, stipulated in his will of February 1498: 'In primis I owe to the hous of saynte Johannes sayntuare in Colchester for my Ladies dettis – whom god pardonn – xxj li the which summe I will be made and spent to the bieng of v chales to be geven to the saide hous of colchestre to praie for my Ladie and for me as procuratoure of this benifete so that the chalesis be Clerely worth xxj li. Beside the facioun the which my will is: to paie of my owne coste and charge': TNA, PROB 11/11 f. 200r. I am grateful to Marie Barnfield for drawing my attention to Lessy's will, throughout which 'my Lady' refers to the Duchess of York.

17. *CPR 1494–1509*, pp. 124, 126.

18. Baldwin, *The Lost Prince*, p. 93.

23. When was the story of the murder of the 'princes in the Tower' put out?

1. *V^{ta} octobris, reverendus in Christo pater episcopus Heliensis, referendarius sanctissimi nostri papae Innocentii Octavi, per Dunensem monasterium iter ad Angliam faciens, dum Calisiam ingressus esset, mortem audivit comitis de Richemont, nuper institute regis.* Baron Kervyn de Lettenhove, ed., *Chroniques relatives à l'histoire de la Belgique sous la domination des Ducs de Bourgogne*, vol. 1, Bruxelles 1870, Adrien de But, *Chroniques*, p. 649.

2. See Ashdown-Hill, *The Dublin King*.

3. Strachey, *Rotuli Parliamentorum*, vol. 6, pp. 272, 289.

4. 'nameinge himself, by usurpacõn, King Richard the III^d'. Strachey, *Rotuli Parliamentorum*, vol. 6, p. 276.

5. R. Lockyer, ed., F. Bacon, *The History of the Reign of King Henry the Seventh*, London 1971, p. 47.

6. PROME, Henry VII, November 1485, vi–276.

7. E. E. Reynolds, ed./trans., T. Stapleton, *The Life of Sir Thomas More* (Douai 1588), London 1966, p. 2, note 3.

24. *How and why was the story promulgated?*

1. It is not certain that the prisoner held in the Tower by Henry VII was the *real* Earl of Warwick, because his father, the Duke of Clarence, is said to have plotted a substitution. See Ashdown-Hill, *The Dublin King*, chapters 4 & 5.

2. E. Hall, *Chronicle*, London 1809, p. 491.

3. For fuller details, see Ashdown-Hill, *The Dublin King*, Appendix 2.

4. 'At the junction with the presently named Shorncliff Road (previously Thomas Street) was the bridge crossing of *St Thomas-a-Watering* over a small brook, which marked a boundary in the Archbishop of Canterbury's authority of the nearby manors in Southwark and Walworth. The landmark pub nearby, the "Thomas a Becket", derives its name from this connection. It was a place of execution for criminals whose bodies were left in gibbets at this spot, the principal route from the southeast to the City of London.' http://en.wikipedia.org/wiki/Old_Kent_Road (consulted December 2013).

5. A. H. Thomas and I. D. Thornley, eds, *The Great Chronicle of London*, London 1938, p. 289.

6. Vergil sometimes misuses the words 'monk' and 'monastery'. In reality there were never Augustinian *monks*. There were Augustinian *canons regular*, and also Augustinian *friars*. Patrick could have been either of those.

7. Sutton/Vergil – my emphasis.

8. R. Lockyer, ed., Bacon, *The History of the Reign of King Henry the Seventh*, London 1971, p. 195.

9. For a full account in this respect, see Ashdown-Hill, *The Dublin King*, chapter 17.

10. Ashdown-Hill, *The Dublin King*, pp. 168–9.

11. D. Seward, *The Last White Rose*, London 2010, pp. 116–7, citing Warwick's nephew, Cardinal Pole.

12. G. A. Bergenroth, ed., *Calendar of State Papers between England and Spain*, vol. 1, *1485–1509*, London 1862, vol. 1, p. 213, January 1500. http://www.british-history.ac.uk/cal-state-papers/spain/vol1/pp213-216 (consulted April 2015).

13. Sylvester, ed., St Thomas More, *The History of King Richard III*, p. 89, note 6.

14. Sylvester/More, *The History of King Richard III*, pp. 88–9.

25. How are the boys said to have been killed?

1. Thomas & Thomley, eds, *The Great Chronicle of London*, London 1938, pp. 236–7. For a quotation of this text, see below, Appendix 2, Tanner page 7, note T1.

2. '*Le Duc de Glaucestre … feit mourir les deux fils dedans la tour de Londres, donnant à entendre aux peuples qu'ils estoient morts par accident s'estans precipitez du hault du pont lequelentre dedans la tour*'. *Les Memoires de Mess Martin du Bellay, Seigneur de Langey*, Paris 1569, p. 6. Cited (briefly, with a small error in the French spelling, and with no precise details of the source) in J. Gairdner, *History of the Life and Reign of Richard the Third* (hereinafter Gairdner, *Richard III*), Cambridge 1898, pp. 125–6, footnote 2.

3. Sylvester/More, *The History of King Richard III*, p. 85.

4. Ellis/Vergil, p. 184; my emphasis.

5. Richard III appears to have had a servant with the name John Green – *CPR 1476–1485*, pp. 434, 462, 513, 544, 551.

6. Sylvester/More, *The History of King Richard III*, pp. 85–6.

7. CCR *1476–85*, no. 1270, p. 373; *CPR 1476–85*, p. 364.

8. Sylvester/More, *The History of King Richard III*, p. 86.

9. Edwards, *Itinerary*, pp. 5–6.

10. i.e. a servant, sleeping on a portable low bed, outside the king's bed chamber.

11. Sylvester/More, *The History of King Richard III*, pp. 86–7.

12. *CPR 1476–85*, pp. 88, 317, 370, 396, 430, 435, 461, 474, 505, 556.

13. His privy (toilet).

14. James' younger brother – later knighted by Henry VII.

15. Sylvester/More, *The History of King Richard III*, p. 87.

16. Sylvester/More, *The History of King Richard III*, p. 87.

17. Sylvester/More, *The History of King Richard III*, pp. 87–8.

18. Miles Forrest was a servant of Richard III. Apparently he died in 1484, because in September of that year the king made a grant to Miles' widow, Joan, and to his son and heir, Edward. *CPR 1476–1485*, p. 473.

19. Richard III granted a John Dighton the office of bailiff of the lordship of Ayton (Staffordshire) on 7 March 1483/4 (*CPR 1476–1485*, p. 436), but the man in question is not named as a servant of the king. In May 1487 a priest called John Dighton was granted the rectorship of St Nicholas' Church, Fulbeck (Lincolnshire) by Henry VII (*CPR 1485–1494*, p. 173), and may have held the rectorship until 1514 (https://en.wikipedia.org/wiki/St_Nicholas%27_Church,_Fulbeck – consulted November 2017). Of course it is not certain that the same person is referred to in both grants. Also, if they were different people, it is also not clear which of them was later named as an alleged murderer by Thomas More.

20. Sylvester/More, *The History of King Richard III*, p. 88.

21. Sylvester/More, *The History of King Richard III*, p. 88.

22. Sylvester/More, *The History of King Richard III*, pp. 88–9.

26. What bones were found at the Tower of London, and when?

1. Sylvester/More, p. 88.

2. Sylvester/More, p. 88.

3. H. Maurer, 'Bones in the Tower: A Discussion of Time, Place and Circumstance', part 1, *The Ricardian*, vol. 8, no. 111, Dec. 1990, pp. 474–93 (p. 488, note 2).

4. *Sic* – it has not been proved that they are the remains of just *two* individuals – see below, chapter 27.

5. *Sic* – this is a misnomer. The Collegiate Church of St Peter at Westminster has not actually been an *abbey* since 1558.

6. Maurer, 'Bones in the Tower', part 1, p. 474.

7. Myers/Buck, *History of Richard III*, pp. 85–6.

8. Maurer, 'Bones in the Tower', part 1, p. 485, citing R. Brooke, *A Catalogue and Succession of the Kings ... of England*, London 1619 (unnumbered pagination).

9. Maurer, 'Bones in the Tower', part 1, p. 478, citing various earlier published sources, but acknowledging that the present whereabouts of the note in question are unknown.

10. Maurer, 'Bones in the Tower', part 1, p. 479, citing the report published by Louis Aubery du Maurier.

11. See, for example, Carson, *Maligned King*, 2013 edition, p. 210.

12. Maurer, 'Bones in the Tower', part 1, pp. 475–6, citing G. Parnell, 'The Roman and Medieval Defences and Later Developments of the Inmost Ward, Tower of London: Excavations 1955–77', *Transactions of the London and Middlesex Archaeological Society*, vol. 36, 1985, pp. 5–7.

13. A. Williamson, *The Mystery of the Princes*, Gloucester 1978, 1981, p. 183; Maurer, 'Bones in the Tower', part 2,, *The Ricardian*, vol. 9, no. 112, March 1991, pp. 2–22 (p. 7).

14. Williamson, *The Mystery of the Princes*, p. 183; Maurer, 'Bones in the Tower', part 2, p. 8.

15. Carson, *Maligned King*, 2013 edition, p. 209, citing C. Wren, *Parentalia*.

16. http://www.westminster-abbey.org/our-history/royals/edward-v (consulted July 2017).

17. Ashdown-Hill, *The Third Plantagenet*, p. 190.

18. Maurer, 'Bones in the Tower', part 2, p. 10, citing R. Davey, *Tower of London*, London 1910, pp. 22–3.

27. What did the 1933 urn opening reveal?

1. Kleyn, *Richard of England*, pp. 43–4. For the full text of the report of the 1933 examinations, see below, Appendix 2.

2. P. Lindsay, *On Some Bones in Westminster Abbey: A Defence of King Richard III*, London 1934, reprinted Bath 1969, pp. 36–7.

3. Appendix 2, Tanner's p. 24.

4. Ashdown-Hill, *The Third Plantagenet*, chapter 17.

5. Appendix 2, Tanner's p. 20.

6. http://www.history.com/news/iron-age-graves-in-britain-yield-hybrid-animals-and-human-sacrifice (consulted August 2017).

7. Kleyn, Richard of England, p. 45.

8. Kleyn, Richard of England, p. 47.

9. T. Molleson, 'Anne Mowbray and the Princes in the Tower: a study in identity', *London Archaeologist* 5 (10) 1987, pp. 258–62 (pp. 258–9), citing *E. Hunt and I. Gleiser, 'The estimation of age and sex of pre-adolescent children' *Amer J Phys Anthrop* 13 (1955) pp. 79–87.

10. Appendix 2, Tanner's p. 24.

11. Appendix 2, Tanner's p. 25.

12. Kleyn, *Richard of England*, pp. 46–7, citing Hammond & Wright, 'The Sons of Edward IV: a re-examination of the evidence on their deaths and on the Bones in Westminster Abbey'.

13. Kleyn, *Richard of England*, pp. 44–5.

14. Molleson, 'Anne Mowbray and the Princes in the Tower: a study in identity', pp. 260–1, citing *J. F. Gravely and D. B. Johnson 'Variation in the expression of hypodontia in monozygotic twins' *Dent Pract dent Rec* 21 (1971) 212–20 and **C. F. A. Moorrees, E. A. Fanmag and E. E. Hunt 'Age variation of formation stages for ten permanent teeth' *J dens Rec* 42 (1963) 1490–1502.

15. Molleson, 'Anne Mowbray and the Princes in the Tower: a study in identity', p. 262.

16. Kleyn, Richard of England, p. 47.

17. Ecclesiastes 12, v. 7; Jeremiah 16, v. 4.

18. 1 Corinthians 15, vv. 36–7, 40, 42–3.

28. Hypodontia?

1. Appendix 2, Tanner's p. 16.

2. Appendix 2, Tanner's p. 18.

3. R. Drewett & M.Redhead, *The Trial of Richard III*, Gloucester 1984, p. 66.

4. Molleson, 'Anne Mowbray and the Princes in the Tower: a study in identity', pp. 259–60, citing *A. H. Brook 'A unifying aetiological explanation for anomalies of human tooth number and size' *Archs oral Biol* 29 (1984) pp. 373–8.

5. Ashdown-Hill, *The Secret Queen*, p. 250.

6. M. A. Rushton, 'The Teeth of Anne Mowbray'. *British Dental Journal*, no. 119, 1965, pp. 335–9.

7. Rushton, 'The Teeth of Anne Mowbray', pp. 335–6.

8. Account of Mathieu d 'Escouchy, cited by S. G. Elkington and R. G. Huntsman, 'The Talbot Fingers: a study in Symphalangism', *British Medical Journal*, 18 February 1967, pp. 407–11 (p. 409).

9. See Ashdown-Hill, *The Secret Queen*, plate 40.

10. Ashdown-Hill, *The Secret Queen*, chapter 20.

11. B. Ross, ed., *Accounts of the Stewards of the Talbot Household at Blakemere 1392–1425*, Keele 2003.

12. J. Ashdown-Hill, 'Carbon Dating of the CF2 bones – are they the remains of Eleanor Talbot?' *Ricardian Bulletin*, December 2017, pp. 35–7.

29. Can DNA now reveal the truth?

1. Ashdown-Hill, *The Last Days of Richard III*, Stroud 2010.

2. Ashdown-Hill, *The Mythology of Richard III*, pp. 148–50.

3. Jacquette de Luxembourg or Jacquette de St Pol is often referred to by English historians as 'Jacquetta'. But the only fifteenth-century sources for a three-syllabled version of her name were written, not in English, but in Latin! She herself used the two-syllabled French version of her name when living in England.

4. Either this is a misprint, or the inscription has been misread. Mary actually died in 1533.

5. *Proceedings of the Suffolk Institute of Archaeology*, vol. 1, 1853, p. 56.

6. *Proceedings of the Suffolk Institute of Archaeology*, vol. 1, 1853, p. 56.

7. Again, this is a mistake. It should read 1533.

8. *Proceedings of the Suffolk Institute of Archaeology*, vol. 1, 1853, p. 55, citing Forster's Stowe Catalogue, Appx. p. 297.

9. *Proceedings of the Suffolk Institute of Archaeology*, vol. 1, 1853, pp. 55–6.

10. G. Moran, 'The mtDNA Sequence of the "Princes in the Tower"' (appendix, published in Ashdown-Hill, *The Private Life of Edward IV*, pp. 234–43 [pp. 235–6]).

11. Personal communication from Elizabeth Roberts, 15 October 2017.

12. The designations of the clan mothers given here are derived from B. Sykes, *The Seven Daughters of Eve*, New York & London 2001, p. 195 and *passim*.

13. J. Ashdown-Hill, 'Margaret of York's Dance of Death – the DNA evidence', *Handelingen van de Koninklijke Kring voor Oudheidkunde, Letteren an Kunst van Mechelen*, 111, 2007, pp. 193–207.

14. *Op. cit.*; P.B. Duncan, *A Catalogue of the Ashmolean Museum*, Oxford 1836, p. 140, no. 378, 'a lock of king Edward the IVth's hair, taken from his head when the body was found in the college chapel, at Windsor, March 1789. [Presented by] Rev. Arthur Onslow, late Dean of Windsor'.

Conclusion

1. This may be related to the coup attempted by Elizabeth Widville. For the evidence on the questionable nature of Edward IV's precise birth date, see Ashdown-Hill, *The Private Life of Edward IV*, chapter 3, and Ashdown-Hill, Cecily *Neville*, chapters 3 & 11.

Appendix 1: The Reign of Edward V

1. 'took to his bed about Easter-time', *Crowland Chronicle Continuations*, p. 151. Commynes says Edward IV fell ill when he received news of the Treaty of Arras (signed 23 December 1482) and the marriage arranged between the Dauphin Charles and Margaret of Austria, and that he died 'shortly afterwards' (Dockray, *Source Book*, p. 146).

2. Davies, *York Records*, pp 142 &. 143, fn.

3. Jean Molinet – see above, chapter 8, note 4.

4. Bishop Thomas Basin – see above, chapter 8, note 5.

5. Davies, *York Records*, pp 142 &. 143, fn.

6. Gairdner, *Richard III*, p. 48.

7. Armstrong/Mancini, p. 59.

8. Colchester Oath Book f.107r (modern foliation).

9. Gairdner, *Richard III*, p. 48, citing Davies, *York Records*, 142.

10. Davies, *York Records*, p. 143, fn.

11. Gairdner, *Richard III*, p. 48. *Crowland Chronicle Continuations* (but no date stated in that source).

12. *HHB*, vol. 2, p. 383.

13. *Crowland Chronicle Continuations*, p. 151 (written 1486); *The Great Chronicle of London* (as cited – but not *quoted* in respect of the *date* – in Dockray, Source Book, p. 146); *Fabyan's Chronicle*, p. 667 (Fabyan died *circa* 1512, however, his Chronicle, as published concludes with the year 1540 – so not contemporary?); Kingsford, ed., *Chronicles of London*, pp. 189, 278 (Vitellius A XVI – not contemporary – the Chronicle continues to the end of the reign of Henry VII); Hall, *Chronicle*, p. 341 (published 1548; 1550 – so not contemporary).

14. Ashdown-Hill, *'Beloved Cousyn'*, p. 83, citing *HHB* – boat fees.

15. Gairdner, *Richard III*, p. 46, but no date cited.

16. Ashdown-Hill, *'Beloved Cousyn'*, p. 83, citing *HHB* – boat fees.

17. Gairdner, *Richard III*, p. 48.

18. Gairdner, *Richard III*, p. 48.

19. Armstrong/Mancini, p. 75 – no date given.

20. Gairdner, *Richard III*, p. 55, states this, citing Patent Rolls. But he gives no specific reference. The word 'protector' does not appear in the only entry I can find for 21 April 1483 in the published *CPR 1476–1485*, (pp. 350–1). However, it might possibly figure in the original manuscript.

21. Armstrong/Mancini, p. 121 – note 64.

22. Armstrong/Mancini, p. 75 – no date given.

23. Gairdner, *Richard III*, p. 49, citing Stevenson, *Records of the Borough of Nottingham*, ii, 394.

24. Gairdner, *Richard III*, p. 51.

25. *Crowland Chronicle Continuations*, p. 157.

26. Armstrong/Mancini, p. 81.

27. *Crowland Chronicle Continuations*, p. 157; Armstrong/Mancini, p. 79.

28. Gairdner, *Richard III*, p. 55, states this, citing Patent Rolls. But again, he gives no specific reference. I cannot find any document in the published *CPR 1476–1485* which bears Gairdner's claim date (2 May 1483).

29. Armstrong/Mancini, p. 119 – note, citing PRO, Ancient Correspondence, xlv, no. 236.

30. *Crowland Chronicle Continuations*, p. 155.

31. Armstrong/Mancini, p. 120 – note, citing *The Great Chronicle of London* & *Fabyan's Chronicle*; *Crowland Chronicle Continuations*, p. 157 (no precise date – just 'a few days later').

32. Armstrong/Mancini, p. 121 – note 64.

33. Armstrong/Mancini, p. 121 – note. 65.

34. Armstrong/Mancini, p. 122 – note 67.

35. Armstrong/Mancini, p. 123 – note 72.

36. Gairdner, *Richard III*, p. 59, citing Nichols, *Grants of Edward V*, 3; Armstrong/Mancini, p. 122 – note 67.

37. Gairdner, *Richard III*, p. 55.

38. Armstrong/Mancini, p. 124 – note 74.

39. *Stonor Letters*, vol. 2, p. 160, no. 330.

40. *Stonor Letters*, vol. 2, p. 160, no. 330.

41. *Stonor Letters*, vol. 2, p. 159, no. 330.

42. *Stonor Letters*, vol. 2, p. 160, no. 330.

43. Hammond & Sutton, *The Road to Bosworth*, p. 104.

44. Gairdner, *Richard III*, p. 61, citing *Paston Letters*, iii, no. 874.

45. Gairdner, *Richard III*, p. 62.

46. *Crowland Chronicle Continuations*, p. 159; *Stonor Letters*, vol. 2, p. 161, no. 331.

47. Hammond & Sutton, *The Road to Bosworth*, p. 103.

48. *Crowland Chronicle Continuations*, p. 159. Different (earlier) date suggested in Mancini and elsewhere (Armstrong/Mancini, p. 124 – note 67. But Gairdner, *Richard III*, p. 78, goes with THIS date, citing Crowland and also 'Stallworth's second (*actually third*) letter (*Stonor Letters*, vol. 2, p. 161, no. 331).

49. *CPR 1476–1485*, p. 352.

50. *CCR 1476–1485*, p. 306.

51. Colchester Oath Book f.107r (modern foliation); *CCR 1476–1485*, p. 306, nos. 1036, 1037 and 1038.

52. Armstrong/Mancini, p. 122 – note 74.

53. *Stonor Letters*, vol. 2, p. 161, no. 331.

54. *Stonor Letters*, vol. 2, p. 161, no. 331.

55. Armstrong/Mancini, p. 123 – note 72.

56. Armstrong/Mancini, p. 123 – note 72. Gairdner, *Richard III*, p. 55, citing *Report VII of Deputy Keeper of Public Records*, app. Ii, p. 212.
57. Gairdner, *Richard III*, p. 73.
58. *Crowland Chronicle Continuations*, p. 159.
59. CPR 1476–1485, p. 360.
60. CCR 1476–1485, p. 304.
61. CCR 1476–1485, p. 328, no. 1108.
62. Horrox & Hammond, eds, *British Library Harleian Manuscript 433*, vol. 2, p. 2
63. Colchester Oath Book, f.107r (modern foliation).
64. TNA, C 66/553 (CPR 1476–1485, p. 375).

Appendix 2: Tanner 1930s Article

1. This is NOT a certain fact – particularly given the claim made later by 'Richard of England'/'Perkin Warbeck'!
2. This is a very big claim. What evidence will be presented by Tanner to prove that the bones all belonged to just TWO individuals?
3. What proof has been presented that the boys were murdered? Where does Tanner explore the possibility that at least one of them may have died naturally?
4. Assuming those points could be proved, would even that prove that Richard III was himself responsible for whatever happened?
5. Why 'ostensibly'? That was definitely the reason why Edward V went to live at the Tower.
6. There is no proof for that assertion.
7. There is no proof that the gates of the Tower closed upon them. Also 'one pathetic glimpse' is incorrect. Tanner himself quotes 'sundry times' (see below).
8. Potential proof that they were not prisoners.
9. Morton was also in a position to REWRITE the story for political reasons!
10. It is naïve to believe that More told the truth. See, for example, his completely mad allegation that the claim was made that Edward IV had been married to a woman called Elizabeth Lucy. No such woman seems to have existed at that time, and the real claim put forward in 1483 was that Edward IV had been married to Lady Eleanor Talbot.
11. As has been shown earlier in the present book, More's account cannot be trusted.
12. It is interesting that this account offers THREE DIFFERENT VERSIONS of how the boys may have been killed.
13. As Tanner notes, the actual place where the bones were found is unclear, based on the surviving source material.
14. Given More's claim that the bodies were reburied on the orders of Richard III, because he was unhappy that the sons of a king should have been interred inappropriately, this suggestion is obviously ridiculous.

15. Presumably this reference is to the first volume of J. Dart, *Westmonasterium; or the History and Antiquities of the Abbey Church of St. Peter's, Westminster*, 2 vols. London, 1742.

16. Presumably De Ros, *Memorials of the Tower of London*, 1866. So the alleged tradition that the boys were murdered in the Bloody Tower can actually only be dated to the mid-nineteenth century.

17. We have already seen that Mancini sometimes makes erroneous statements (e.g. when he suggests that Richard of Shrewsbury was with Edward V in Stony Stratford in April 1483), and he makes no claim regarding what happened to Richard later, though he does suggest that Edward died.

18. J. Nichols, *The Progresses, Processions and Magnificent Festivities of King James the First*, 4 vols., London 1828.

19. It is good to see that, here at least, Tanner acknowledges that everything is uncertain. Unfortunately, the rest of his account assumes that he knows the truth.

20. Tanner's words 'If this was really so' acknowledge the fact that in reality nothing is certain.

21. It has already been pointed out that precisely the same conclusion was traditionally assigned to the bones lying in the Clarence vault at Tewkesbury. They too were assumed to belong to TWO individuals because there were two fairly intact skulls present. However, the scientific examination of the Clarence vault remains, organised by the present writer in 2013, proved that in reality parts of more than two skeletons were present.

22. Regarding Tanner's allegation that Richard III had 'designs on the crown', see above, chapters 9 & 14.

23. I consulted the Ashmolean Museum once again on this matter in August 2017, but I received the following answer: 'I can confirm that we don't possess (and to our knowledge, never have possessed) the bones.'

24. Wright's decision to apply the names 'Edward' and 'Richard' from this point onwards is unfortunate and unscientific. It would be better if he referred to the two skulls and teeth in a similar way to that used by me. I refer to the skulls as 'TL1' and 'TL2'.

25. Is it really likely that suffocation would cause blood staining of the *bones* of a person who died in that way? Surely if someone was suffocated, and if there was associated bleeding, that would stain the *surface tissue* (which would not have survived hundreds of years of burial).

26. There is no proof that Humphrey of Lancaster, Duke of Gloucester was murdered. Nor is there proof that he was murdered in this way. Citing Shakespeare as a source is pointless. Shakespeare was writing a PLAY, and he was writing more than a century after Humphrey's demise.

27. It is hard to explain why a prince who was OFFERED the throne by the three estates of the realm should be called 'usurping'.

28. Where is the evidence for an 'elm chest'?

29 Wright appears to take no account of the possibility that bones were lost or stolen AFTER the remains were discovered in 1674.

30. Wright appears to assume that the bones were not found – as is elsewhere reported – *buried beneath a staircase*. He assumes they were always buried in the open.

31. Wright has now absolutely proved that the urn in the Henry VII chapel did not only contain the bones of two boys!

32. It sounds as though in 1933, after the examination, only the HUMAN bones were replaced in the urn. So what was then done with the animal remains, nails, and other finds? Where are they today?

33. Now, of course, thanks to the Looking For Richard Project, the remains of Richard III have been found, scientifically identified with the help of mtDNA, and honourably reburied!

34. It is very interesting to note that Wright acknowledges that there were some human bones present in the urn which could not be clearly attributed to either of the skull owners.

35. I think this claim was disproved by the evidence presented earlier in the present book.

36. But, as we saw earlier, according to More's account they were supposed to have been removed from that site on the orders of Richard III. So how could they be found there in 1674?

37. Plus fish, ducks, chickens, rabbits, sheep, pigs, and oxen – and possibly other human beings (because some bones could not be associated with either of the skull owners).

38. Does smothering usually cause bleeding?

Appendix 3: The meaning of the Latin word nuper

1. Ellis/Vergil, p. 119.

2. PROME, Henry VII, November 1485.

3. PROME, Richard III, January 1483/4.

4. All from PROME, Edward IV, October 1472.

5. W. Smith, *A Latin–English Dictionary*, London 1868, p. 739; S.C. Woodhouse, *The Englishman's Pocket Latin–English and English-Latin Dictionary*, London 1952, p. 114; D.A. Kidd, ed., *Collins Latin Gem Dictionary*, London 1957; 1972, p. 218.

6. CPR *1466–1476*, p. 279.

BIBLIOGRAPHY

Original Documents

Anlaby Cartulary, Fitzwilliam Museum, Cambridge, Ms. 329

Edward V's letter to Cardinal Bourchier, The National Archives, SC 1/45/236

Esex Record Office, Colchester Oath Book, D/B 5 R1

Howard Household Accounts, Soc. Ant., MS 77

Patent Rolls, Richard III to William Daubeney, The National Archives, C 54/337

Close Rolls, Thomas Ormond & William Catesby, The National Archives, C 66/553

Books

Adams N and Donahue C, eds, *Select Cases from the Ecclesiastical Courts of the Province of Canterbury, c. 1200–1301*, London 1981

André – *see* Sutton

Armstrong C A J, ed., Mancini D, *The Usurpation [sic] of Richard III*, Gloucester 1989

Arthurson I, *The Perkin Warbeck Conspiracy 1491–1499*, Stroud 1994; 1997

Ashdown-Hill J, *Richard III's 'Beloved Cousyn': John Howard and the House of York*, Stroud 2009

Ashdown-Hill J, *The Third Plantagenet, George, Duke of Clarence, Brother of Richard III*, Stroud 2014

Ashdown-Hill J, *The Dublin King*, Stroud 2015

Ashdown-Hill J, *The Mythology of Richard III*, Stroud 2015

Ashdown-Hill J, *The Wars of the Roses*, Stroud 2015

Ashdown-Hill J, *The Secret Queen*, Stroud 2016

Ashdown-Hill J, *The Private Life of Edward IV*, Stroud 2016

Ashdown-Hill J, *Cecily Neville Mother of Richard III*, Barnsley/Havertown PA 2018

Aurelius C, *Divisiekroniek* – see internet

Bacon F – see Lockyer

Basin T – see Quicherat

Bergenroth G A, ed., *Calendar of State Papers between England and Spain*, vol. 1, *1485–1509*, London 1862 – see internet

Benham W G, ed., *The Red Paper Book of Colchester*, Colchester 1902

Benham W G, ed., The Oath Book, or Red Parchment Book of Colchester, Colchester 1907

Bentley S, ed, *Excerpta Historica*, London 1831

Buchon J-A, ed., *Chroniques de Jean Molinet*, vol. 2, Paris 1828

Buck G, – see Myers

Calendar of Charter Rolls, vol. 6, *1427–1516*, London 1927

Calendar of Close Rolls, 1468–1476, London 1953

Calendar of Close Rolls, 1476–1485, London 1954

Calendar of Papal Registers, vol. 13, part 1, Papal Letters 1471–1484, London 1955

Calendar of Patent Rolls, 1467–1477, London 1900

Calendar of Patent Rolls, 1476–1485, London 1901

Calendar of Patent Rolls, 1485–1494, London 1914

Carson A, *Richard III The Maligned King*, Stroud 2008; 2013

Carusi E, ed., Jacopo Gherardi da Volterra, *Il Diario Romano dal 7 Settembre 1479 al 12 Agosto 1484*, Castello 1904

Cheetham A, *The Life and Times of Richard III*, London 1972

Commynes P de, *Memoirs* – see Jones

Crawford A, ed., *The Household Books of John Howard, Duke of Norfolk, 1462–71, 1481–83*, Stroud 1992

Davies R, *Extracts from the Municipal Records of the City of York during the Reigns of Edward IV, Edward V and Richard III*, London 1843

Davis N, ed., *Paston Letters and Papers of the Fifteenth Century*, 2 vols., Oxford 1971 and 1976.

Dockray K, *Edward IV, a source book*, Stroud 1999

Drewett R & Redhead M, *The Trial of Richard III*, Gloucester 1984

Duncan P B, *A Catalogue of the Ashmolean Museum*, Oxford 1836

Edwards R., *The Itinerary of King Richard III 1483–1485*, London 1983

Ellis H, ed., Fabyan R, *The New Chronicles of England and France*, London 1811

Ellis H, ed., *Three Books of Polydore Vergil's English History*, London 1844

Fabyan – see Ellis

Fleetwood W, alleged editor (but the book in question was produced anonymously 85 years after his death) – see *Les Reports des Cases en les ans des Roys Edward v. Richard iij. Henrie vij & Henrie viij.*

Gairdner J, *Letters and Papers of the Reigns of Richard III and Henry VII*, London 1861

Gairdner J, ed., *The Historical Collections of a Citizen of London in the Fifteenth Century* [Gregory's Chronicle], London 1876

Gairdner J, ed., *Letters and Papers, Foreign and Domestic: Henry VIII*, vol. 6, London 1882

Gairdner J, *History of the Life and Reign of Richard the Third*, Cambridge 1898 Gairdner J, ed., *The Paston Letters*, Gloucester 1983

Given-Watson C, ed., *The Parliament Rolls of Medieval England*, Leicester 2005

'Gregory's Chronicle' – see Gairdner

Gudenus, *Codex Diplomaticus*, vol. 4, Frankfurt & Leipzig 1758

Hall E, *Chronicle*, London 1809

Halsted C A, *Richard III as Duke of Gloucester and King of England*, 2 vols., London 1844

Hammond P.W., & Sutton A.F., *Richard III: The Road to Bosworth*, London 1985 Hammond P W, ed., H. Walpole, *Historic Doubts on the Life and Reign of King Richard the Third*, (originally published 1768) Gloucester 1987

Hanham A, ed.,*The Cely Letters 1472–1488*, London 1975

Hanham A, *Richard III and his Early Historians 1483–1535*, Oxford 1975

Hanham A, *The Celys and their World*, CUP, Cambridge 1985

Hicks M, *Richard III*, Stroud, 2000

Horrox R. and Hammond P.W., eds., *British Library Harleian Manuscript 433*, vol. 1, London/Gloucester 1979; vol. 2, London/Gloucester 1980; vol. 3, London/Gloucester, 1982; vol. 4, London/Gloucester 1983

Jones M, ed., Philippe de Commynes, *Memoirs*, Harmondsworth 1972

Jones M, *Bosworth 1485: Psychology of a Battle*, Stroud 2002

Kendall P M, *Richard the Third*, London 1955; 1976

Kidd D A, ed., *Collins Latin Gem Dictionary*, London 1957; 1972

Kleyn D M, *Richard of England*, Oxford 1990

Kingsford C L, ed., *Chronicles of London*, Oxford 1905

Kingsford C L, ed., *The Stonor Letters and papers*, vol. 2, Camden third series, XXX, London 1919

Laynesmith J.L., *The Last Medieval Queens*, Oxford 2004

Les Reports des Cases en les ans des Roys Edward v. Richard iij. Henrie vij & Henrie viij., London 1679

Lindsay P, *On Some Bones in Westminster Abbey: A Defence of King Richard III*, London 1934, reprinted Bath 1969

Lockyer R, ed., Bacon F, *The History of the Reign of King Henry the Seventh*, London 1971

Lyell L & Watney F D, eds, Acts of Court of the Mercers' Company 1453–1527, Cambridge 1936

Mancini D, – see Armstrong

Maxwell-Lyte H C, ed., *The Registers of Robert Stillington, Bishop of Bath and Wells 1466–1491 and Richard Fox, Bishop of Bath and Wells 1492–1494*, Somerset Record Society 1937

Metcalf D M, *Sylloge of Coins of the British Isles 23. Ashmolean Museum, Oxford. Part III. Coins of Henry VII*, London, 1976

Mitchiner M, *Jetons, Medalets and Tokens*, vol. 1, *The Medieval Period and Nuremberg*, London 1988

Molinet J – see Buchon

More T – see Sylvester

Mortimer I, *The Fears of Henry IV*, London 2007

Myers A R, ed., Buck G, *The History of the Life and Reigne of Richard the Third*, London 1973

Nicolas N H, ed., *Privy Purse Expenses of Elizabeth of York & Wardrobe Accounts of Edward IV*, London 1830

Pollard A J, *Richard III and the Princes in the Tower*, Stroud, 1991

Proceedings of the Suffolk Institute of Archaeology, vol. 1, 1853

Pronay N & Cox J, eds, *The Crowland Chronicle Continuations*, London 1986

Quicherat J, ed., T. Basin, *Histoire des règnes de Charles VII et de Louis XI*, vol. 3, Paris 1857

Rawcliffe C, *The Staffords, Earls of Stafford and Dukes of Buckingham 1394–1521*, Cambridge 1978

Reynolds E E, ed./trans., Stapleton T, *The Life of Sir Thomas More*, (Douai 1588), London 1966

Rolls of Parliament/*Rotuli Parliamentorum* – see Given-Watson (PROME); Strachey

Ross B, ed., *Accounts of the Stewards of the Talbot Household at Blakemere 1392–1425*, Keele 2003

Sandford F, *A Genealogical History of the Kings and Queens of England*, London 1707

Scofield C., *The Life and Reign of Edward the Fourth*, 2 vols, London 1923, 1967

Seward D, *The Last White Rose*, London 2010

Smith J J, *Essentials of Early English*, Oxford 1999, 2005

Smith W, *A Latin–English Dictionary*, London 1868

Stapleton – see Reynolds

Stow J, *Annales, or a General Chronicle of England*, London 1631

Strachey J, ed., *Rotuli Parliamentorum; ut et Petitiones, et Placita in Parliamento*, vol. 6, London 1777

Stevenson J, ed., *Letters and Papers Illustrative of the Wars of the English in France during the Reign of Henry the Sixth*, vol, 2, part 2, London 1864

Sutton A F & Hammond P W, *The Coronation of Richard III: the Extant Documents*, London 1984

Sutton D F, ed., Bernard André, *De Vita atque Gestis Henrici Septimi Historia*, on-line 2010

Sutton D F, ed., Polydore Vergil, *Anglica Historia* (1555 version), on-line 2005, 2010

Sykes B, *The Seven Daughters of Eve*, New York & London 2001

Sylvester R S, ed., St Thomas More, *The History of King Richard III*, New Haven & London 1976

Thomas A.H. and Thornley I.D., eds, *The Great Chronicle of London*, London 1938

Toulmin Smith L, ed., Ricart R, *The Maire of Bristowe is Kalendar,* London 1872

Tudor-Craig P, *Richard III* (catalogue for the National Portrait Gallery exhibition June – October 1973)

Twining A G, *Our Kings and Westminster Abbey*, London 1907

Vergil P, – see Ellis; Sutton

Walpole H, *Historic Doubts on the Life and reign of Richard the Third*, London 1768 – see Hammond

Williamson A, *The Mystery of the Princes*, Gloucester 1978, 1981

Woodhouse S C, *The Englishman's Pocket Latin–English and English–Latin Dictionary*, London 1952

Worcester W, *Annales* – see Stevenson, *Letters and Papers*

Wroe A, *Perkin a story of deception*, London 2003

Articles

Ashdown-Hill J, 'Norfolk Requiem: the Passing of the House of Mowbray', *The Ricardian*, vol. 12, March 2001, pp. 198–217

Ashdown-Hill J, 'The Inquisition *Post Mortem* of Eleanor Talbot, Lady Butler, 1468 (PRO C 140/29/39)', *The Ricardian*, vol. 12, No. 159, December 2002, pp. 563–573

Ashdown-Hill J, 'The Death of Edward V – new evidence from Colchester', *Essex Archaeology & History* 35 2004, pp. 226–30 – see below: Internet – http://cat.essex.ac.uk/reports/EAS-report-0002.pdf

Ashdown-Hill J, 'The Endowments of Lady Eleanor Talbot and of Elizabeth Talbot, Duchess of Norfolk, at Corpus Christi College Cambridge', *The Ricardian*, vol. 14, 2004, pp. 82–94

Ashdown-Hill J, 'Margaret of York's Dance of Death — the DNA evidence', *Handelingen van de Koninklijke Kring voor Oudheidkunde, Letteren an Kunst van Mechelen*, 111, 2007, pp. 193–207

Ashdown-Hill J, 'The Full Intinerary of Edward IV – see below, Internet

Ashdown-Hill J, 'Carbon Dating of the CF2 bones – are they the remains of Eleanor Talbot?' *Ricardian Bulletin*, December 2017, pp. 35–37

Blunt C E, 'The medallic jetton of Perkin Warbeck', *British Numismatic Journal*, 26 (1949–51), pp. 215–16

Britnell R H, 1982 'The Oath Book of Colchester and the Borough Constitution, 1372–1404', *EAH*, 14, pp. 94–101

Davies C S L, 'A Requiem for King Edward', *Ricardian*, vol. 9, no. 114, September 1991, pp 102–05

Dolley M, '*Tre Kronor Trí Choróin*, a note on the date of the "three crown" coinage of Ireland', *Numismatiska Meddelanden*, vol. 30 (1965), pp. 103–12

Elkington S G and Huntsman R G, 'The Talbot Fingers: a study in Symphalangism', *British Medical Journal*, 18 February 1967, pp. 407–11

Fahy C, 'The marriage of Edward IV and Elizabeth Woodville: a new Italian source', *English Historical Review*, vol. 76 (1960), pp. 660–72

Hammond P W, 'Richard III: Dutch Sources', *The Ricardian*, vol. 3, no. 46, September 1974, pp. 12–13

Hicks M, 'Unweaving the Web: The Plot of July 1483 against Richard III and its Wider Significance', *The Ricardian*, vol 9, no. 114 (September 1991) pp. 106–109

Longpérier A de, 'Perkin Werbecque', *Revue Numismatique* (1860), pp. 384–95

Longstaffe W H D, 'Misplaced Coins – Richard IV's Groat', *Numismatic Chronicle*, 3rd series, vol. 9 (1889), pp. 363–4

Marques A S, 'Álvaro Lopes de Cheves [*sic*]: A Portuguese Source', *Ricardian Bulletin*, Autumn 2008, pp. 25–7

Maurer H, 'Bones in the Tower: A Discussion of Time, Place and Circumstance', part 1, *The Ricardian*, vol. 8, no. 111, Dec. 1990, pp. 474–93

Milles Rev. Dr, 'Observations on the Wardrobe Account', *Archaeologia*, vol. i (1770), pp. 364–79

Molleson T, 'Anne Mowbray and the Princes in the Tower: a study in identity', *London Archaeologist*, 5 (10) 1987, pp. 258–62

Moran G, 'The mtDNA Sequence of the "Princes in the Tower" – see Ashdown-Hill, *The Private Life of Edward IV*

Richmond, 'The Death of Edward V'

Richmond C F, 1989, 'The Death of Edward V', *Northern History*, 25, pp. 278–80 Rushton M A, 'The Teeth of Anne Mowbray'. *British Dental Journal*, no. 119, 1965, pp. 335–9

Sheppard Routh P, '"Lady Scroop Daughter of K. Edward": an Enquiry', *The Ricardian*, vol. 9, no. 121, June 1993, pp. 410–16

Smith G, 'Lambert Simnel and the King from Dublin', *Ricardian* 10 (December 1996), pp. 498–536

Symonds H, The Irish Silver Coinage of Edward IV', *Numismatic Chronicle*, series 5, no. 1 (1921), pp. 108–25

Unpublished material

Ashdown-Hill L J F, 'The client network, connections and patronage of Sir John Howard (Lord Howard, first Duke of Norfolk) in north-east Essex and south Suffolk', PhD thesis, University of Essex 2008

Internet

Ashdown-Hill J, 'The Death of Edward V – new evidence from Colchester' – http://cat.essex.ac.uk/reports/EAS-report-0002.pdf (consulted September 2017)

Ashdown-Hill, 'The Full Intinerary of Edward IV', https://www.amberley-books.com/community-john-ashdown-hill

Aurelius C, *Divisiekroniek*, http://resources.huygens.knaw.nl/retroboeken/divisiekroniek/#page=842&accessor=thumbnails&source=1&view=imagePane (consulted October 2017)

G.A. Bergenroth, ed., *Calendar of State Papers between England and Spain*, vol. 1, *1485–1509*, London 1862, http://www.british-history.ac.uk/cal-state-papers/spain/vol1/pp213-216 (consulted April 2015)

https://en.wikipedia.org/wiki/Commanderies_of_the_Order_of_Saint_John (consulted October 2017)

https://en.wikipedia.org/wiki/John_Fogge (consulted September 2017) https://en.wikipedia.org/wiki/John_Scott_(died_1485) (consulted September 2017)

https://en.wikipedia.org/wiki/John_Talbot,_3rd_Earl_of_Shrewsbury (consulted October 2017)

https://en.wikipedia.org/wiki/Order_of_Saint_John_(Bailiwick_of_Brandenburg) (consulted October 2017)

https://en.wikipedia.org/wiki/St_Nicholas%27_Church,_Fulbeck (consulted November 2017)

https://en.wikipedia.org/wiki/Walter_Devereux,_7th_Baron_Ferrers_of_Chartley (consulted September 2017)

https://fr.wikipedia.org/wiki/Angelo_Catho_de_Supino (consulted August 2017)

http://www.medievalcoinage.com/earlydated/ (consulted September 2017)

http://www.irishcoinage.com/HAMMERED.HTM **(consulted August 2017)**

G. McKelvie, 'The Bastardy of Edward V in 1484: New Evidence of its Reception in the Inquisitions Post Mortem of William, Lord Hastings', *Royal Studies Journal*, 3, 2016, pp. 71–9 [p. 74] – http://www.rsj.winchester.ac.uk/index.php/rsj/article/view/75 (consulted August 2017).

Spink, auction sale report, 31 March 2004: http://www.coinarchives.com/w/lotviewer.php?LotID=148309&AucID=121&Lot=86 (consulted October 2008).

Sutton/André – *see* Books – Sutton

Sutton/Vergil – *see* Books – Sutton

PROME – see Books – Given-Watson

ACKNOWLEDGEMENTS

As usual, I am very grateful to my old friend, Dave Perry, for his proofreading. Hopefully he has managed to prevent me from making obvious typos – but if there are any errors the fault is mine, not his!

I am also very grateful to the staff of both The National Archives, and the Essex Record Office, for the valuable help they gave me in researching the original Richard III reign documentation referring to Edward V as 'bastard' and 'late'.

I was very grateful to my friend Philippa Langley for her reading of the text, for her comments, and for sometimes drawing my attention to other sources, and additional points that I might make. Other members of Philippa's 'princes' project also helped me. They include David and Wendy Johnson; also the Dutch researchers Wim Wis, Nathalie Nijman, Jean Roefstra and A. J. de Rooij. And I should like to thank my dear cousin Jacqueline Enkelaar for her help in translating medieval Dutch source material, because, sadly, my own linguistic skills do not include that language.

I was very grateful to Gill Hawkins and other staff of the Moyse's Hall Museum in Bury St Edmunds for trying very hard to help me extract hair samples of Mary, Queen of France and Duchess of Suffolk from the sealed locket held in that museum, and for then sending the locket to my friend Philip Wise, of the Colchester and Ipswich Museums, so that he too could try to safely have some hair extracted for testing. Unfortunately, in the end we all had to give up on that because the Suffolk locket proved to be firmly soldered shut.

However, I was then enormously grateful to the Rt Hon. the Earl of Derby, and his curator, Emma McCarthy, for agreeing to allow me to have strands of hair from another locket, at Knowsley Hall. Also to Emma's successor, Stephen Lloyd, for photographing the locket for me (plate 23). And I am very grateful to Professor Jean-Jacques Cassiman for the testing he did on some of the hair samples which this time had been successfully extracted.

I was very grateful to Glen Moran, who disagreed with a tentative conclusion which I had reached, to the effect that there were no traceable living all-female lines of descent from the family of Elizabeth Widville. He questioned my conclusion in that respect, asked me to help him with some sixteenth-century Latin texts, and eventually traced living female-line descendants from one of Elizabeth Widville's sisters!

I am also very grateful to one of those descendants – Elizabeth Roberts – who then kindly agreed to provide samples for DNA testing, allowed me to publish the results, and who has also helpfully provided her photograph and her thoughts for this book.

And although Professor Cassiman has now retired, I am also grateful to his successor, Professor Ronny Decorte, for testing the mtDNA samples provided by Elizabeth Roberts, and for retesting my final samples of the hair I was given from the Knowsley Hall locket.

Finally I am tremendously grateful to Alex Bennett, my editor at Amberley, for the wonderful work he has done – both on this book, and all my previous Amberley publications.

INDEX

*Nobles are listed under surnames, but titles are cross-referenced.
Women are listed under maiden surnames, but married names are
cross-referenced.*

Admiral, Lord 45
Alcock, John, Bishop of Rochester,
  Bishop of Worcester, Bishop of Ely
  29, 30, 33, 62
allegations
  re. coins – see 'England, Richard of'
  re. marriage plans – see Richard III
  re. murderers (identity) – see
  Dighton; Forrest
  re. servant at the Tower of London –
  see Slaughter
  re. usurpation – see usurpation
Allyngton, William, speaker of the
  House of Commons 29, 32
André, Bernard (historian) 27, 129,
  154
Anjou, Margaret of, consort of Henry
  VI 30
Anlaby Cartulary, the 42, 108, 272
Aragon, Catherine of, Princess of
  Wales, later consort of Henry VIII
  157, 158, 161–2
Archdeacon of London – see Martyn,
  Richard
Argentine, Dr John, Edward V's
  physician 34, 107–8, 114
arrest 48, 49, 51, 54, 58, 59, 64, 68, 72,
  73, 81, 83, 93, 120, 148, 218, 220
Arthur, Prince of Wales, son of Henry
  VII 157, 158, 161–2, 214
Arundel, Countess of – see Widville,
  Margaret
Aurelius, Cornelius (chronicler) 96–7,
  133, 282

Baldwin, David (historian) 147–50
Basin, Bishop Thomas (chronicler) 42,
  117–8, 124
Bath and Wells, Bishop of – see
  Stillington, Robert
'bastard' erasure of (Colchester Oath
  Book) 101–2, 105
bastardy decision for children of
  Edward IV and Elizabeth Widville
  4, 5, 15–6, 20, 30, 64, 65, 73, 80,
  81, 83, 84, 88, 97, 126, 147–8, 164,
  192, 211, 213
'bastardy myth' in respect of Edward
  IV- see Edward IV 'bastardy myth'
Baynard's Castle, London 53, 74, 79,
  80, 83, 219, 220
Beauchamp, Margaret, Countess of
  Shrewsbury 190
Beaufort, Henry, Cardinal 8
  Henry, Duke of Somerset 10
  Margaret, Countess of Richmond
  39, 94
  Margaret, Countess of Stafford 94
  Thomas, Duke of Exeter 201
Bedford, Duchess of – see St Pol,
  Jacquette de
Berkeley, William, Lord, later Earl of
  Nottingham 40, 113–4
Bermondsey Abbey 129
Bishop, John, Colchester bailiff 101–2,
  278
Bishop of London's Palace 52–3, 54, 79
bones 4, 16, 17, 162, 168, 172–85,
  192–3, 195, 209, 214–6, 224, 226,

232–37, 239, 241–3, 245–57, 289, 293–5

Bonville, Cecily, Marchioness of Dorset 69

Booth, Lawrence, Bishop of Durham, Archbishop of York 29, 30

Bosworth, battle of 19, 31, 58, 67, 82, 99, 125, 145, 148, 149, 150, 151, 155, 165, 213, 242

Boteler, Lady – see Talbot, Eleanor
Sir Thomas 10

Bourchier, Thomas, Cardinal Archbishop of Canterbury 30, 54, 56, 115, 218, 219

Brackenbury, Sir Robert, constable of the Tower 155, 165, 167, 169, 171, 231

Brandon, Charles, Duke of Suffolk 197

Bristol local government records 42, 112

Brittany 52

Brooke, Ralph (antiquarian) 173

Brown (Ibsen), Joy 194–5, 208

Buck, George (antiquarian) 15–6, 99, 258

Buckingham, Duchess of – see Widville, Catherine
Duke of – see Stafford, Henry

Buckingham Palace 2, 3, 21

'Buckingham's Rebellion' 32, 58, 95, 98, 112, 117, 131

Burgundy, Duchess of – see York, Margaret of
Duke of – see Charles the Bold

Bury St Edmunds 82, 196, 200, 247
Abbey 197
Moyse's Hall Museum 196, 201
St Mary's Church 197, 198

Calais 69, 153

calendar 6, 99

Cambridge, Richard of, Duke of York 8, 10

Canterbury, Archbishop of – see Bourchier; Morton

Carlisle, Bishop of – see Story, Edward

Cassiman, Professor Jean-Jacques (human genetics) 204, 262, 264, 266

Castillon, battle of 191

'Cat(te)' – see Catesby

Catesby, William (the 'Catte') 67, 106, 125, 155, 166

Cato, Angelo, Archbishop of Vienne 14, 107

Caversham, shrine of Our Lady of 118

Cely, George 75–7

CF2 remains, Norwich 193
- see also Talbot, Eleanor

chancellor 29, 30, 34, 41, 62, 64, 76, 77, 83, 115, 120, 122, 124, 218, 219, 221, 225, 229
servant of – see Stallworthe, Simon

Chapuys, Eustace (diplomat) 20

Charles II 175, 177, 224, 233, 235

Charles the Bold, Duke of Burgundy 35, 138, 283

Chichester, Bishop of – see Story, Edward

Chokke, Sir Richard, lawyer 29, 32

Clarence, Duchess of – see Neville, Isabel
Duke of – see York, George of
Edward of, Earl of Warwick 5–6, 27, 84, 149, 157–61, 278, 286
vault at Tewkesbury – bones found in 175, 180, 185, 294

coins, history of 134–44
English medieval royal 'portraits' 135–6
introduction of closed crown 139–40
introduction of dating 134, 139
- see also 'England, Richard of'; 'Edward VI'

Colchester 33, 201, 262, 278, 285
Abbot of – see Stansted, Walter
local government records (Oath Book) 42, 99–107, 108, 258
St John's Abbey 149–50, 284, 285

coronation 3, 4, 11, 18, 21, 43, 50, 52, 54, 60–1, 63–4, 67, 70, 80, 86–9, 91, 93, 94, 95, 210, 218, 219, 220, 230

Coytemore, Geoffrey 30

Cristemesse, Thomas, Colchester bailiff 101–2, 278

Crosby's Place, Bishopsgate 119, 123–4, 221, 277, 281

Crowland Chronicle Continuations 4–5, 14, 46, 47, 49, 52, 55, 72, 112, 115, 117, 122, 124, 280, 291

Cullum, Sir John (antiquarian) 198, 199, 200, 201, 202

Daubeney, William (diplomat & courtier) 104–5

Davy, William, pardoner of Hounslow 118

De But, Adrien (chronicler) 153

Decorte, Professor Ronny (human
genetics) 206, 209, 264
Derby, Earl of – see Stanley, Edward
Devereux of Ferrers, Walter 29, 31
Dighton, John, bailiff(?), priest(?),
alleged murderer 162, 168, 169, 231,
232, 287
DNA – see mtDNA; Y chromsome
Dorset, Marchioness of – see Bonville,
Cecily
Marquess of – see Grey, Thomas
Dudley, John, Duke of
Northumberland 41, 42
Durham, Bishop of – see Booth,
Lawrence

'Eastwell, Richard of' 145–51
Edward III 38, 44, 47, 90, 135, 195,
283
Edward IV 3, 5, 8, 9, 10, 12, 15, 18–9,
22, 24, 28, 29, 31, 32, 33, 34, 35,
36, 37, 38, 39, 40, 51, 52, 53, 57,
60, 62, 69, 70, 77, 80, 83, 84, 85,
86, 88, 96, 97, 102–3, 105, 106,
113, 114, 115, 116, 117, 118, 119,
120, 121, 122, 123, 124, 129, 130,
131, 132, 136, 137, 138, 140, 149,
151, 153, 154, 155, 156, 158, 159,
161, 162, 163, 166, 167, 170, 172,
173, 176, 179, 182, 183, 184, 190,
193, 200, 210, 214, 215, 216, 219,
221, 226, 227, 239, 258, 261
'bastardy myth' 81
death of 41–3, 45, 46, 47, 68, 77,
87, 92, 100, 110–1, 217–8
hair of 25, 208
marriages of 10–1, 15–6, 18–9, 20,
24, 30, 61, 63–6, 71, 74, 81, 91, 93,
125–8, 147, 148, 192, 211–2, 213,
260
will of (1475) 13–4, 23–4, 26, 77
Edward V 4–6, 12, 15, 18, 21, 31–2,
34, 41, 43, 44, 46, 47, 49, 50, 51,
52, 53, 54, 55, 56, 60, 62, 68, 70,
73, 74, 77–8, 79, 83, 87–8, 93,
95–6, 113, 114, 117, 118, 131, 156,
167, 171, 172, 174, 175, 182, 183,
189, 190, 196, 197, 201, 207, 210,
217–22, 223, 226, 232, 233, 241,
245, 249, 253, 256, 257
'bastard' 19, 61, 63–5, 71, 80–1,
102–6, 147, 148, 211
birth of 11

coins of? 135–7
depressed? 21, 24, 168
hair colour? 21, 22, 25, 200, 204
'late' 98–102, 104–11, 147, 153,
157, 212, 258
religious? 24
restored as 'prince' (& rightful king)
by Henry VII 128
sickly? 21, 23, 26
trust in his mother 48
'Edward VI' (1486–87) 27, 129, 154,
157, 158, 278
coins of 136–8, 283
Edward VI (1547–53) 41–2
Elizabeth of York – see York, Elizabeth of
Ely, Bishop of – see Alcock, John;
Grey, William; Morton, John
'England, Richard of' 5–6, 27–8, 84–5,
124, 129–30, 131, 155, 159
alleged groats 138–41
alleged jetton 141–3
movements in 1495 133
erasure of 'bastard' (Colchester records /
Oath Book) – see 'bastard', erasure of
Estates General of France 213, 225
Eve – see 'Mitochondrial Eve'
Exeter, Duke of – see Beaufort, Thomas

Fabyan, Robert (chronicler) 163, 272,
291
factions, opposing 52, 71
feast – see Michaelmas; St Anne; St
John the Baptist
Fenys [Fiennes] of Dacre, Richard 29,
30, 31
Fog[ge], (Sir) John 29, 31–2, 98, 151
Forest, Miles, servant of Richard III;
alleged murderer 168
Fowler, Richard 29
Foxley Norris, William, Dean of
Westminster 178, 241
Framlingham Castle 35

Gairdner, James (historian) 17, 225,
228, 230, 287, 292
Gherardi. Iacopo (chronicler) 109
Gloucester, Duke of – see Lancaster,
Humphrey of; York, Richard of
Goldwell, James, Bishop of Norwich 38
Grafton, Richard (chronicler) 92, 172
Green, John, servant of Richard III 165–6
Grey, Lady Jane ('nine-days queen') 41,
197, 207

Sir John 48
Lady – see Widville, Elizabeth
Sir Richard 47, 48, 49, 51, 58, 93, 218
Thomas, Marquess of Dorset 39, 44,
45, 46, 51, 52, 58, 59, 69, 96, 130,
230
William, Bishop of Ely 76
Guildhall of London, the 19, 65, 70,
71, 81

hair colour – see Cambridge, Richard
of; Edward IV; Edward V; Richard
III; Shrewsbury, Richard of; Widville,
Anthony, Earl Rivers
Halsted, Caroline (historian) 17, 87
Hanham, Alison (historian) 121
Hardyng, John (chronicler) 92, 240
Hastings, William, Lord 24, 30, 31,
68–73, 76, 81, 82, 83, 92, 93, 219,
220, 239, 240
enmity re. the Widvilles 45–7, 52,
69–70, 218
Haute, (Lady Fogge) Alice 31, 151
esquire, Richard 30, 32
Henry IV 8, 19, 260
Henry V 19, 140, 260
Henry VI 3, 10, 12, 44, 61, 105, 106,
130, 140, 247, 261, 284
rex de facto, non de iure 19
Henry VII 3, 25, 27, 32, 39, 42, 52,
67, 87, 99, 108, 112, 128, 132, 134,
136, 137, 140, 141, 144, 148, 150,
157, 170, 196, 213–4, 225
French royal connections 7, 139
imprisonment & execution of other
'princes in the Tower' 5, 129–30,
133, 161–2
legislation of first parliament 20, 102,
126–7, 154–5, 164, 259
marriage plans 20, 126–7, 147
motivation for disposing of 'the princes
in the Tower' 84–5, 125, 131, 213
report of his death (October 1485) 153
rewriting of history 6, 7, 15, 66, 73, 81
surname? 8
- see also 'Richmond, Earl of'
Henry VIII 15, 66, 87, 92, 130, 136,
196, 197, 207, 209
Hereford, Bishop of – see Millyng,
Thomas
Hervy, John, Colchester town clerk
100–1, 278
Holcombe, Robert, London vinter 104

Hospital of St John – see St John,
Hospital of
Howard, Sir John, Lord, later Duke
of Norfolk 33, 40, 45, 53, 76, 78,
82, 95, 97, 110, 111, 113–4, 116,
118–9, 122–4, 149–50, 154, 217–8,
241, 278, 281, 285
servant of – see St Clare, Giles
hypodontia 184, 188–93, 215, 289

Ibsen, Joy – see Brown, Joy
illegitimate – see bastardy
invention – see 'Lucy, Elizabeth';
'Princes in the Tower'
Ireland 27, 28, 32, 45, 157
Stephen, wardrober 118
Irish arms 136
coins 135, 136, 137, 283

James I of Scotland 3
James I of England 238, 240
'Jasmine' – see mtDNA
jetton – see 'England, Richard of'
alleged jetton
John, Edward 104, 106

King's Lodgings – see Tower of London
knighthood 60–1, 219
Knowsley Hall 203–4, 209, 264

Lambert (Shore), Elizabeth ('Jane') 69,
220
Lancaster, Humphrey of, Duke of
Gloucester 53, 247, 294
Latin language / translation / meaning
19, 49, 101, 103, 105, 106, 107,
122, 136, 139, 142, 175, 204, 230,
248, 258–61, 270, 279, 290
Leuven, the Catholic University of 204,
206, 209, 262–5
Lincoln, Bishop of – see Russell, John
Earl of – see Pole, John de la
London, Tower of – see Tower of
London
Longpérier, Adrien Prévot de
(numismatist) 141–3
lord protector 44, 46, 53, 55, 68, 71,
80, 211–2
Lovell, Francis, Viscount 149, 150, 285
'Lucy, Elizabeth' – invented woman 15,
16, 66, 127, 282, 293
Ludlow 33, 43, 44, 70, 218
Castle 21, 33, 43, 50

Luxembourg, Jacquette of – see St Pol
Lyne-Pirkis, Dr Richard (anatomist) 183

Mancini, Domenico (diplomat &
  chronicler) 14, 42, 43, 45, 49, 55,
  63, 71, 72, 73, 82, 100, 107, 108,
  114, 239, 240, 274, 275, 276, 279,
  292, 294
March, Earl of – see Edward IV
Martyn, Richard, Archdeacon of London
  (later Bishop of St David's) 29, 32
Mary, Queen of France & Duchess of
  Suffolk 196–201, 203–4, 208, 209,
  262, 264–6, 290
  hair colour 200
McCarthy, Emma (curator, Knowsley
  Hall) 203
Meadway, Christine (dental expert) 193
Michaelmas (feast of St Michael)
  101–2, 226
Middleham 45, 47, 68, 92
  Castle 46, 50
Milles, Rev, Dr (historian) 87
Millyng, Thomas, Abbot of
  Westminster, Bishop of Hereford 29,
  30, 226
'Mitochondrial Eve' 207
Molinet, Jean de (chronicler) 42, 114,
  115, 232, 272, 280
Molleson, Dr Theya (osteologist) 179,
  181–2, 184, 189–90
Moran, Glen 204
More Sir (St) Thomas 15, 69, 73, 92,
  96, 155–6, 162–8, 171, 214, 216,
  229, 230–1, 232, 239, 240, 255,
  257, 287, 293
Morton, John, Bishop of Ely, later
  Cardinal Archbishop of Canterbury
  71, 73, 83, 93–4, 96, 99, 131, 153,
  155–6, 214, 220, 230, 293
Mowbray, Anne 36, 37, 39, 40, 113,
  181, 188–93, 215
  Elizabeth – see Talbot
  family / inheritance 33, 35, 36, 39,
  40, 45, 113, 114, 219
  John, 4th Duke of Norfolk 35, 39, 113
mtDNA 185, 194–7, 200–1, 204–9,
  216, 263, 295
  'Jasmine' 208
  'Ursula' 207–8

Nedeham, Sir John, lawyer 29, 32

Nesfield, John, servant of Richard, Duke
  of Gloucester (Richard III) 122, 147
Neville, Anne, consort of Richard III
  39, 58, 118, 119, 219
  Catherine, dowager Duchess of
  Norfolk 37, 191
  Cecily, dowager Duchess of York 37,
  53, 83, 150, 208–9
  George, Archbishop of York,
  Chancellor 62
  Isabel, Duchess of Clarence 39
  (Talbot), Maud, Furnival heiress
  189–90
  Richard, Earl of Warwick 68, 165
Norfolk, Duchess of – see Mowbray,
  Anne; Neville, Catherine; Talbot,
  Elizabeth
  Duke of – see Howard, John;
  Mowbray, John; Shrewsbury,
  Richard of
Northampton 44, 47, 50, 51, 93, 218
Northumberland, Duke of – see
  Dudley, John
  Earl of – see Percy, Henry
Norwich 10, 35, 37, 192, 193
  Bishop of – see Goldwell, James
Nottingham 47, 218
  Earl of – see Berkeley, William, Lord
nuper (Latin word and its use) 101, 102,
  103, 105, 106, 221, 258–61, 274, 285

Oath Book – see Colchester
oaths of fealty 47, 52

Palace of Westminster 3, 19, 37, 38,
  52, 60, 61, 64, 66, 71, 217, 218
parliament 6, 15, 19, 20 32, 40, 60, 62,
  65, 66, 67, 80, 126, 127, 128, 147,
  149, 150, 154, 216, 219, 220, 259,
  260, 278, 285
Paston, John II 35–6
  John III 36, 82
Paul's Cross, London, preaching at 73,
  81, 127
Percy, Henry, Earl of Northumberland
  59
Persall [?Persivall], servant of the Duke
  of Buckingham 92
'Plantagenet, Rychard' – see Eastwell,
  Richard of'
Plumpton, Edward 74
  Sir Robert 74

Pole, Edmund de la, Duke (later Earl) of Suffolk 157, 158, 161, 162
John de la, Earl of Lincoln 38, 149
Richard de la ('the last White Rose') 158, 161
William de la 5
Pontefract 47, 95
Pope – see Sixtus IV
Portugal, Infanta Joana of 58, 274
Poynes, ... (in the service of Richard of Shrewsbury) 116
prince – meaning of the word
prisoners in the Tower of London 2, 5, 6, 18, 21, 130, 141, 158, 161, 168, 173, 210, 216, 220, 257, 286
protector of the realm, lord – see lord protector

Raleigh, Sir Walter 173, 257
Ratcliffe (Radcliff), Richard, servant of Richard, Duke of Gloucester (Richard III) 155
Reading 111, 118, 221
Regency 51, 212
requiem mass 41, 109–10, 153, 217, 221
Ricart, Robert, Recorder of Bristol 112, 278
Richard III 3, 4, 5, 6, 7, 8, 15, 16, 17, 19, 31, 32, 56–9, 66–7, 73–4, 77, 79, 81–5, 87–9, 94–100, 102, 103, 104, 106, 107, 109, 110, 111, 113, 114, 116, 117–22, 125–6, 128–32, 135, 137, 145–49, 151, 153–6, 161–7, 171, 175, 181, 190–3, 195, 195, 208, 209, 211–6, 220, 221, 222, 225, 226, 231, 232, 235, 247, 249, 256, 260, 283, 287, 293, 294, 295
alleged marriage plans with Elizabeth of York 147–8
hair colour plate 4
servants of – see Forrest; Green; Nesfield; Ratcliffe
Portuguese royal marriage plans 58, 125
– see also York, Richard of, Duke of Gloucester
'Richard IV' – see 'England, Richard of'
Richmond, Countess of – see Beaufort, Margaret
'Richmond, Earl of' 32, 52, 58, 73, 96, 99, 148, 213
and see Henry VII

Rivers, Earl – see Widville, Anthony
Roberts, Elizabeth 205–6, 208–9, 216, 265–6
Rochester, Bishop of – see Alcock, John; Russell, John
Ross, Dr Jean 188–9
Rotherham, Thomas, Archbishop of York 41, 71, 73, 77, 83, 218, 220
royal council, the 18, 53, 56, 61, 62, 64, 65, 68, 70, 71, 72, 73, 80, 83, 93, 120, 123, 125, 212, 220
royal treasury 52, 272
Russe, Robert, sergeant of London 118
Russell, John, Bishop of Rochester; Bishop of Lincoln, chancellor 64, 115, 123, 219

St Alban's Abbey 52, 218
St Anne, feast of 119
St Clare, Giles, servant of John Howard 119, 123–4
St David's, Bishop of – see Martyn, Richard
St George's Day 43, 47
St John's Abbey – see Colchester
St John, Elizabeth, Lady Scrope 12, 226
St John, Hospital of 54
Knights of 133, 148, 282
St John the Baptist, feast of 60
St Michael the Archangel, feast of – see Michaelmas
St Paul's Cathedral 52, 80
St Pol, Jacquette de, Duchess of Bedford 197, 209, 290
Salisbury, Bishop of – see Widville, Lionel
sanctuary 11, 21, 50, 52, 54–7, 67, 83, 88, 113, 122, 149–50, 218, 219, 226, 227, 284
Sandford, Francis (historian) 16, 177, 198, 199, 233, 235, 236, 241, 243
Scot[te], John 29, 32
Scrope, Cecily – see York, Cecily of
Elizabeth, Lady – see St John, Elizabeth
Ralph 58
Thomas, Baron 58
seal, the 28, 50, 61, 62, 80, 140, 270
Shaa (Shaw), Edmund, lord mayor of London 73, 241
Ralph, Friar 73, 81, 220
Shakespeare, William 15, 66, 247, 294
Sheriff Hutton Castle 132
sheriffs 60

Shore, Elizabeth ('Jane') – see Lambert William 69
Shrewsbury, Countess of – see Beauchamp, Margaret
Earl of – see Talbot, John
Richard of, Duke of York 16, 19, 21, 31, 36, 41, 45, 52, 77–8, 88–9, 113, 114, 128, 129, 154, 156, 157, 183, 188, 189, 190, 196, 201, 210, 211, 212, 215
  archer? 116
  birth of 12, 227, 271
  cheerful? 115
  hair colour? 25–6
  healthy? 26
  images of 25–6
  sent from sanctuary to Tower by mother 54–6, 115
  story of his arrest at Stony Stratford 49, 294
  survived to adulthood? 27, 28, 112, 114, 147–51, 155
Sixtus IV, Pope 37, 109
Slaughter, William ('Black Will'), alleged servant at the Tower of London 168
Smith, John, said to have been groom of Edward IV 118
Somerset, Duke of – see Beaufort, Henry
Stafford,Countess of – see Beaufort, Margaret
Henry, Duke of Buckingham 39, 47–9, 52, 54, 55, 58, 65, 70, 72, 73, 79, 90, 92–8, 112, 131, 153
  enmity re. Widvilles 93
  guardian of the bastard 'princes'? 97
  servant of – see Persall [?Persivall]
Stallworthe, Simon, canon, servant of the chancellor, Bishop Russell 64, 115, 292
Stanley, Rt. Hon. Edward, Earl of Derby 203–4, 209
Stansted, Walter, Abbot of Colchester 149–50, 285
Stillington, Robert, Canon; Bishop of Bath and Wells 18–20, 29, 30, 34, 56, 60–65, 67, 68, 70, 80, 93, 125, 164, 219
Stonor, Sir William 64, 115
Stony Stratford 48–50, 51, 54, 218, 294
Story, Edward, Bishop of Carlisle, Bishop of Chichester 29, 30

Stow, John (historian / antiquarian) 118, 124
Suffolk, Duchess of – see Mary, Queen of France
Duke (later Earl) of – see Brandon, Charles; Pole, Edmund de la
Sulyard, John, lawyer 30, 33

Talbot, (Boteler) Eleanor 10–1, 15, 16, 18, 30, 35, 61, 63, 64, 67, 71, 91, 93, 94, 110, 125, 192, 193, 211, 212, 293
  expunged from history by Henry VII 20, 127, 213
  - see also CF2 remains
(Mowbray) Elizabeth, Duchess of Norfolk 35, 36, 37, 39, 40, 67, 94, 127, 189–90, 191, 192
John, 1st Earl of Shrewsbury 10, 35, 189–90, 191, 211
John, 3rd Earl of Shrewsbury 29, 30, 33, 36
Maud, Lady – see Neville
Tanner, Lawrence (historian) 17, 173, 178–81, 183–4, 187–8, 223–57, 293–4
teeth 178, 181–4, 187–91, 193, 200, 215, 244–7
three estates of the realm, the 19, 56, 65, 66, 70–1, 73, 81, 83, 100, 147, 164, 211, 216, 294, 30
Tower of London 1–5, 14, 39, 61, 71, 72, 80, 83, 107, 112, 114, 115, 117, 118, 120, 122, 124, 130, 131, 155, 159, 161, 165, 210, 214, 218, 219, 224, 238
  bones found at 17, 162, 168, 172–5, 178, 180, 187, 237, 243, 256
  functions of 3, 21, 54, 141
  King's Lodging 4, 5, 54, 56, 83, 173, 219, 233, 236, 257
Tudor-Craig, Pamela (medieval art historian) 120–1
Tyrell, Sir James 147, 158, 162, 166–8, 214, 231–2

'Ursula' – see mtDNA
usurpation of Henry VII 125, 140, 157, 213
  alleged, of Richard III 128, 154, 175, 213, 247, 285, 294

Va[u]ghan, Thomas 32

Vergil, Polydore (chronicler / historian)
  15, 27, 46, 81, 85, 159–60, 164–5,
  259, 286
Vienne, Archbishop of – see Cato, Angelo

Walpole, Horace (historian) 17, 86–8,
  200, 202, 203, 225
Wales, Prince of – see Arthur; Edward V;
  Westminster, Edward of
'Warbeck, Perkin' – see 'England,
  Richard of'
Warwick, Anne of – see Neville, Anne
  Earl of – see Clarence, Edward of;
  Neville, Richard
Welles (Wellis), Avice, Edward V's nurse
  34
Westminster, Dean of – see Foxley Norris
  Edward of, Prince of Wales (son of
  Margaret of Anjou) 30, 130
  Palace of – see Palace of Westminster
Westminster Abbey
  Henry VII Chapel 172, 177, 187,
  214, 295
  sanctuary 11, 21, 50, 52, 54–7, 67, 83,
  88, 113, 122, 218, 219, 226, 227
  Abbot of – see Millyng, Thomas
  Widville , Anthony, Earl Rivers 21,
  22, 24, 29, 30, 33, 37, 43, 44, 47,
  48, 49, 51, 54, 58, 59, 69, 70, 93,
  218, 220, 230
    hair colour 25
  Catherine, Duchess of Buckingham 91
  Edward 45, 52, 218, 219, 220, 272
  (Grey) Elizabeth 9, 16, 23, 28, 30, 31,
  32, 33, 35, 36, 37, 38, 39, 47, 48, 58,
  60, 61, 62, 63, 67, 69, 71, 77, 80, 84,
  91, 102, 113, 114, 122, 128, 129, 130,
  147, 151, 154, 159, 196–7, 204, 207,
  208, 216, 219, 260
    entrusted daughters to Richard III
  56–7, 83
    plot / coup attempt of 41, 43–6, 51,
  212, 218, 290
    royal marriage questioned 11,
  15–6, 18–20, 24, 64–5, 81, 83, 88,
  125–7, 147–8, 164, 211
    sent youngest son to Tower 21,
  54–5, 115, 220
  Lionel, Bishop of Salisbury 52

Margaret, Countess of Arundel 205,
  206, 209
Wilford, Ralph, Yorkist pretender,
  possibly motivated by Henry VII's
  regime 158, 160, 161
Woodstock, Palace of 120
Worcester, Bishop of – see Alcock, John
  William (chronicler) 30, 91, 277
Wren, Christopher 174, 234
  Sir Christopher 174, 177, 237, 239
Wright, Dr / Professor William 178, 180,
  181, 183, 184, 187–8, 223, 224, 225,
  236, 241, 242, 255, 256, 294, 295

Y chromosome 182, 194–6
York 41, 47, 62, 65, 82, 92, 95, 148,
  217, 218, 219, 220
  Archbishop of – see Booth,
  Lawrence; Neville; Rotherham,
  Thomas
  city records 41
  (Scrope) Cecily of 38, 57–8
  Duchess of – see Mowbray, Anne;
  Neville, Cecily
  Duke of – see Cambridge, Richard
  of; Shrewsbury, Richard of
  Elizabeth of (junior), consort of
  Henry VII 20, 38, 57, 125, 148, 164,
  196, 200, 201, 207, 209
    bastard 20, 58, 126, 147
    'heiress of the house of York'
  127–8, 213
  Elizabeth of (senior), Duchess of
  Suffolk 5, 130, 161
  George of (junior) 12, 23
  George of (senior), Duke of Clarence
  3, 5, 11, 27, 29, 39, 43, 45, 62, 63,
  64, 66, 84, 91, 129, 130, 149, 158,
  163, 211, 258, 278, 286
  Margaret of (junior) 23
  Margaret of (senior), Duchess of
  Burgundy 7, 35, 195
  Mary of 23
  Richard of, Duke of Gloucester 33,
  39, 44, 45–50, 51–3, 55, 61, 65,
  68–72, 76, 80, 90, 92, 93, 101, 217,
  259, 270
    loyalty of 46
  – see also Richard III